Progress in Mathematics
Vol. 21

Edited by
J. Coates and
S. Helgason

Birkhäuser
Boston · Basel · Stuttgart

Ergodic Theory and Dynamical Systems II

Proceedings
Special Year, Maryland 1979-80

A. Katok, editor

1982

Birkhäuser
Boston • Basel • Stuttgart

Editor:

A. Katok
Department of Mathematics
University of Maryland
College Park, Maryland 20742

Library of Congress Cataloging in Publication Data (Revised)

Main entry under title:

Ergodic theory and dynamical systems.

(Progress in mathematics ; 10, 21)
Bibliography: p.
Includes index.
1. Ergodic theory--Addresses, essays, lectures. 2. Differentiable dynamical systems--Addresses, essays, lectures.
I. Katok, A. II. Series: Progress in mathematics (Cambridge, Mass.) ; 10.
QA611.5.E73 1981 515.4'2 81-1859
ISBN 3-7643-3036-8 (v. 1)

CIP-Kurztitelaufnahme der Deutschen Bibliothek

Ergodic theory and dynamical systems : proceedings, special year, Maryland 1979 - 80 / A. Katok, ed. - Boston ; Basel ; Stuttgart : Birkhäuser

NE: Katok, Anatole (Hrsg.)

2 (1982)
(Progress in mathematics ; Vol. 21)
ISBN 3-7643-3096-1

NE: GT

ISBN 3-7643-3096-1
Printed in USA

CONTENTS

PARTICIPANTS OF THE SPECIAL YEAR IN ERGODIC THEORY AND DYNAMICAL SYSTEMS

(Other than permanent faculty of University of Maryland)

University of Maryland
College Park
1979-80

J. Aaronson - IHES, Bures-sur-Yvette - August 1979

R. Adler - IBM - November-December 1979

S. Alpern - London School of Economics - January 1980

M. Brin - University of Maryland - the whole year

C. Conley - University of Wisconsin - Madison, March 1980

E. Coven - Wesleyan University - April 1980

R. Devaney - Tufts University - Spring semester 1980

J. Feldman - University of California, Berkeley - Fall semester 1979

S. Foguel - Hebrew University - September 1979

J. Ford - Georgia Institute of Technology - March 1980

J. Franks - Northwestern University - November 1979

H. Furstenberg - Hebrew University, Jerusalem - November 1979, January-February 1980

M. Gerber - NSF Postdoctoral Fellow - the whole year

A. del Junco - Ohio State University - October 1979

S. Kakutani - Yale University - November 1979

Y. Katznelson - Hebrew University, Jerusalem - August-September 1979

M. Keane - University of Rennes - April 1980

A. Lasota - Sylesian University, Poland - April-May 1980

D. Lind - University of Washington, Seatle - Fall semester 1979

B. Marcus - University of North Carolina - Fall semester 1979

H. Masur - University of Illinois, Chicago Circle - April 1980

J. Mather - Princeton University - January 1980

J. Moser - Courant Institute, NYU - February 1980

S. Newhouse - University of North Carolina - November 1979

Z. Nitecki - Tufts University - April 1980

D. Ornstein - Stanford University - November 1979

J. Palmore - University of Illinois, Urbana - May 1980

K. Peterson - University of North Carolina - November 1979

P. Rabinowitz - University of Wisconsin, Madison - March 1980

M. Ratner - University of California, Berkeley - September 1979

C. Robinson - Northwestern University - February 1980

D. Rudolph - Stanford University - Fall semester 1979, March 1980

D. Ruelle - IHES, Bures-sur-Yvette - December 1979

J.-M. Strelcyn - University of Paris - North - January - February 1980

M. Stuart - Northeastern University - March 1980

L. Swanson - Texas A & M University - Fall semester 1979

W. Szlenk - University of Warsaw - September 1979

W. Veech - Rice University - March-May, 1980

R. Williams - Northwestern University - January 1980

P. Winternitz - University of Montreal, April 1980

Graduate Students

A. Fisher - University of Washington, Seattle - Fall semester 1979

B. Kitchens - University of North Carolina - Fall semester 1979

S. Williams - Yale University - November 1979

PROGRAM OF THE SPECIAL YEAR IN ERGODIC THEORY AND DYNAMICAL SYSTEMS

A. SPECIAL COURSES AND SEMINARS

Fall semester 1979

J. Feldman - Orbit structure in Ergodic Theory.

A. Katok - Constructions in Ergodic Theory.

D. Lind - *D. Rudolph* - Finitary Isomorphism of Measure-preserving transformations.

B. Marcus - Horocycle Flows.

Spring semester 1980

R. Devaney - Non-integrable Classical Dynamical Systems.

W. Veech - Interval Exchange Transformations.

B. SERIES OF LECTURES

H. Furstenberg - Mildly Mixing Transformations.

M. Gerber, A. Katok - Smooth Models for Thurston's Pseudo-Anosov maps.

D. Ruelle - Characteristic Exponents and Invariant Manifolds in Hilbert space.

C. TALKS

J. Aaronson - Infinite Measure Preserving Transformations.

R. Adler - Cross Section for Geodesic Flows and Continuous Fractions.

S. Alpern - Ergodic Properties of Measure-preserving Homeomorphisms.

M. Brin - Topology and Spectrum of Anosov Diffeomorphisms.
Topology and Ergodicity of Frame Flows.

C. Conley - On Limiting for Directal Families of Flows with no Limit Flow and a New Way of Codifying Algebraic Properties of Flows. (2 talks)

J. Feldman - Amenable and Anti-Amenable Group Actions.

S. Foguel - Asymptotic Behaviour of Iterates of a Harris Operator.

J. Ford - Computer Models of Dynamical Systems. (2 Talks)

J. Franks - Symbolic Dynamics and Knot Theory. Anomalous Anosov Flows.

H. Furstenberg - Some Dynamical Systems Connected with Number Theory.

M. Gerber - A Zero-entropy Mixing Transformation Whose Cartesian Products are Loosely Bernoulli.

A. del Junco - Finitary Coding for $\mathbb{Z}^n$-actions.

S. Kakutani - Proof of Maximal Ergodic Theorem.

Y. Katznelson - An Ergodic Approach to the Szemeridi Theorem and its Generalizations.

M. Keane - Continuous Homomorphisms of Bernoulli Shifts.

A. Lasota - Exactness for One-dimensional Maps.

An Application of a Fixed Point Theorem to Ergodic Theory.

H. Masur - Strict Ergodicity of Measured Foliations.

J. Mather - Caratheodory Theory of Prime Ends.
Invariant Subsets for Area-preserving Homeomorphisms.

J. Moser - Isospectral Deformations and Separation of Variables.

S. Newhouse - Modern Bifurcation Theory for Smooth Dynamical Systems.

Z. Nitecki - Non-wandering Points for Maps of the Interval.

D. Ornstein - Automorphism Non-equivalent to the Direct Product of Bernoulli and Zero Entropy.

Orbit Equivalence with Additional Structures.

J. Palmore - New Stable Configurations and Relative Equilibria of Interacting Vortices by a Topological Method.

P. Rabinowitz - Periodic Solutions of Hamiltonial Systems.

Critical Points of Indefinite Functionals.

M. Ratner - Horocycle Flows and the Loose Bernoulli Property.

C. Robinson - Non Absolutely Continuous Invariant Foliations.

D. Rudolph - Measure-preserving Maps with Minimal Self-joinings and Some Applications.

Non-isomorphic Flows with Isomorphic Automorphisms. (2 talks)

J.-M. Strelcyn - Dynamical Systems with Singularities and Billiard Systems. (2 talks)

L. Swanson - Minimal Self-joinings and an Example of Chacon.

W. Szlenk - Dynamics of One-dimensional Maps.

R. Williams - Lorentz Attractors and Knotted Periodic Orbits. (2 talks)

P. Winternitz - Quadratic Hamiltonians in Phase Space and Their Eigenfunctions.

TOPOLOGICAL DYNAMICS ON THE INTERVAL

Zbigniew Nitecki
Tufts University

Introduction

A great deal has been written about maps of the interval, especially in recent years. In addition to many detailed mathematical papers, there have been a number of numerical studies and descriptive works (Co, Fe, GM, HoH, Ma2, MeS, Mr) and studies relating one-dimensional dynamical systems to models in the biological (GOI, HLM, La5-6, Mal, MaO, WL) and physical (CE, GM1, La3,6, LaR, Lo1-3) sciences. The subject is appealing because it is easy to talk about - very little technical apparatus is needed to pose many problems in the field - and yet one-dimensional systems can exhibit surprizingly complex dynamic behavior.

I began work on this paper with the intention of writing a survey of rigorous results in this area, but became preoccupied with trying to understand geometrically the structure theorems of Jonker-Rand and Hofbauer. The paper that has resulted is much narrower in scope and more concerned with certain technical details than a survey should be. Nevertheless, I have tried to write an expository work about the topological theory of continuous (and especially piecewise-monotone) maps of a compact interval into itself. I assume a basic familiarity with dynamical systems theory in general, but no specific knowledge of one-dimensional systems.

This paper has five sections. The first is a unified and fairly detailed exposition of ideas developed by Li, Yorke, Block, Misiurewicz and others on the relation of symbolic dynamics to the periodic behavior of interval maps. This includes the elegant proof published recently by

Block et. al. of Šarkovskiĭ's theorem, the minimal period examples of Štefan and Misiurewicz, and results of Block and Misiurewicz on the structure of maps with all periods powers of 2 and on the behavior of periods under perturbation. The second section treats unstable sets of periodic orbits, and includes Block's theorem on homoclinic points and odd periods. Much of this section is concerned with technical results to be used in section 4. The third section briefly summarizes general results about nonwandering points of continuous maps of the interval. The fourth section is the heart of the paper, a new proof of a kind of spectral decomposition theorem for an arbitrary continuous piecewise-monotonic map of the interval. The fifth and final section is a brief discussion of topological entropy for piecewise-monotonic maps of the interval.

The result (theorem 4.17) in section 4 extends a theorem for C^1 maps with a single critical point proved by Jonker-Rand (JoR 3,5), and is closely related to a result recently announced by Hofbauer (Hof 5, cf. Hof 3,4) for piecewise-continuous, piecewise-monotone maps with a generating partition. The methods of both of these proofs are based on symbolic dynamics, whereas our analysis is more geometric.

We treat a map $f: I \to I$ which is continuous and *piecewise-monotonic,* which means there exist finitely many *turning points* separating intervals on which f is alternately increasing and decreasing. (Note that all real-analytic maps satisfy this hypothesis.) The one-sided unstable sets of periodic orbits (2.1) provide a pseudo-filtration (4.5) for the nonwandering set $\Omega(f)$, and a resulting finite or countable decomposition of $\Omega(f)$ into closed invariant sets whose pairwise intersections are empty or finite. With the exception of finitely many of these sets, each is contained in the Birkhoff center, and is either a single orbit attracting or repelling from at least one side, a degenerate "block" of monotone-equivalent periodic orbits, or is (up to identification of some pairs of nonperiodic orbits) a topologically transitive one-sided subshift of finite type. Each of the exceptional sets contains the ω-limit of some turning point of f. If the decomposition is infinite, then there exist "limit" exceptional sets which are (up to identification of pairs of orbits) generalized "adding machine" minimal sets (4.14). When an actual identification of orbits takes place, such a limit set can contain an infinite nonwandering orbit outside the Birkhoff center (4.18). Aside from the limit exceptional sets a piece of the decomposition which contains the ω-limit of a turning point may contain finitely many points outside the Birkhoff center, and the rest of the points satisfy a topological mixing property (4.23).

In narrowing the scope of this paper, I have omitted many important topics in one-dimensional dynamics, which can be classified in three groups: (i) the more analytic theory associated with the quadratic map; (ii) ergodic theory on the interval, and (iii) the analogous theory on the circle.

The study of the quadratic maps on the interval, $f_a(x) = ax(1-x)$, goes back to Myrberg (My), and has given rise to a rich theory of smooth maps with one turning point under various hypotheses on the derivative. At the end of section 4, in discussing the result of Jonker-Rand, we make brief mention of the kneading calculus of Milnor-Thurston (MiT) and the negative Schwartzian condition introduced by Singer (Sg). However, we make no mention of the general theory of bifurcations on the interval discussed by Guckenheimer (G 1-3) and Gumowski-Mira (GM, Mr) or the extensive recent work on universal properties initiated by the brilliant speculative work of Feigenbaum (Fe) and carried out by Collet-Eckmann-

Lanford (CE2, CEL), Derrida-Gervois-Pomeau (DGP), and Campanino-Epstein Ruelle (CaE). A leisurely survey of this area is the monograph by Collet-Eckmann (CE1); some aspects are treated in a basic paper by Guckenheimer (G4). A different result on the quadratic map is given by Henry (Hn).

The ergodic theory has two aspects: existence theorems for invariant measures, and the analysis of specific classes of ergodic transformations with a natural presentation on the interval. Many theorems about the existence of various kinds of invariant measures have been proved by, among others, Lasota-Yorke (La 1-4, LaY 1-2), Li-Yorke (Li, LiY2) Pianigiani (Pi 1-3), Adler (Ad), Ruelle (R), Bowen (Bo 3), Walters (Wa), Misiurewicz (Mi 5), Szlenk (Sz 1,2) and Jakobson (Ja). Interval-exchange transformations are treated by Keane-Rauzy (Kea, KeaR), Katok (Ka) and Veech (Ve). The β-transformations $f(x) = \beta x + \alpha \pmod 1$ are studied by Renyi (Re), Parry (Pa 1), Hofbauer (Hof 1,7), Smorodinsky (Sm), Takahashi (Ta) and Wilkinson (Wi). Other results on the ergodic theory of one-dimensional systems are given by Adler-Weiss (AW), Bowen (Bo 1-2), Boyarsky et. al. (By, ByC, ByS), Hofbauer-Keller (HK), Jabłonski-Malczak (JM), Keller (Kel), Kowalski (Kow), Kołodziej (Kol), Ledrappier (Le), Li-Schweiger (LiS), Mayer (May) and Wong (Wo). See also (Key, Mas).

Finally, the theory of continuous maps on the circle has some features distinct from those of the corresponding theory on the interval. The classical theory of homeomorphisms of the circle was surveyed in 1935 by van Kampen (vK); a recent developemt is the celebrated thesis of M. Herman (He), solving the conjecture of Arnold (Ar). L. Block has established an extension to the circle of Šarkovskiĭ's theorem (Bℓ 10, 12, cf. Ll). Block et. al. have established lower bounds on entropy from periodic data (BGMY, BCN). Various classes of continuous maps on the circle have been analyzed by Markley (Mar), Auslander-Katznelson (AuK) and Block-Franke (Bℓ 1-5, BℓF, Fr), Bunimovič (Bu), Yano (Ya), Żołądek (Zo) and myself (Ni 1-3). A study of a class of maps of the interval closely related to maps of the circle is carried out by Keener (Kee).

The lists above serve merely as indications of the literature on the subject; there are undoubtedly many omissions, and the survey I originally intended still needs to be written. The present paper has benefitted greatly from several stimulating conversations I had with Ethan Coven, whom I would like to thank for his interest and help.

1. *Periodic behavior*

Recall that the dynamic behavior of a homeomorphism of the interval to itself is very simple. Either the map preserves orientation, and every periodic (in fact every chain-recurrent) point is fixed, or the map reverses orientation, there is a single fixedpoint, and all other periodic (chain-recurrent) points have least period 2. In either case, the α- and ω- limit sets of any point are each contained in a single periodic orbit. The only complication that can occur is the degeneracy arising from the fact that any closed set can be the fixedpoint set of some homeomorphism. This description works equally well if f is simply *monotone:* $x < y < z$ implies $f(y)$ lies between $f(x)$ and $f(z)$ (possibly at one of these points).

When a continuous map $f : I \to I$ is not monotone, this simple picture breaks down in general. However, a good deal can be said; the first and best-known theorem of this type was proved in 1964 by A. Šarkovskiĭ (Sa):

(1.1) *Šarkovskiĭ's Theorem (Sa, BGMY):*

Write the positive integers in the following order:

(1.1a) $1 = 2^0,\ 2 = 2^1,\ 2^2,\ \cdots,\ \cdots,\ 2^2\cdot 3,\ \cdots,\ 2\cdot 5,\ 2\cdot 3,\ \cdots\ 9,\ 7,\ 5,\ 3$

That is:

(i) ascending powers of 2 come first

(ii) descending odds > 1 come last

(iii) each sequence of descending odds > 1 times a fixed power of 2 comes between, with higher powers of 2 coming earlier.

Then, for any continuous map of the interval to itself (or the line) the existence of a periodic point with least period n implies the existence of periodic points with least periods m for each m preceding n in (1.1a).

We shall refer to (1.1a) as the "Šarkovskiĭ order" and say that f "possesses period n" when some periodic point of f has least period n.

Šarkovskiĭ's proof of his remarkable theorem was published in Russian and became known to English-speaking readers by way of Štefan's exposition (St) thirteen years later. In between, parts of this result were independently rediscovered by Li and Yorke (LiY 1) and Nathanson (Na). An elegant and natural proof of (1.1) was published recently by L. Block, J. Guckenheimer, M. Misiurewicz and L. Young (BGMY). This proof uses symbolic techniques developed earlier by Li - Yorke (LiY 1), L. Block (Bℓ 6-9) and Misiurewicz (Mi 2-4), and used again more recently by Li et. al. (LiMPY). The proof itself has even been rediscovered independently by Ho - Morris (HoM) (see also (Str)).

Suppose we are given a finite set of points $P = \{0 = p_0 < p_1 < \cdots < p_n = 1\}$; then an orbit of $f : I \to I$ can be described by specifying the sequence of intervals $J_i = [p_{i-1}, p_i]$ $i = 1, \cdots, n$ through which it passes. A finite or countable sequence a_i, $i = 0, \cdots$ of integers, $0 \leq a_i \leq n$ is an *itinerary* (also called an "f-expansion") of x relative to P if for each $i \geq 0$ $f^i(x)$ belongs to interval number a_i. Note that the intervals are not quite disjoint, so that there is some ambiguity about which itinerary should be assigned to an orbit hitting some partition point p_i, $0 < i < n$. This ambiguity is analogous to the ambiguity in the decimal expansion of 1/10 as $0.100 \cdots = .0999 \cdots$. (The analogy is an identity when $f(x) = 10x \bmod 1$ and $p_i = i/10$.) We will nonetheless refer to P as a partition of I, and deal with this ambiguity as it comes up.

The analysis of itineraries on the interval is based on two simple technical observations:

(1.2) *<u>Fixedpoint lemma</u>: If $J \subseteq I$ is a closed interval and $f : J \to I$ is continuous, then the existence of points $x, y \in J$ with $f(x) \leq x$ and $f(y) \geq y$ implies the existence of a fixedpoint of f in J.*

(1.3) *<u>Itinerary lemma</u> (LiY 1): Suppose $J_0, J_1, \cdots$ is a finite or countable sequence of closed intervals $J_i \subset I$, and f is continuous on each J_i and satisfies $f(J_i) \supset J_{i+1}$ for each i. Then this sequence represents the itinerary of some orbit of f:*

$$(\exists x \in I)\ f^i(x) \in J_i \qquad i = 0, \cdots$$

The proof of (1.2) is just the Darboux property of $f(x) - x$, while the proof of (1.3) is based on the observation that for each i, some component of $J_0 \cap f^{-1}J_1 \cap \cdots \cap f^{-i}J_i$ maps onto J_i under f^i. In particular, the fixedpoint lemma has two useful reformulations. Suppose $f : J \to I$ is continuous, where $J \subset I$ is an interval (not necessarily closed):

(1.2a) *If J contains no fixedpoints of f, then simultaneously for all points $x \in J$ either $f(x) > x$ or $f(x) < x$.*

(1.2b) If J is closed and either contains or is contained in its image $f(J)$, then J contains a fixedpoint of f.

Given a finite partition P as above and a continuous map $F : I \to I$, we construct a directed graph with vertices J_i and an edge $J_i \to J_i$ iff $f(J_i) \supset J_j$. Then the itinerary lemma insures that every path in the graph corresponds to the itinerary of some point. One can use the graph as the transition graph of a topological Markov chain (= one-sided subshift of finite type), and if we identify sequences corresponding to a single orbit under the ambiguity noted above, this system is a factor (image of a semiconjugacy) of some invariant set of f. We shall refer to this graph as the *Markov graph* of the partition. The idea of using topological Markov chains to study maps of the interval originated with Parry (Pa 2), but has received new impetus from the work of Li - Yorke, L. Block, and Misiurewicz (and, in a different language, Milnor-Thurston and Guckenheimer).

The fixedpoint lemma insures that every loop in the Markov graph represents a periodic orbit of f. We would like to use the length (= number of vertices or of edges) of the loop to measure the least period of this periodic orbit. Of course, we should check that the loop in question is not simply the multiple traversal of one proper subloop (i.e. it is *irreducible*). We must also insure that the periodic orbit in question is interior to each of the intervals in its itinerary, lest the ambiguity allow a different, shorter loop to represent the same orbit.

We consider a partition P of some subinterval $[p_0, p_{n-1}] \subset I$ by the orbit segment $P = \{x, f(x), f^2(x), \ldots, f^{n-1}(x)\}$ of a point satisfying

(1.4) $f^n(x) \leq x < f(x)$

or the "mirror-image" condition obtained by replacing "less" by "greater" in (1.4). The numbering of the points p_i corresponds to their order on the line, not their iteration order; let us assume $x = p_a$. The condition (1.4) yields certain properties of the Markov graph of P. Since $f(p_a) > p_a$ and $f(p_{n-1}) < p_{n-1}$ there exists at least one interval, $J_i = [p_{i-1}, p_i]$, with $p_{i-1} \geq p_a$, $f(p_{i-1}) \geq p_i$ and $f(p_i) \leq p_{i-1}$. Denote the corresponding vertex in the Markov graph by S_1. Then

(1.5a) The Markov graph contains the loop $S_1 \to S_1$.

Thus by (1.2b), J_i contains a fixedpoint z of f. Since some image of p_i is $f^{n-1}(x)$, the next image of J_i contains both $f^n(x) \leq p_a$ and $z > p_a$. Thus, some image of J_i contains $[p_a, z]$. Now, the images of p_a include both endpoints of $[p_0, p_n]$, so that the images of J_i include $[p_0, z]$ and $[z, p_n]$. Since every interval other than J_i is contained in one of these, we have

(1.5b) The Markov graph contains a path from S_1 *to every other vertex.*

Now, suppose for a moment that we also had

(1.5c) The Markov graph contains a path ending at S_1 *and starting at some other vertex.*

Then (1.5b,c) would give an irreducible loop of length ℓ, $2 \leq \ell \leq n$ with (1.5a) not a subloop. The loop of length ℓ followed by k traversals of (1.5a) is an irreducible loop of length $\ell + k$ for every $k \geq 1$. With one possible exception (if p_{i-1} or p_i is periodic) these loops represent periodic orbits interior to their itinerary, and we have

(1.5) __Lemma:__ (1.5a-c) imply that f *possesses every period greater than or equal to n.*

We apply (1.5) by means of a condition equivalent to the failure of (1.5c). We formulate the notion more generally, as we will use it again later. Suppose X is a set of points, not necessarily f-invariant; a *separation* of X under f is a point $\inf X < z < \sup X$ such that for each $x \in X$, $f(x) \geq z$ iff $x \leq z$. A separation, if it exists, can be achieved by a fixedpoint.

(1.6) Lemma: If P is an orbit segment satisfying (1.4), then either (1.5c) holds or every point of S_1 separates P under f.

This is clear: if $f(p_{j-1}) < z$ and $j \leq i - 1$, then since $f(p_{i-1}) > z$, we can pick j so that the above holds and $f(p_j) > z$. Since $f(p_{j-1}) \leq p_{i-1}$ and $f(p_j) \geq p_i$, $f(J_j) \supset J_i = S_1$.

Lemmas (1.5) and (1.6) give a variation of the statement that the decreasing odds come at the end of the Šarkovskiĭ order:

(1.7) Proposition (LiMPY)

If $f : I \to I$ is continuous and x satisfies (1.4) for some odd n (in particular, if f possesses an odd period $n > 1$) then f possesses period k for

(i) each $k \geq n$, and

(ii) every even $k < n$.

Proof of (1.7)

If x is periodic, so that $f^n(x) = x$, the set P is permuted by f and, having the odd number n of elements, cannot be separated. If $f^n(x) < x$, a separation requires $x \leq z$ (since $f(x) > x$) and the fact that $f^n(x) < x \leq z$ allows us to use the same counting argument as in the periodic case to rule out a separation of P. Since P is not separated, (1.6) gives a subgraph for P of the form

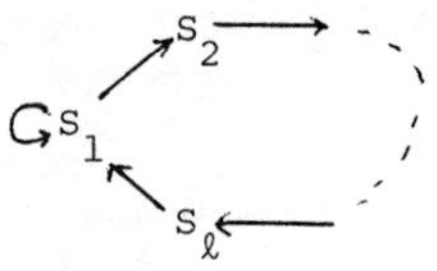

with $2 \leq \ell \leq n - 1$. Then (1.5) implies (i): f possesses all periods $k \geq n$. In particular, f possesses a periodic orbit of least period n.

Thus, to prove (ii), we can assume x is periodic with least period n, and that f possesses no odd period between 1 and n. This implies

$\ell = n - 1$ and the long loop has no short cuts $S_i \to S_j$ with either $j > i + 1$ or $j = 1$ and $i \neq 1, n - 1$. In particular, if S_1 represents J_i, then $f(J_i)$ contains J_i and one of the adjacent intervals, S_2, and no others. Assuming for a moment that $S_1 = J_i$, $S_2 = J_{i-1}$, we are forced to have $f(p_i) = p_{i-2}$ and $f(p_{i-1}) - p_i$. Then in turn, $f(S_2)$ must contain S_3 and no other intervals, and necessarily $S_3 = J_{i+1}$, $f(p_{i-2}) = p_{i+1}$. Continuing this argument, we see that the images of p_{i-1} move outward from S_1, separated by S_1, up to $f^{n-1}(p_{i-1})$, which is forced by our initial choice $S_2 = J_{i-1}$ to be p_0, and must map to p_{i-1}. (The other choice, $S_2 = J_{i+1}$, would lead to the mirror-image pattern and thus force the mirror image of 1.4.) This last observation forces $f(S_{n-1}) = f([p_0,p_1])$ to contain $[f(p_0), f(p_1)] = [p_{i-1},p_{n-1}]$ which is the union of all the odd-numbered S_i. Thus, the Markov graph has subgraph

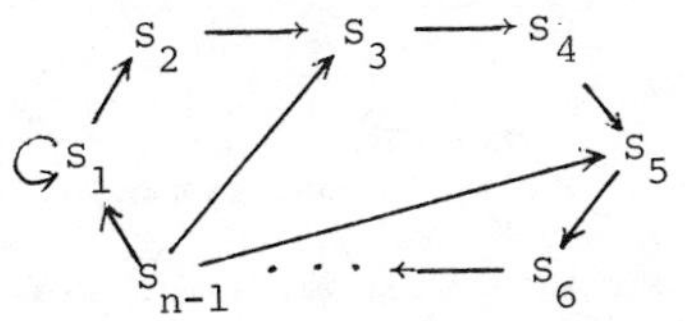

in which the loops at S_{n-1} exhibit all even periods below n. ∎

The argument above tells us how to construct, for any odd $n > 1$, a map f possessing only the periods k specified by (1.7). We set up a periodic orbit of odd period n according to

$$x_{n-1} < \cdots < x_4 < x_2 < x_0 < x_1 < x_3 < \cdots < x_{n-2}$$

and $f(x_i) = x_{i+1}$ $(i + 1 \bmod n-1)$ and extend f linearly to the intervals between. For example, $n = 5$ gives

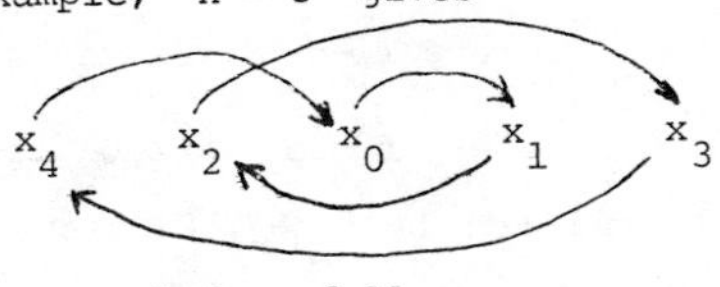

and the map f can be graphed as follows:

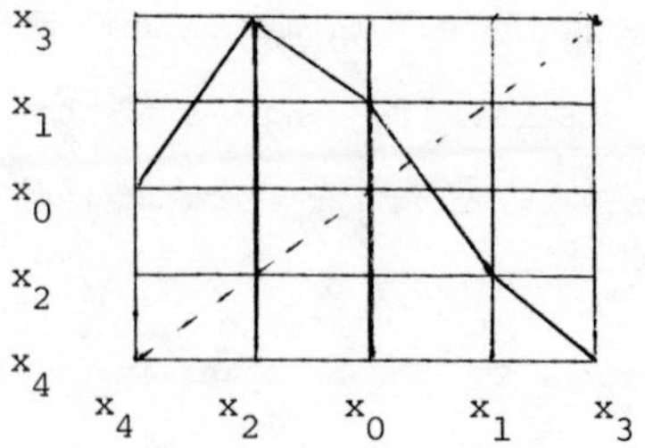

This structure was noted by Štefan (St).

Now, suppose f possesses only even periods (with the exception $1 = 2^0$, which is always understood). The arguments for (1.5) and (1.6) imply that any fixedpoint in $[p_0, p_{n-1}]$ belongs to J_i. Furthermore, the separation of P makes each half of P an orbit segment under f^2, and unless the f^2-orbits of x and $f(x)$ are monotone up to $n/2$ (which fails if x has even period n) the hypothesis (1.4) applies to f^2 in $[p_0, p_i]$, to give us a periodic point of least period 2 in $[p_0, p_i]$. Thus,

(1.8) *<u>Lemma</u>:* *If $f : I \to I$ is continuous and possesses only even periods, then any orbit segment P satisfying (1.4) for some even n is separated by a fixedpoint of f. If $f^n(x) = x$ in (1.4), there is a periodic orbit of least period 2 separating each half of P under f^2.*

In general, if f possesses only periods divisible by some fixed power of 2, say $2^N (N \geq 1)$, (with the understood exception of 2^k, $k = 0, \cdots, N - 1$), the structure of periodic orbits is described by an inductive application of (1.8). A set P is *separated to order one* if it is separated as before; denote the two halves under this separation by P_0, P_1. Then P_0 and P_1 are f^2-orbit segments. Inductively, say P is *separated to order* k under f for $k > 0$ if P is separated to order $(k - 1)$ under f and each half P_0, P_1 is separated to order $(k - 1)$ under f^2. Note that unless P is itself periodic of period 2^{ℓ}, $\ell < k$, a separation to order k (if it exists) can be accomplished by a collection of periodic orbits with least periods $2^0, 2^1, 2^2, \cdots. 2^{k-1}$.

(1.8a) Corollary: If $f: I \to I$ is continuous and every period possessed by f is either a power of 2 or is divisible by 2^N ($N \geq 2$), then every periodic orbit with least period not 2^k for some $k < N$ is separated to order N under f. In particular, f possesses periods 2^k, $k = 0, \cdots, N$.

(1.7) and (1.8) are special cases of Šarkovskiĭ's theorem, and easily give the full theorem:

Proof of (1.1)

(1.7) gives (1.1) for n odd. Suppose f possesses period $n = 2^N \cdot m$, m odd, and assume it possesses no period $2^{N-1} \cdot p$, $p > 1$ odd. By (1.8a), f possesses period 2^k for $k = 0, \cdots, N$. If $m = 1$, we are done; if $m > 1$, apply (1.7) to f^r, where $r = 2^N$. Thus f^r possesses all periods $q \geq m$ and $2q$, $q < m$. Noting that a point of least period k under f has least period $k \div \gcd(k,r)$ under f^r, we see that f possesses all periods $r \cdot q$ for $q \geq m$ and $2r \cdot q$ for $q < m$, giving (1.1). ∎

The notion of separation suggests an algorithm for constructing examples of maps possessing only periods preceding a specified n in (1.1a). Given m odd, we have seen how to construct f_m possessing no odd period below m except $1 = 2^0$. To construct a map f possessing no period $2k$ with $1 < k < m$ odd, we employ the return-time doubling (or "square root") trick of Štefan (St). Re-scale f_m so that $\tilde{f}_m : [0, 1/3] \to [0, 1/3]$, and define f_{2m} on $[0, 1]$ by $f_{2m}(x) = \tilde{f}_m(x) + 2/3$ for $0 \leq x \leq 1/3$, $f_{2m}(x) = x - 2/3$ for $2/3 \leq x \leq 1$, and extending linearly to $(1/3, 2/3)$. All f_{2m}-pre-images of (1/3, 2/3) are contained in this interval, where f_{2m} is a homeomorphism and hence possesses only periods 2^0 and 2^1. On the other hand, f_{2m} interchanges [0, 1/3] with [2/3, 1], and on each, $(f_{2m})^2 = \tilde{f}_m$. Thus, the periods of f_{2m} are precisely 2^0, 2^1, and 2q, where q ranges over periods of f_m.

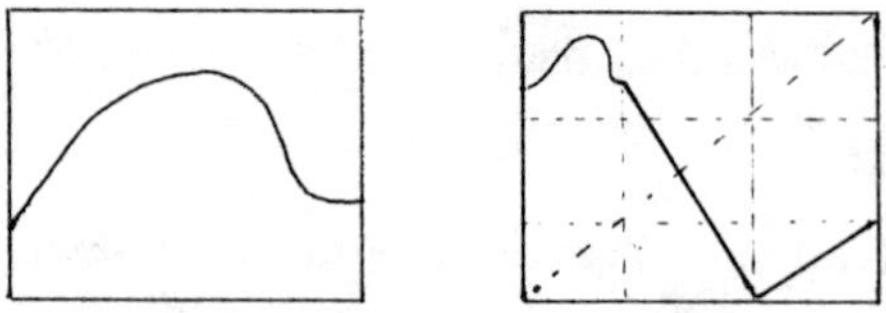

f_m $\qquad$ f_{2m}

An inductive application of this procedure, forming f_{4m} from f_{2m}, etc. gives examples of maps f_n, for any n, possessing precisely the periods specified by (1.1). (f_1 a homeomorphism gives f_n for $n = 2^N$.)

We note further that the sequence of maps starting from any g_0 and constructing g_{i+1} from g_i by the square-root trick satisfies $g_i(x) = g_j(x)$ whenever $x \geq 2/3^n$ and $i, j \geq n$; thus the functions g_i converge uniformly on any interval $[\varepsilon, 1]$ $\varepsilon > 0$, to a continuous function g_∞, which one easily sees must satisfy $g_\infty(0) = 1$. It is easy to see that g_∞ has precisely one periodic orbit of least period 2^n for each $n = 0, 1, \cdots$, and no other periodic orbits. Also, the set M_n complementary to the intervals $(1/3^k, 2/3^k)$, $k = 1, \cdots, n$ and their translates by multiples of $2/3^k$ is invariant and separated to order n under g_i for all $i \geq n$, hence by g_∞. Thus, the middle-third cantor set $M_\infty = \bigcap_{n=1}^{\infty} M_n$ is an invariant set for g_∞, separated to all orders.

The dynamics on M_∞ is that of the "*adding machine*" or 2-adic minimal set (GoH), which can be described as follows: points of M_∞ are labelled by sequences $\underline{k} = k_0, k_1, \cdots$ where each k_i is 0 or 1, and the point labelled $\underline{k}$ maps to the point labelled $\underline{k} + 1$, defined by adding 1 to k_0 and carrying (base 2): if $i \geq 0$, $k_i = 0$ and $k_j = 1$ for $j < i$, then

$$\underline{k} + 1 = (1, \cdots, 1, 0, k_{i+1}, \cdots) + 1$$
$$= (0, \cdots, 0, 1, k_{i+1}, \cdots) .$$

The correspondence between M_∞ and sequences $\underline{k}$ is obtained by labelling the right component of M_1 by 0, the left component by 1, then labelling each component C of M_n by a sequence $k_0 \cdots k_{n-1}$ with $k_0 \cdots k_{n-2}$ the label of the component C' of M_{n-1} containing C, and $k_{n-1} = 0$ for C = the right third ($k_{n-1} = 1$ for C = the left third) of C'.

The example described above is due to Misiurewicz, and shows that there exist maps possessing all powers of 2 and no other periods. On the other hand, an immediate corollary of Šarkovskiĭ's theorem is

(1.9) <u>*Remark:*</u> *If $f: I \to I$ possesses some period not a power of 2, it possesses infinitely many periods.*

L. Block (Bℓ 6-9) and Misiurewicz (Mi 2-4) have analyzed the structure of maps possessing only powers of 2 as periods (which is equivalent, as shall see in section 5, to having topological entropy zero). Block (Bℓ 9) noted that in such a map all periodic orbits are separated to all orders ("simple" in his terminology; note that an orbit of period 2^k has trivial separation of order beyond k) while Misiurewicz (Mi 3) has shown further that any topologically transitive invariant set of such a map is separated to all orders and essentially modelled by the adding machine described above. We state this result in a slightly refined form, using the language of order of separation:

(1.10) <u>*Theorem*</u> *(cf (Mi 3)): Suppose $f: I \to I$ continuous, $N \geq 2$, and every period possessed by f is a power of 2 or is divisible by 2^N.*

Any topologically transitive invariant set K *for* f *either*

(i) consists of a single periodic orbit of period 2^k, $k < N$,

or (ii) contains no periodic orbit of period 2^k, $k < N - 1$, *and is separated by* f *to order* N.

In particular, if every period possessed by f *is a power of 2, then* K *is either a single periodic orbit or is a minimal set mapping continuously onto the adding machine by a map that is injective except possibly for identifying a countable number of pairs of points.*

We will not prove this here, but note that one uses (1.8a), where P is a segment of a dense orbit.

We saw earlier that if f possesses odd period $n > 1$ and no odd periods between n and 1, then the points of the n-orbit are traversed in a pattern determined up to mirror images by the argument in (1.7). One might suspect that, when all periods are powers of 2, the separation arguments of (1.8) and (1.8a) might similarly determine the pattern of all 2^n-orbits. While true for $n = 0, 1, 2$, this is false for $n \geq 3$, as shown (Bℓ 9) by the following pair of patterns of period 8, both separated to order 3:

$$x_1 < x_5 < x_7 < x_3 < x_2 < x_6 < x_8 < x_4$$

$$x_1 < x_5 < x_7 < x_3 < x_2 < x_6 < x_4 < x_8 .$$

Here as before, $f(x_i) = x_{i+1}$ $(i + 1 \bmod 8)$. The two patterns differ only in the reversal of the order of x_4 and x_8, and are clearly not mirror-images of each other. It is of course possible to further limit the patterns for a piecewise monotone map from knowledge of the location of the turning points. One can check that the first pattern above is possible with a single turning point, located between x_7 and x_2 (it can be on either side of x_3), whereas the second requires at least two turning points, one between x_5 and x_3, the other between x_6 and x_8. However, this indeterminacy makes it extra difficult to enumerate the patterns of orbits of period $2^n \cdot m$, $m > 1$ odd and $n > 1$, when this is the last period for f in the Šarkovskiĭ order. I understand C. W. Ho has done some work on this problem, but I am not familiar with his results. I have formulated the separation results above for maps possessing only periods divisible by 2^n with an eye toward this problem.

We will see another characterization of maps possessing only powers of 2 when we consider homoclinic phenomena in the next section. We close this section with some results of L. Block and M. Misiurewicz concerning the behavior of this picture under perturbation.

(1.11) <u>*Theorem*</u> *(Bℓ 11) : If $f : I \to I$ is continuous and possesses period n, then every map in some C^0 neighborhood of f possesses each period preceding n in (1.1a).*

The proof, which we only sketch, proceeds by noting, in case n is odd, that the itinerary of the orbit of period $n + 2$ given in (1.7) defines an interval J with n disjoint images and $f^{n+2}J = S_1$, which contains J in its interior; a nearby map g will still exhibit n disjoint images of J and $g^{n+2}J \supset J$. In the case of $n = 2^N$, $N \geq 2$, (1.10) gives a point y fixed for $f^{n/2}$ and not for $f^{n/4}$ and separating two adjacent points $p_i < y < p_{i+1}$ of the 2^N-orbit under $f^{n/2}$. For g near f, $g^{n/2}(p_i) > y > g^{n/2}(p_{i+1})$ and so some fixedpoint near y persists.

The lower-semicontinuity result (1.11) does not have an upper-semicontinuity analogue for C^0 perturbations (a fixedpoint can be changed into an invariant interval possessing period 3), but there is a partial analogue for C^1 perturbations, due to Misiurewicz (Mi 4):

(1.12) <u>*Theorem*</u> *(Mi 4): If* $f: I \to I$ *is* C^1 *and possesses only finitely many periods* $2^0, 2^1, \cdots, 2^N$, *then no map sufficiently* C^1*-close to* f *can possess period* 2^{N+2}.

The techniques of this proof are quite different from what we have been doing here. An interesting consequence of (1.12) is that any C^1-continuous parametrized family of maps (for example, the quadratic maps $f_a(x) = 4ax(1 - x)$, $0 \le a \le 1$) possessing finitely many periods for one parameter value and infinitely many for another necessarily possesses precisely the powers of 2 for some parameter value between.

2. *Homoclinic behavior*

This section concerns the behavior of unstable sets for periodic orbits. Such sets have been used by L. Block (Bℓ 8) to characterize maps possessing only powers of 2 as periods (theorem (2.4) below) and by Coven and myself (CN) in studying the nonwandering points of a continuous map which wander under some power. Similar ideas appear in Lℓibre [Lℓ].

For a periodic source in a smooth dynamical system, the unstable manifold is the set of points which lie on orbits originating arbitrarily near the source. The notion of unstable set modifies this in three ways: we assume no non-degeneracy for the periodic orbit, we take the closure of the set described above, and we distinguish orbits originating on different sides of the periodic point.

Given a point $x \in I$, a full neighborhood *(F-neighborhood)* of x can be given in the form $N(x, \varepsilon, F) = (x - \varepsilon, x + \varepsilon)$ for some $\varepsilon > 0$; we distinguish the two sides of this as the *L-neighborhood* of size ε

$$N(x, \varepsilon, L) = (x - \varepsilon, x]$$

and the *R-neighborhood* of size ε

$$N(x, \varepsilon, R) = [x, x + \varepsilon).$$

We can speak of any one of the three types of neighborhood as an *S-neighborhood* where the side $S = R, L$, or F.

Suppose $p \in Per(f)$, $f: I \to I$ continuous. We define the *S-unstable set* of the f orbit of p ($S = R, L$, or F) by

$$(2.1) \quad U(p, f, S) = \bigcap_{\varepsilon>0} clos \{\bigcup_{n\geq 0} f^n[N(p, \varepsilon, S)]\}$$

When p is fixed under f, it is clear that $U(p, f, S)$ is a closed interval containing p — possibly equal to $\{p\}$, in which case we call it *trivial*, — and equals its image under f, which we refer to as *strong invariance*. If p is periodic under f with least period n, then each point $f^k(p)$ of the orbit of p is fixed under f^n; one can see that given S a side at p, there exist sides $f^k(S)$ at $f^k(p)$ such that

$$(2.2a) \quad f^k[U(p, f^n, S)] = U(f^k(p), f^n, f^k(S))$$

and

$$(2.2b) \quad U(p, f, S) = \bigcup_{k=0}^{n-1} U(f^k(p), f^n, f^k(S))$$

Of course, $f^k(F) = F$ for any k. When $S = R$ or L, the situation can be slightly more complicated; however, we note that in (2.2b) there are two possibilities: either $U(p, f^n, R) = U(p, f^n, L)$, in which case every choice of $f^k(S)$ can be made arbitrarily, or else the choices $f^k(R)$ and $f^k(L)$ are distinct for any k. The second case means that for at least one of the two choices, $f[N(f^k(p), \varepsilon, f^k(S))]$ is contained in an $f^{k+1}(S)$-neighborhood of $f^{k+1}(p)$. In any case, we always have

$$(2.2c) \quad U(p, f, F) = U(p, f, R) \cup U(p, f, L).$$

When n is not the least period of p, (2.2) needs a slight modification. Let us say a map g *respects side S* at a fixedpoint if the image of every sufficiently small S-neighborhood of p is contained in an S-neighborhood of p (this includes the possibility that some S-neighborhood collapses to p); g *flips side* S if the image of every sufficiently small S-neighborhood of p is a T-neighborhood of p, where $T \neq S$. A map which flips both sides *exchanges sides* at p. In general, a continuous map may neither respect nor flip some side, but map every one-sided neighborhood onto a full neighborhood. However, a piecewise monotone map respects or flips each side at p, giving three possibilities: (i) both sides respected, (ii) one side flipped onto the other, which is respected, or (iii) both sides flipped - that is, exchange of sides. If g exchanges sides at p, then g^2 respects both sides, and then

$$U(p, g, R) = U(p, g, L) = U(p, g^2, R) \cup U(p, g^2, L)$$

and the last two sets may be distinct. Thus, if the least period f^m exchanges sides at p, then for n any even multiple of m a choice of $f^k(S)$ in accordance with (2.2a) leads to $f^m(R) = L$ and vice versa, so that $f^k(S)$ and $f^{k+m}(S)$ represent opposite sides of the same point, $f^k(p)$. The reader can check that this is the only modification needed to make (2.2a,b) valid for any n with $f^n(p) = p$.

The considerations above easily give us

(2.3) <u>*Remark:*</u> *If $f^n(p) = p$ and $S = F$, L or R, then $U(p, f, S)$ is strongly f-invariant; it is a finite union of closed intervals permuted by f. An endpoint of one of these intervals either belongs to a periodic orbit consisting of endpoints, or else is the image under f^k $(k \leq n)$ of a point interior to $U(p, f, S)$, and hence belongs to f-orbits originating arbitrarily near p.*

Before proceeding further with a technical analysis of S-unstable sets, I would like to present another characterization, due to L. Block (Bℓ 8), of maps with all periods a power of 2: the lack of homoclinic points. Recall that an orbit is homoclinic to a fixedpoint p if it is distinct from p but has α- and ω-limit equal to p. In our language in this context, a fixedpoint p of f has a *homoclinic point* if some point interior to one of the sets $U(p, f, S)$, $S = R$ or L hits p under f. A periodic point has a homoclinic point if it has one as a fixedpoint at some power of f.

(2.4) <u>*Theorem*</u> *(Bl 8): If* $f: I \to I$ *is continuous then* f *possesses some period not a power of 2 if and only if some periodic point (which can be chosen with period a power of 2) has a homoclinic point.*

One direction in (2.4) follows from the proof of (1.7) The other direction is a consequence of the following refinement of Block's argument, which we shall use again later:

(2.5) <u>*Lemma:*</u> *If* x *lies between two of its forward images, say* $f^n(x) \leq x < f^m(x)$, $m \neq n > 1$, *then there exists* z, *fixed under* f^2, *such that* $x \in U(z, f, F)$.

<u>*Proof of (2.5)*</u>:

If x has period 1 or 2, $z = x$ works, so assume x, $f(x)$ and $f^2(x)$ are distinct. By adjusting m and n and taking mirror images if necessary, we can assume $f^k(x) > x$ for $k = 1, \cdots, m$, and $n = m + 1$. As in (1.6), take $P = \{f^k(x); k = 0, \cdots, m\}$ partitioning an interval. Some interval $J = [p_L, p_R]$ of the partition satisfies $J \subset f(J)$. Let $z_L \leq z_R \in J$ be the fixedpoints of f^2 nearest the ends of J for which $f(z_i) \in J$. $f(y) - y$ has constant sign on $[p_L, z_L)$ and on $(z_R, p_R]$. Thus, either (i) $f(p_L) < p_L$ so that $f(z_L) = z_L$ and $p_L \in U(z_L, f, L)$, (ii) $f(p_R) > p_R$, so $f(z_R) = z_R$ and $p_R \in U(z_R, f, R)$, or (iii) $f(p_L) \geq p_R$, $f(p_R) \leq p_L$. In the last case, there exist intervals $J_L = [q_L, z_L)$, $J_R = (z_R, q_R]$ such that $f(q_L) = p_R$, $f(q_R) = p_L$ and $f(J_L), f(J_R) \subset J$. In particular, J_L and J_R contain no fixedpoints of f^2, and $f^2(J_L) \supset J_L$, so that

$p_L \in U(z_L, f, L)$.

In any case, $p_S \in U(z_S, f, S)$ for $S = R$ or L, and hence $f^n(x)$, which is an image of x, also belongs to $U(z_S, f, S)$. Since $f^n(x) \leq x < z_S$, $x \in U(z_S, f, S)$. ∎

(2.5a) Remark: *In the argument above, if x is periodic with period exceeding 2, then at least one and hence all of the points on the orbit of x are actually interior to $U(z_S, f, S)$.*

The rest of this section is concerned with the relation between the unstable set $U(p, f, S)$ of a periodic orbit of f and the unstable sets $U(f^k(p), f^n, f^k(S))$ of its individual points, regarded as fixed-points of f^n, and then with the consequences of equality of unstable sets for different points. Much of this is very technical, and is gathered here so that the overall argument in section 4 will be easier to follow. The reader might skim this section and return to it in light of section 4. Because of the central role of the distinction between the two sides of a point, we shall be dealing with pairs (p, S), $p \in \text{Per}(f)$, $S = R$ or L; let us denote the set of these pairs by

$$\Sigma = \text{Per}(f) \times \{R, L\}$$

Note that (2.2a) defines an action of f on Σ.

We begin with a characterization of the components of the unstable set of a periodic orbit. First note

(2.6) Remark: *If $f^n(p) = p$ and $U(f^k(p), f^n, f^k(S)) \subset U(p, f^n, S)$, then these two sets are equal. In particular, this holds if $f^k(p)$ is interior to $U(p, f^n, S)$.*

(2.6) is a simple consequence of (2.2a) together with the strong f^{kn}-invariance of both sets.

(2.7) Proposition: *Suppose $f^n(p) = p$. There exists $r > 0$ such that*

$U(f^k(p), f^n, f^k(S)) = U(f^m(p), f^n, f^m(S))$ if and only if $k \equiv m \bmod r$. The components of the unstable set of the f-orbit of p, $U(p, f, S)$, are described by precisely one of the following:

either (i) each component of $U(p, f, S)$ agrees with $U(f^k(p), f^n, f^k(S))$ for every k in some residue class mod r,

or (ii) $r = 2s$ is even, each component of $U(p, f, S)$ has the form

$$U(f^k(p), f^n, f^k(S)) \cup U(f^{k+s}(p), f^n, f^{k+s}(S)),$$

and the intersection of these two sets separates any f^s-orbit segment in their symmetric difference.

Proof of (2.7):

Since f permutes the sets $U(f^k(p), f^n, f^k(S))$ by (2.2a), the existence of r is clear. Denote the distinct sets $U(f^k(p), f^n, f^k(S))$, $k = 0, \cdots, r-1$ by U_k. (2.6) says that $U_i \subset U_j$ implies their equality. We claim $U_i \cap U_j \neq \phi$ and $U_j \cap U_k \neq \phi$ cannot occur for i, j, k distinct. To see this, note that we can pick i, j, k so that U_i is to the left of U_j and U_k and intersects nothing to its own left. Thus, U_j is between U_i and U_k. But then the power of f taking U_j to U_i takes U_i and U_k to sets which both intersect U_i and lie to its right. Thus, one of these is interior to the union of the others. Since this includes an image of p, (2.6) again says U_i, U_j and U_k are not distinct. Thus, if $U_i \cap U_j \neq \phi$, their union is a component of $U(p, f, S)$ and so $f^s(U_i) = U_j$, $f^s(U_j) = U_i$. In particular, $U_i \cap U_j$ is f^s-invariant and hence separates f^s-orbits in $U_i \triangle U_j$. ∎

(2.7a) Remark: The second case occurs either when s is the least period of p, f^s exchanges sides of p, and each component of $U(p, f, S)$ has the form $U(f^k(p), f^r, R) \cup U(f^k(p), f^r, L)$, or else

when $U_i \cap U_{i+s}$ *is a closed interval whose f-orbit is disjoint from the f-orbit of* p.

For the rest of this section, we find it convenient to adopt the following:

(2.8) *Standing hypothesis:* $f : I \to I$ *is continuous and piecewise monotone.*

Given (2.8), we call two pairs $(p_i, S_i) \in \Sigma$ $(i = 1, 2)$ *m-equivalent* (m = "monotone") if there exists an interval $J \subset I$ which contains an S_i-neighborhood of p_i $(i = 1, 2)$ and such that f^k is monotone on J for every $k > 0$. This is equivalent to saying that all points of J can be assigned the same itinerary with respect to the partition by turning points of f. Note that p_i itself can hit a turning point of f, but in this case one of the sides of p_i is not m-equivalent to any other pair in Σ. Given $(p, S) \in \Sigma$, let $[(p, S)]$ denote the convex hull of periodic points m-equivalent on some side to (p, S). We see that $[(p, S)]$ is an interval with periodic end-points satisfying the properties of J above. In particular, if $[(p, S)]$ is nontrivial, then some power f^r of f maps $[(p, S)]$ monotonically onto itself, and hence f^r exhibits the dynamical behavior described at the start of section 1.

The local behavior of an arbitrary continuous map near a fixedpoint can be quite involved, but as we will see, (2.8) insures that most degeneracies are contained in some m-equivalence class, and hence are relatively simple.

Recall that we have noted already, when $f(p) = p$ and (2.6) holds, that if either side is flipped, then $U(p, f, R) = U(p, f, L)$. Thus, unless f exchanges sides, one can always pick $\tilde{S}$ for any S such that $\tilde{f} = f$ respects S and $U(p, \tilde{f}, \tilde{S}) = U(p, f, S)$. If f exchanges sides, then $\tilde{f} = f^2$ respects both sides: we pick $\tilde{S} = R$ and note that $U(p, f, \tilde{S}) = U(p, f, S) = U(p, \tilde{f}, R) \cup U(p, \tilde{f}, L)$. We distinguish three types of fixedpoint pair:

(2.9) *__Definition:__* *Suppose* $(p, S) \in \Sigma$, $f(p) = p$. *With notation* $\tilde{f}$, $\tilde{S}$ *as above,*

(i) (p, S) *is __degenerate__ if* $[(p, \tilde{S})]$ *is non-trivial.*

(ii) (p, S) *is an __attractor__ if* $[(p, \tilde{S})]$ *and* $U(p, \tilde{f}, \tilde{S})$ *are both trivial.*

(iii) (p, S) *is a __repellor__ if* $[(p, \tilde{S})] = \{p\}$ *and* $U(p, \tilde{f}, \tilde{S})$ *is non-trivial.*

Note that if (p, S) is degenerate, then $U(p, f, S) \subset [(p, \tilde{S})]$. The significance of the terms in (2.9a) is explained by

(2.10) *__Proposition:__* *Assuming (2.6),* $f(p) = p$, *and* f *respects* S *at* p, *there exists an S-neighborhood* V *of* p *such that*

(i) if (p, S) *is an attractor,*

(a) $f(\overline{V}) \subset V$

(b) $\bigcap_n f^n(V) = \{p\}$

(c) V *contains either an endpoint of* I *or a turning point of* f

(ii) if (p, S) *is a repellor,*

(a) $f(V) \supset \overline{V}$

(b) for any $N(p, \delta, S) \subset V$, $U(p, f, S) = \operatorname{clos} \bigcup_n f^n N(p, \delta, S)$.

(c) V *contains a turning point of* f.

__Proof of (2.10)__:

Assume without loss of generality that $S = R$, and let (p, q) be largest subject to the requirement that it contains no turning points of

f. Then q is a turning point of f unless $q = 1$. Any fixedpoint of f in $[p, q]$ is m-equivalent to p, so if p is non-degenerate, $f(x) < x$ or $f(x) > x$ simultaneously for all $x \in (p, q]$. In the first case, $f(q) \in [p,q)$ and so (i) is clear for V some slight enlargement, to the right, of $[p, q]$. In the second case, $q < f(q) \leq 1$ and (iia,c) are clear for $V = [p, q + \varepsilon)$, $0 < \varepsilon < f(q) - q$. To see (iib), we note that as long as $f^{n-1}(p + \delta) \leq q$, we have $p + \delta < f(p + \delta) < \cdots < f^{n-1}(p + \delta) < f^{n}(p + \delta)$, so that $\bigcup_{k\geq 0} f^k N(p,\delta,R) = \bigcup_{k\geq 0} f^k(V)$ for all small δ, and so $U(p,f,S) = \bigcup_{k>0} f^k(V) = \bigcup_{k} f^k N(p,\delta,R)$. ∎

We see from (2.10) that a fixed attractor or repellor behaves topologically like the corresponding hyperbolic fixedpoint, except that some interval may collapse to a point under f and one side may flip onto the other. In the case of an attractor, (b) justifies defining the *basin of attraction* $B(p, S)$ as the largest interval B containing an S-neighborhood of p such that $f(B) \subset B$ and $\bigcap_{n\geq 0} f^n(B) = \{p\}$.

When $(p, S) \in \Sigma$ and p is not fixed, we call (p, S) degenerate, an attractor or a repellor according to which part of (2.9) applies to a power of f fixing p. In the case of a periodic attractor (p, S), the basin of attraction of the f-orbit of (p, S) is the union $B(p, f, S)$ of basins for the points $(f^k(p), f^k(S))$ along that orbit, regarded as fixedpoints of a power of f.

If we recall that a turning point x of f^n is any point such that $f^k(x)$ is a turning point of f for some $k \leq n - 1$, we easily see the following:

(2.10a) *<u>Remarks:</u>* *Assume (2.8).*

(i) If $(p, S) \in \Sigma$ is a periodic attractor (resp. repellor), then $B(p, f, S)$ (resp. $U(p, f, S)$) contains a turning

point of f.

(ii) *If* $(p, S) \varepsilon \Sigma$ *is a periodic repellor of least period* N, *set* $g = f^N$ *unless* f^N *exchanges sides at* p, *in which case set* $g = f^{2N}$. *For any sufficiently small* S*-neighborhood* V *of* p, $g^{n+1}(V) \supset \text{clos}\, g^n(V)$ *for each* $n > 0$.

The second statement above tells us that any interior point q of $U(p, f, S)$ for (p, S) a fixed repellor belongs to all sufficiently high g-images of any S-neighborhood of p. The same need not be true of q an endpoint, if it is periodic (recall (2.3)). However, this restricts the unstable set of q:

(2.11) <u>*Lemma:*</u> *Assume (2.8),* $f(p) = p \neq q \varepsilon \text{Per}(f)$, *and suppose* $U(p, f, S)$ *contains a* T*-neighborhood of* q. *Then either* $U(q, f, T)$ *is trivial or* q *is the image of some interior point of* $U(p, f, S)$.

<u>*Proof of (2.11)*</u>:

We can assume q is an endpoint of $U(p, f, S)$, and taking f^2 or f^4 if necessary, that f respects $S = R$ and $T = L$, and $q > p$ is also fixed. As in the proof of (2.10), take $\varepsilon > 0$ small so that $(q - \varepsilon, q)$ contains no turning points. Reducing $\varepsilon > 0$ further, assume that no turning point of f, $c \varepsilon (p, q)$, satisfies $f(c) \varepsilon (q - \varepsilon, q)$. For all n sufficiently large, (ii) tells us that $f^n [p, q - \varepsilon) \cap (q - \varepsilon, q] \neq 0$. Let $x_n \varepsilon (q - \varepsilon, q]$ denote the right endpoint of this set. If $x_n < q$, then $f(x_n) < x_n$. But if $f(x_n) \neq x_{n+1}$, then $x_{n+1} = f(c)$ for some turning point $c \varepsilon [p, q - \varepsilon)$. Thus, either $x_n = q$ as desired, or else $f^{n+1}[p, q - \varepsilon) = [p, x_{n+1}) \neq [p, x_n)$, contradicting (2.10a ii). ∎

The arguments of section 4 will involve the notion of *h-equivalence*, which holds between two elements of Σ if their unstable sets are equal (h $\simeq$ "homoclinic" à la Newhouse (Ne)). We denote h-equivalence by $(p, S) \sim (q, T)$. The following result, a kind of specification property, will give us a mixing result for the closure of an h-class:

(2.12) ***Proposition:*** *Assume (2.8), and suppose* $p \neq q \in Per(f)$, *p is a fixedpoint, f respects S at p, and*

$$U(p, f, S) = U(q, f, T).$$

Then for any S-neighborhood V of p and any full neighborhood W of q, there exists $N > 0$, *depending on V and W, such that for every* $n \geq N$, *some* $x \in Per(f)$ *satisfies* $x \in V$, $f^n(x) \in W$.

Proof of (2.12):

Note that since (p, S) and (q, T) are h-equivalent elements of different orbits, they must be repellors. Also, we note that either $U(p, f, S)$ is a T-neighborhood of q or else some power of f fixes q and flips T, so that $(q, R) \sim (q, L)$. Thus, we can assume that $S = R$, $V = [p, p + \varepsilon)$, $q > p$, and $W_1 \subset W$ is a T-neighborhood of q contained in $U(p, f, S)$.

Now, assuming $\varepsilon > 0$ small, $f(z) > z$ for every $z \in V$ $(z \neq p)$, and we can decompose V into fundamental domains

$$(p, p + \varepsilon) = \bigcup_{i=1}^{\infty} [p + \varepsilon_{i+1}, p + \varepsilon_i) \underset{\text{def}}{=} \bigcup_{i=0}^{\infty} V_i$$

where $f(V_i) = V_{i-1}$ for $i \geq 1$. By (2.11) some $p_0 \in V_0$ satisfies $f^N(p_0) = q$, and $f^N(V_1)$ contains a T-neighborhood $W_2 \subset W_1$ of q. Similarly, for some $t > 0$ $f^t(W_2) \supset [p, q] \supset V$. Pick $C \subset W_2$ an interval such that $F^t(C) = V$.

Now, for any $k \geq 0$, consider the sequence of intervals

$$\bar{V}_k, \bar{V}_{k-1}, \cdots, \bar{V}_0, f(\bar{V}_0), \cdots, f^{N-1}(\bar{V}_0), C, f(C), \cdots, f^{t-1}(C).$$

The f-image of each contains the next, and $f^t(C) \supset \overline{V}_k$, so by (1.3) and (1.2) there exists $x \in \text{Per}(f)$ such that

$$\begin{aligned} f^i(x) &\in \overline{V}_{k-i} \quad i = 0, \cdots, k \\ f^{j+k}(x) &\in f^j(\overline{V}_0) \ j = 0, \cdots, N-1 \\ f^{m+N+k-1}(x) &\in f^m(C) \quad m = 0, \cdots, t-1. \end{aligned}$$

In particular, $x \in \text{Per}(f)$, $x \in \overline{V}_k \subset V$, and $f^{N+k-1}(x) \in C \subset W$, so (2.12) holds for $n = N + k - 1$, $k = 1, 2, \cdots$. ∎

3. *Nonwandering points*

In this section, we consider some general properties of the nonwandering set $\Omega(f)$ of a continuous map $f : I \to I$. We will not need to assume piecewise monotonicity except in one place. Theorems will be quoted without proof.

Recall that for any dynamical system, a nonwandering point is one that belongs to its own prolongational limit set: $x \in \Omega(f)$ iff there exist $x_n \to x$ such that a subsequence of $\{f^n(x_n)\}$ converges to x. On the interval, "converges" can be replaced by "equals" in this definition, an observation first made by Young (Y 1) in the piecewise-monotone case.

(3.1) <u>*Lemma*</u> *(CN): $x \in \Omega(f)$ for $f : I \to I$ continuous if and only if there exist $x_n \to x$ such that $f^n(x_n) = x$ for a subsequence $n = n_i \to \infty$.*

Of course, $x_n = x$ gives $\text{Per}(f) \subset \Omega(f)$ for any f, and so $\overline{\text{Per}(f)} \subset \Omega(f)$. On the other hand, examples exist [Bℓ 2, Y 1] with $\Omega(f) \neq \overline{\text{Per}(f)}$. One example works as follows: a point x maps to $p > x$, with $f(p) = p$. An R-neighborhood $J_\perp$ of x maps into [p, 1], which is invariant. On the other hand, (p, L) is a repellor with (U(p, f, L) = [x, p]. This means some turning point $c \in U(p, f, L)$ of

f satisfies $f^k(c) = x$. Finally, an L-neighborhood J_- of x maps onto an L-neighborhood $f(J_-) = (p - \varepsilon, p]$ of p, with $p - \varepsilon$ to the right of J_+. Thus, an orbit of J_- returns to $J_- \cup J_+$ at most once, and this image lies in J_+, whose images are far from $J_- \cup J_+$. Hence $x \notin \overline{Per(f)}$, but $x \in f^n J_+$ for all large n, so $x \in \Omega(f)$. We sketch the graph of the map f below:

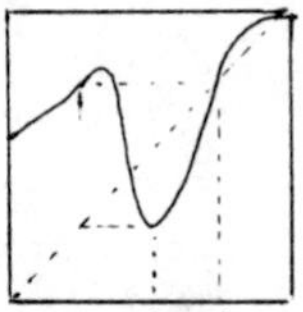

This example can be modified (4.18) so that the orbit of x is infinite (i.e., is not eventually periodic). On the other hand, two things can be said about $x \in \Omega(f) \setminus \overline{Per(f)}$ in some generality:

(3.2a) <u>*Proposition*</u> *(Bℓ 6): If $f : I \to I$ is continuous, then $\Omega(f) \subset \text{clos } EP(f)$, where $EP(f) = \{x | f^k(x) \in Per(f), \text{ some } k \geq 0\}$.*

(3.2b) <u>*Proposition*</u> *(Ni 4): If $f : I \to I$ is continuous and piecewise monotone, and $x \in \Omega(f) \setminus \overline{Per(f)}$, then there are half-neighborhoods J_+ and J_- of x such that $f^n J_+ \cap [J_+ \cup J_-] = \phi$ and $f^n J_- \cap [J_+ \cup J_-] \subset J_+$ for all $n > 0$.*

Even when $\Omega(f) \neq \overline{Per(f)}$, the set $\overline{Per(f)}$ plays an important role. Recall that the *Birkhoff center* of a dynamical system is the limiting set of the transfinite sequence defined by: $\Omega^{\alpha+1} = \Omega(f|\Omega^\alpha)$, $\Omega^0 = \Omega(f)$, and $\Omega^\beta = \bigcap_{\alpha<\beta} \Omega^\alpha$ at limit ordinals. In general, the Birkhoff center is the closure of the recurrent points, and contains $\overline{Per(f)}$; on the interval, these are equal, as shown by Coven-Hedlund:

(3.3a) <u>*Theorem*</u> *(CH 2): For $f : I \to I$ continuous, the Birkhoff center equals $\overline{Per(f)}$.*

The following result, a corollary of (3.26) when (2.8) holds, has recently been shown in general by A. Block (Kharkov), according to M. Jakobson:

(3.3b) <u>*Theorem*</u> *((Ni 4) for piecewise monotone, A. Block in general):* $\overline{Per(f)} = \Omega(f|\Omega(f))$ *for any* $f : I \to I$ *continuous.*

On the other hand, generically the sets $\overline{\mathrm{Per}(f)}$ and $\Omega(f)$ are equal. For $r = 2$, this is a special case of a powerful approximation theorem proven by Jakobson on the circle:

(3.4) <u>*Theorem*</u> *(Ja 1): A* C^2*-dense, open set of maps of the circle and interval satisfy Axiom A and are* C^2*-structurally stable.*

Much more recently, Young (Y 1), via a careful analysis of $\Omega(f) \setminus \overline{\mathrm{Per}(f)}$ for piecewise monotone maps (like 3.26, but predating it), proved the C^r genericity of $\Omega(f) = \overline{\mathrm{Per}(f)}$ for $r \geq 1$. The C^0 case requires slightly different techniques (see (CMN)):

(3.5) <u>*Theorem*</u> *(Ja 1, Y 1, CMN): Every element* f *of a* C^r*-residual set of* C^r *maps* $f : I \to I$*, for every* $r \geq 0$*, satisfies* $\Omega(f) = \overline{Per(f)}$*.*

I would like to mention a result concerning the return-times of a neighborhood of $x \in \Omega(f)$ to itself. It is known in general that a recurrent (resp. periodic) point of f is also recurrent (resp. periodic) under any power of f (i.e., if some subsequence of $f^n x$ converges to (resp. equals) x, this subsequence can be chosen from the multiples of any given positive integer), but examples exist with $\Omega(f^2) \neq \Omega(f)$. One such example (CN) can be obtained from the earlier example by having the R-neighborhood of x collapse to p, the L-neighborhood of x map onto an R-neighborhood of p, and having p exchange sides, again with x a left endpoint of U(p, f, R):

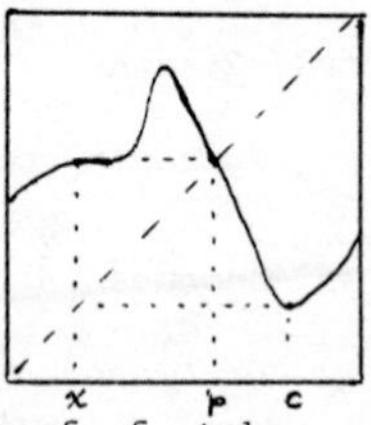

Here, every even iterate of f takes a neighborhood of x into [p, 1], so $x \notin \Omega(f^2)$. The phenomena in this example are for the most part typical of such examples:

(3.6) ***Theorem*** *(CN): Suppose* $f : I \to I$ *continuous and* $x \in \Omega(f)$.

(i) If $x \notin EP(f)$, *then* $x \in \Omega(f^n)$ *for every* n.

(ii) If $x \in EP(f)$, *then* $x \in \Omega(f^n)$ *for every odd* n

Given (i), which is shown by analyzing three successive intersections of a neighborhood of $x \in \Omega(f)$ that wanders under some power of f, (ii) proceeds from the observation that by (3.1) if $x \in \Omega(f)$ and $f^k(x) \in$ (Per(f), then $x \in U(f^k(x), f, S)$ for some side S. If $f^k(x)$ is fixed, we use the analysis of (2.10a), and the general case is reduced to this via an analogue of (2.7).

Related to the observation concerning unstable sets is the following more general result, a corollary of (3.1) and (2.5):

(3.7) ***Proposition****; For* $f : I \to I$ *continuous and any* $x \in \Omega(f)$, *there exists* p *with* $f^2(p) = p$ *and* $x \in U(p, f, F)$.

4. *A spectral decomposition for piecewise-monotone maps*

In this section we analyze the nonwandering set $\Omega(f)$ of a map $f : I \to I$ satisfying the piecewise-monotonicity hypothesis (2.8). This analysis will be carried out by means of a decomposition of the periodic points of f.

We combine the two notions of equivalence for $(p_i, S_i) \in \Sigma$, m-equivalence (when $[(p_1, S_1)] = [(p_2, S_2)]$ is a non-trivial interval on which each power of f is monotone) and h-equivalence (when $U(p_1, f_1 S_1) = U(p_2, f, S_2))$ by defining (p_1, S_1) to be *equivalent* to (p_2, S_2) if either $[(f^k p_1, f^k S_1)] = [p_2, S_2]$ is non-trivial for some k or $U(p_1, f, S) = U(p_2, f, S)$. Note that (p, S) and $(f(p), f(S))$ are equivalent, but (p, R) and (p, L) need not be. Denote the set of equivalence classes in Σ by $\underline{A}$, and if $(p, S) \varepsilon \alpha \varepsilon A$, define the set *accessible* from α as the subset of I

$$A(\alpha) = \{U(p, f, S)\} \cup \{\bigcup_k [f^k(p), f^k(S)]\}.$$

We see from section 2 that at least one of the sets in curly brackets is simply the f-orbit of p. Furthermore, the accessible set $A(\alpha)$ is a finite union of closed intervals, strongly invariant under f. The character of two elements of α in definition (2.9) is the same, so that using (2.10a) we can characterize a class α as an *attractor* if $A(\alpha)$ is trivial, a *repellor* if $A(\alpha)$ contains a turning point of f in its interior, and *degenerate* if the interior of $A(\alpha)$ is nonempty and contains no turning points of f.

(4.1) *__Remarks:__* *(i) If $\alpha \neq \beta$ and $A(\alpha) \supset A(\beta)$, then α is a repellor.*

(ii) The number of attractors is less than or equal to the number of turning points of f.

The second remark is a consequence of (2.10a).

Given $\alpha \varepsilon A$, call the minimum of the least periods of elements of α the *period* of α. Using (2.5a), we obtain

(4.2) *__Lemma:__* *(i) For every $\alpha \varepsilon A$, there exists $\beta \varepsilon A$ with $period(\beta) \leq 2$ and $A(\alpha) \subset A(\beta)$.*

(ii) If $A(\alpha) \subset A(\beta)$, then $period(\beta) \leq 2\, period(\alpha)$.

Proof of (4.2):

(i) is a direct consequence of (2.5a). To see (ii), it suffices to show that period(α) = 1 implies period$(\beta) \leq 2$, that is: if $U(p, f, S)$ contains a fixedpoint of f, then there exists (q, T) equivalent to (p, S) with $f^2(q) = q$. To see this, we look at the proof of (2.5). If J contains a fixedpoint x which belongs to $U(p, f, S)$, then it is easy to see that $p_L \leq z_L \leq x \leq z_R \leq p_R$ implies $z_L, z_R \in U(p, f, S)$. But $p \in U(z_T, f, T)$ for $T = R$ or L, so $z_T = q$. ∎

As a consequence, we have

(4.3) Lemma: *(i) For each n, the set of $\alpha \in A$ with period $\alpha = n$ is finite.*

(ii) For each $\alpha \in A$ there exist only finitely many $\beta \in A$ with $A(\alpha) \subset A(\beta)$.

The first part is the corresponding statement about m-equivalence classes, which we have seen using itineraries with respect to the turning points, while the second follows from (4.2 ii) and (4.3 i).

(4.3) allows us to define a *filtration ordering:* we number the elements of A $\alpha_1, \alpha_2, \cdots$ so that

(4.4) $A(\alpha_i) \supset A(\alpha_j)$ *implies* $i \leq j$.

Now, define a nested sequence of sets M_i, $i = 1, \cdots$, by

(4.5a) $M_i = \bigcup_{j \geq i} A(\alpha_j)$.

It is easy to see the following:

(4.5b) Lemma: *(i)* $\Omega(f) \subset M_1$

(ii) M_i is a finite union of closed intervals, strongly invariant under f.

(iii) If $M_i = M_{i+1}$, then either α_i is an attractor or $M_i = \phi$.

(iv) For each $p \in Per(f)$, *the set of* i *such that* $p \in M_i$ *is finite.*

(v) If M_i *contains no turning points, then there exists* k *finite such that* $M_{i+k} = \phi$, *and* α_{i+j}, $j = o, \cdots, k-1$ *are degenerate or attracting.*

If there are infinitely many elements in A, we define

(4.5c) $M_\infty = \bigcap_{i=1}^{\infty} M_i$

and note:

(4.6) Lemma: *If* A *is infinite, then*

(i) M_∞ *is a nonempty closed invariant set*

(ii) $M_\infty \cap Per(f) = \phi$

(iii) M_∞ *contains the orbit of a turning point of* f.

The sets M_i form something like a filtration, except that the sets M_i map onto themselves, not into their interior. We will use a variant of the difference sets $M_i \setminus M_{i+1}$ to decompose $\Omega(f)$.

(4.7) Remark: *For* $i < \infty$, *if* $p \in Per(f) \cap [M_i \setminus M_{i+1}]$, *then* $(p, S) \in \alpha_i$ *for* $S = R$ *or* L.

Proof of 4.7:

Since M_i and M_{i+1} are intervals, each component of $M_i \setminus M_{i+1}$ is a nontrivial interval. Thus, $M_i \setminus M_{i+1}$ contains an S-neighborhood of p for $S = R$ or L. Since M_i is invariant, $A(p, S) \subset M_i$ and so $(p, S) \in \alpha_j$ with $j \geq i$. If $j > i$, then $p \in A(\alpha_i) \subset M_{i+1}$, contradicting the hypothesis. ∎

The converse is true with the exception that an endpoint p of M_{i+1} might belong to α_i, either if α_i is an attractor so that $M_i = M_{i+1}$, or if one side S of p points into the interior of $M_i \setminus M_{i+1}$ and $(p, L) \neq (p, R)$, with $(p, S) \in \alpha_i$.

(4.8) Remarks: (i) *If p is an endpoint of M_i and $M_i \setminus M_{i+1}$ is an S-neighborhood of p, then either $(p, S) \in \alpha_i$ or else $p = f^k(c)$ for some $k > 0$ and some turning point $c \in M_i \setminus M_{i+1}$ of f.*

(ii) *If p is an endpoint of M_{i+1} and $M_i \setminus M_{i+1}$ is an S-neighborhood of p, then either $(p, S) \in \alpha_i$ or else there exists an S-neighborhood $V(p)$ of p such that $f^k(V(p)) \subset M_{i+1}$ for some $k > 0$, and $f^i(V(p)) \subset V(f^i(p))$ for $i < k$.*

Proof of (4.8):

In light of (2.3), the only part of (i) that needs proof is that $c \in M_i \setminus M_{i+1}$. But invariance of M_i and $f^k(c) = p$ implies $c \in M_i$, while invariance of M_{i+1} and $p \notin M_{i+1}$ implies $c \notin M_{i+1}$. To prove (ii), suppose $(p, S) \notin \alpha_i$. If $p \notin \text{Per}(f)$, then some image of p is interior to M_{i+1}, and taking k the least such, a choice of $V(p)$ is easy. If $(p, S) \in \alpha_j$ for some $j > i$, then either α_j is an attractor and $V(p)$ is given by (2.10), or $f^k(p) = p$ and f^k flips a small S-neighborhood into the interior of M_{i+1}. ∎

Now, define

(4.9) a) $\text{Per}(i) = \{p \mid (p, S) \in \alpha_i \text{ for } S = R \text{ or } L\}$

b) $\Omega_i = \text{clos Per}(i)$

c) $N_i = M_i \setminus [M_{i+1} \cup \bigcup\{V(p) : p \in \partial M_{i+1} \setminus \text{Per}(i)\}] \cup \text{Per}(i)$

Definitions (a) and (b) are clear; in (c) N_i is a closed subset of $M_i \setminus \text{int } M_{i+1}$ containing Per(i) and excluding a neighborhood of any endpoint of M_{i+1} which is not in Per(i). From (4.8 ii) we see that $f(N_i) \supset N_i$. Define

(4.9 d) $K_i = \bigcap_{n \geq 0} f^{-n} N_i = \{x \mid f^n(x) \in N_i \text{ for } n = 0, 1, \cdots\}$.

Clearly,

(4.10) $\Omega_i \subset \Omega(f) \cap N_i = \Omega(f) \cap K_i$.

We would like to establish the extent to which (4.10) is an equality:

(4.11) <u>*Proposition:*</u> *If* $x \in \Omega(f)$ *and* x *is interior to* $M_i \setminus M_{i+1}$, *then* $x \in \Omega_i$.

<u>*Proof of (4.11):*</u>

By (4.7), $x \in \Omega_i$ iff $x \in \overline{\text{Per}(f)}$. If $x \notin \overline{\text{Per}(f)}$, then (3.2b) gives $J = J_+ \cup J_- \subset M_i \setminus M_{i+1}$ a neighborhood of x such that $f^n J_+ \cap J = \phi$ for all $n > 0$ and $f^n J_- \cap J = J_+$ for infinitely many $n > 0$. Consider the set $G = \bigcup \{f^n J_-; n > 0\}$ and note that $x \in G$ is an endpoint of the component G_0 of G containing it. G_0 is a closed nontrivial interval, and $f^n G_0 \subset G_0$ whenever $f^n G_0 \cap G_0 \neq \phi$. Note that $G_0 \subset M_i$. Since this occurs for many $n > 0$, there exists $N > 0$ (the least such n) such that $f^k G_0 \cap G_0 = \phi$ if k is not multiple of N. Thus, $x \in \Omega(f^N | G_0)$, and by (3.7) some periodic point $p \in G_0$ satisfies $x \in U(p, f^N, S)$. Since $x \notin M_{i+1}$, $p \in \alpha_i$, so that $J_- \subset M_i \setminus M_{i+1} \subset U(p, f^N, S)$. But p is the image of some $q \in J_-$, with a one-sided neighborhood of q inside J_- mapping onto an S-neighborhood of p. But then J_- eventually maps across itself, and $J_- \cap \text{Per}(f) \neq \phi$, a contradiction. ∎

(4.11a) <u>*Corollary:*</u> $\Omega(f) \cap N_i = \Omega_i$ *unless* $M_i \setminus M_{i+1}$ *contains a turning point of* f. *If equality does not hold for some* i, *the points of* $\Omega(f) \setminus \Omega_i$ *in* N_i *are endpoints of* M_i *not in* M_{i+1}. *Thus,* $M_\infty \cup \bigcup_{i<\infty} \Omega_i$ *contains all but a finite number of points in* $\Omega(f)$.

We would like to say something about the structure of the sets Ω_i. Note that each such set is closed and invariant, and $\Omega_i \cap \Omega_j$ is empty unless some endpoint of M_j has $(p,S) \in \alpha_j$, $(p,T) \in \alpha_i$ for $T \neq S$; in particular, $\Omega_i \cap \Omega_j$ is finite. If α_i is degenerate or an attractor, it is clear that $\Omega_i = \mathrm{Per}(i)$, and that in this case Ω_i consists only of points of least period equal to n = period α_i, unless α_i is degenerate and f^n exchanges sides for some $(p, S) \in \alpha_i$, in which case every orbit in Ω_i other than that of p has least period $2n$.

When α_i is a repellor, it may consist of a single orbit, or it may have a "chaotic" structure. When $M_i \setminus M_{i+1}$ is nontrivial and contains no turning points in its interior, this structure is easy to see. Note that in this case each component of N_i maps monotonically onto any component intersecting its image, and so using the components of N_i as vertices, we can set up a Markov graph describing all itineraries in K_i. Thus, we have a topological Markov chain as a factor of K_i, via a semi-conjugacy which is a one-to-one correspondence between components of K_i and sequences. Since no two points of $\mathrm{Per}(i)$ are monotone equivalent and the interior of an interval disjoint from its images wanders, this semi-conjugacy is one-to-one over eventually periodic points and at most two-to-one over infinite orbits. Thus:

(4.12) Proposition: There are at most finitely many i such that $M_i \setminus M_{i+1}$ contains a turning point of f in its interior. For any other finite i, Ω_i is either (i) degenerate, (ii) a non-degenerate periodic orbit, or else (iii) a cantor set with a semi-conjugacy onto a nontrivial subshift of finite type which is at most two-to-one, and is injective on $\mathrm{Per}(i)$.

(4.12a) Remark: This last statement also holds when every turning point in $M_i \setminus M_{i+1}$ eventually maps into the interior of M_{i+1}; note that then α_i is not degenerate.

When N_i contains the orbit of a turning point, then a component of N_i may map across part but not all of some component, or may be non-monotone, and we cannot claim (4.12). Nonetheless, something can be said.

We will show Ω_i is topologically transitive, in fact we will prove a mixing property. These proofs are independent of (4.12), so will clarify the character of the irreducible parts of the Markov chain in (4.12 iii).

(4.12) *Proposition:* *Each set* Ω_i *for which* α_i *is nondegenerate has a finite decomposition into closed disjoint sets*

$$\Omega_i = \Omega_{i1} \cup \cdots \cup \Omega_{in}$$

which are permuted cyclically by f, *and* $f^n|\Omega_{ij}$ *is topologically transitive. Furthermore, either* f^n *is topologically mixing on each set* Ω_{ij}, *or else there is a further decomposition of each* Ω_{ij} *into two parts*

$$\Omega_{ij} = \Omega_{ij}^1 \cup \Omega_{ij}^2$$

which intersect at a single point, are exchanged by f^n, *and* f^{2n} *is topologically mixing on each* Ω_{ij}^k.

Proof of (4.13):

First suppose Ω_i contains a fixedpoint (p, S) for which f respects S. We know that $U(p, f, S)$ is a single interval; we want to show f topologically mixing on Ω_i: that is, given $x, y \in \Omega_i$, and neighborhoods V, W of x and y, we need to find N such that $f^n[V \cap \Omega_i] \cap W \cap \Omega_i$ is nonempty for every $n \geq N$. Note that V and W contain points of $\mathrm{Per}(i)$, so we can assume x and $y \in \mathrm{Per}(i)$. If $x = p$, then $y = q$ in (2.12) gives us the required N, since the periodic points given by (2.12) must belong to $\mathrm{Per}(i)$ (hence to Ω_i) in light of (4.7). If $y = p$, then taking $x = q$ in (2.12) and noting that these same periodic orbits satisfy $z \in C \subset W$, $f^t(z) \in \overline{V}_k \subset V$, $f^{t+k}(z) \in \overline{V}_0 \subset V$, we have the required intersection with $N = t$. Finally, note that for any $n > 0$ and $\tilde{V}$ an S-neighborhood of p, $f^{n+1}(\tilde{V} \cap \Omega_i) \supset f^n(\tilde{V} \cap \Omega_i)$, and exercising a little care, we can also insure that given q, the f^k-image of $V \cap \Omega_i$ contains $\tilde{V} \cap \Omega_i$ for some k. Thus, given $x, y \in \alpha_i$, we find that given V and W, $f^k(V \cap \Omega_i) \supset \tilde{V} \cap \Omega_i$, and for all $n > N$, $f^n(\tilde{V} \cap \Omega_i) \cap W \cap \Omega_i \neq \phi$, so that mixing follows.

In case Ω_i contains a fixedpoint p but f exchanges sides at p, we consider $U(p, f^2, S)$ for $S = R$ and L. If they are the same, then the argument above still gives mixing; if they are different, then they intersect only at p and we let Ω_i^k, $k = 1, 2$ be the intersection of Ω_i with each. Then f^2 respects each side and so is mixing on Ω_i^k.

In general, we pick $p \in \mathrm{Per}(i)$ with smallest period, say n. Note that f^{2n} respects some side S of p with $(p, S) \in \alpha_i$. Consider the components of $U(p, f, S)$ in light of (2.7). If each component agrees with $U(f^k(p), f^{2n}, f^k(S))$ for some k (case (i) in 2.7), we define Ω_{ij}, $j = 1, \cdots, r$ as the intersection of Ω_i with the components of $U(p, f, S)$. If each component has the form $U(f^k(p), f^{2n}, f^k(S)) \cup U(f^{k+s}(p), f^{2n}, f^{k+s}(S))$, then we ask about the intersection of these sets, using remark (2.7a). If the intersection is disjoint from the orbit of p, we note that any periodic point in this intersection has period less than that of p, and hence does not belong to α_i. We can therefore assert that the intersection contains or is contained in an open set disjoint from Ω_i, so that we obtain again $r = 2s$ disjoint sets Ω_{ij}, each equal to $\Omega_i \cap U(f^k(p), f^{2n}, f^k(S))$ for some k. In both these cases, f^{2n} has a fixedpoint in Ω_i for which it respects a side. But the number of pieces is r, which is in general not $2n$, and we must show f^r mixing. In the final case, when two unstable sets intersect in an image of p whose sides are exchanged, the components of $U(p, f, S)$ define Ω_{ij} $j = 1, \cdots, s$ and the two pieces Ω_{ij}^1 and Ω_{ij}^2 are the intersections with unstable sets under f^{2n}.

To show f^r mixing in case $r < 2n$ in the first case above, note that we know $2n = kr$, and setting $g = f^r$, can show that $g^{k\ell}(V \cap \Omega_i) \cap W \cap \Omega_i \neq \phi$ for all large ℓ. Note, however, that this is true for $V_0 = V$, $V_1 = g(V)$, $\cdots$, $V_{k-1} = g^{k-1}(V)$ and any W simultaneously, so that really for every $m = k\ell + j$, $0 \leq j < k$ and any ℓ sufficiently large, we have

$$\phi \neq g^{k\ell}(V_j \cap \Omega_i) \cap W \cap \Omega_i = g^{k\ell+j}(V \cap \Omega_i)$$

and thus $g = f^r$ is mixing.

Finally, of course, topological transitivity is an easy consequence of mixing. ∎

Next, we turn to the structure of M_∞, when A is infinite. Note that f acts on the components of each M_i as a permutation π_i, and so we can decompose M_i into disjoint closed invariant subsets M_{ij}, each a union of components of M_i on which π_i is transitive. Considerations as in (4.5 v) say that any M_{ij} which contains no turning point of f must be disjoint from M_∞. Suppose there are t turning points for f; then for any i, at most t of the sets M_{ij} intersect M_∞; we can ignore the rest, or simply assume they don't exist, for purposes of analyzing M_∞. Furthermore, since the number of "pieces" in M_{i+1} is at least that in M_i, there must be some i_0 such that the number of relevant pieces M_{ij} is independent of i provided $i \geq i_0$. We can assume $i_0 = 1$, let n be the number of relevant pieces,

$$M_i = M_{i1} \cup \cdots \cup M_{in}$$

and assume the numbering is such that $M_{(i+1)j} \subset M_{ij}$ for every i and j. We decompose M_∞ into sets $M_{\infty j}$ according to

$$M_{\infty j} = \bigcap_i M_{ij}.$$

We note that each M_{ij} contains the orbit of a turning point of f, for $i = 1, 2, \cdots$, and hence for $i = \infty$. We will analyze a single set $M_{\infty j}$; thus, we drop the subscript j for convenience.

Note that the number of components of M_{i+k} inside a given component of M_i depends only on i and k, not the component. This number must grow without bound as k grows for i fixed, otherwise it is eventually constant and some power of some permutation, π_j^n, fixes all components of M_j, for $j = j_0$ and also for all $j > j_0$. This would imply that M_∞ has a periodic point, contrary to (4.6). Thus, we can pick a subsequence $i_k \to \infty$ such that $M_{i_{k+1}}$ has $n_k \geq 2$ components inside each component of M_{i_k}. We can take $i_k = k$. Note that n_k may well vary with k.

We will model the dynamics of M_∞ by generalizing the "adding machine" example in section 2.

Start by numbering the components of M_1

$$C_0^1, C_1^1, \cdots, C_{n_1-1}^1$$

in such a way that $f(C_i^1) = C_{\pi(i)}^1$, $\pi(i) = i + 1 \mod n_1$. Now, each C_i^1 contains $n_2 \geq 2$ components of M_2. These will be labelled by pairs of numbers, C_{ij}^2, where $0 \leq j \leq n_2 - 1$. The numbering is done as follows: pick

$$C_{00}^2 \subset C_0^1$$

arbitrary. Now, for $i = 1, \cdots, n_1 - 1$,

$$f^i(C_{00}^2) \subset C_i^1;$$

let this component of M_2 be labelled with $j = 0$

$$f^i(C_{00}^2) = C_{i0}^2 .$$

Now,

$$f(C_{n_1-1,\,0}^2) \subset C_0^1$$

is distinct from C_{00}^2, so label it C_{01}^2.

We proceed with this numbering so that

$$f(C_{ij}^2) = \begin{cases} C_{i+1,\,j}^2 & \text{if} \quad i < n_1 - 1 \\ C_{0,\,j+1}^2 & \text{if} \quad i = n_1 - 1 \text{ and } j < n_2 - 1 \\ C_{00}^2 & \text{if} \quad i = n_1 - 1,\ j = n_2 - 1 . \end{cases}$$

This defines a cyclic map ϕ_2 on pairs

$(i, j) \in \{0, \cdots, n_1 - 1\} \times \{0, \cdots, n_2 - 1\}$

$$\phi_2(i, j) = \begin{cases} i + 1, j & i < n_1 - 1 \\ 0, j + 1 & i = n_1 - 1, j < n_2 - 1 \\ 0, \quad 0 & i = n_1 - 1, j = n_2 - 1 . \end{cases}$$

In general, having labelled the components of M_k with k-tuples $\underline{g} = g_1, \cdots, g_k$, $0 \le g_i \le n_i - 1$, so that $f(C^k_{\underline{g}}) = C^k_{\phi_k(\underline{g})}$, we label the components of M_{k+1} by (k+1)-tuples $\underline{g}, j$ so that

$$C^{k+1}_{\underline{g}\, j} \subset C^k_{\underline{g}} \qquad \text{for all } j$$

$$f\, C^{k+1}_{\underline{g}\, j} = C^{k+1}_{\phi_{k+1}(\underline{g},\, j)}$$

where

$$\phi_{k+1}(\underline{g}, j) = \begin{cases} \phi_k(\underline{g}), j & \text{if } \phi_k(\underline{g}) \neq 0, \cdots, 0 \\ 0, j + 1 & \text{if } \phi_k(\underline{g}) = 0, \cdots, 0 \end{cases}$$

and $j + 1$ is taken mod n_{k+1}.

The map ϕ_k is a cyclic permutation on $N_k = n_1 \cdot n_2 \cdot \ldots \cdot n_k$ objects, and so can be regarded as a translation in the cyclic group $G_k = \mathbb{Z}/N_k\mathbb{Z}$. The maps $p_k : G_k \to G_{k-1}$, defined by taking initial strings of coordinates, are surjective homomorphisms commuting with the ϕ's. Thus, we have an inverse limit system

$$\begin{array}{ccccc} & \vdots & & \vdots & \\ & \downarrow & & \downarrow & \\ & G_k & \xrightarrow{\phi_k} & G_k & \\ p_k & \downarrow & & \downarrow & p_k \\ & G_{k-1} & \xrightarrow{\phi_{k-1}} & G_{k-1} & \\ p_{k-1} & \downarrow & & \downarrow & p_{k-1} \\ & \vdots & & \vdots & \\ p_2 & \downarrow & & \downarrow & p_2 \\ & G_1 & \xrightarrow{\phi_1} & G_1 & \end{array}$$

whose inverse limit $\phi : G_\infty \to G_\infty$ is a translation on an infinite group. When $n_k = 2$ for all k, this is the "adding machine" we saw before; we call this general model the *generalized adding machine* (or abacus?). Elements of G_∞ are infinite sequences

$$\underline{g} = g_1, g_2, \cdots$$

where $0 \le g_i \le n_i - 1$ for each i, $n_i \ge 2$. The map ϕ is defined by the following rule: given $\underline{g}$, let i, $1 \le i \le \infty$ be the first place in which $g_i < n_i - 1$. Then

$$\begin{aligned} \phi(\underline{g}) &= \phi(n_1 - 1, n_2 - 1, \cdots, n_{i-1} - 1, g_i, g_{i+1}, \cdots) \\ &= (0, 0, \cdots, 0, g_i + 1, g_{i+1}, \cdots). \end{aligned}$$

It is evident that this map reflects the action of f on components of M_∞, which can be labelled by

$$C^\infty_{\underline{g}} = \bigcap_{k=1}^{\infty} C^k_{g_1 \cdots g_k} .$$

In fact, G_∞ can be given the topology of the cantor set by taking the inverse limit of the discrete topologies on the G_k; then the map assigning $\underline{g}$ to every $x \in C^\infty_{\underline{g}}$ is a semiconjugacy of $f|M_\infty$ onto $\phi|G_\infty$. Thus, we have shown

(4.14) <u>Theorem:</u> If A is infinite, then M_∞ has a decomposition into disjoint closed sets

$$M_\infty = M_{\infty 1} \cup \cdots \cup M_{\infty k} .$$

For each j, $M_{\infty j}$ is an invariant set containing some turning point of f which has a generalized adding machine

$$\phi_j : G_{\infty j} \to G_{\infty j}$$

as a factor. The semiconjugacy is bijective on components.

The properties of the model $\phi_j|G_{\infty j}$ have been studied by Eberlein (Eb): he shows that ϕ_j is a homeomorphism which is minimal (every orbit is dense) and uniquely ergodic (there is a unique ϕ_j invariant Borel probability measure on $G_{\infty j}$).

We note that the semiconjugacy $h: M_{\infty j} \to G_{\infty j}$ is injective on components, and since the forward images of any component in this set are disjoint, any component of M_∞ which is not a single point is an interval with wandering interior. Thus,

$$\Omega_{\infty j} = M_{\infty j} \cap \Omega(f)$$

is mapped at most $2:1$ to $G_{\infty j}$ by h. Furthermore, we note that any component of M_i contains a periodic point of f; this implies the observation below:

(4.15) Lemma: (i) Each component of M_∞ has at least one endpoint in $\overline{Per(f)}$.

We will see an example shortly with $\Omega_\infty \setminus \overline{Per(f)}$ infinite. However, we can say the following:

(4.16) Proposition: For each j:

(i) $\Omega_{\infty j} = M_{\infty j} \cap \Omega(f)$ is a cantor set containing the ω-limit set of some turning point of f (in M_∞);

(ii) If $M_{\infty j}$ is totally disconnected (so $\Omega_{\infty j} = M_{\infty j}$) or if there are no endpoints common to a subsequence of the $M_{\infty j}$, then $\Omega_{\infty j} \subset \overline{Per(f)}$.

(iii) In particular, if (ii) holds for each j, then $\Omega(f) \setminus \overline{Per(f)}$ is finite.

The preceding results are summarized in

(4.17) Decomposition Theorem (c.f. (JoR 3, 5, Hof 3-5))

Suppose $f: I \to I$ is continuous and piecewise monotone. Then the nonwandering set $\Omega(f)$ has a finite or countable decomposition into closed invariant sets

$$\Omega(f) = \tilde{\Omega}_1 \cup \cdots \cup \tilde{\Omega}_N, \qquad N \leq \infty.$$

The pairwise intersections in this decomposition are finite.

Let $\Omega_i = \tilde{\Omega}_i \cap \overline{Per(f)}$, $F_i = \tilde{\Omega}_i \setminus \Omega_i$.

1. *For each* $i < \infty$

a) F_i *is finite*

b) Ω_i *has a finite decomposition*

$$\Omega_i = \Omega_{i1} \cup \cdots \cup \Omega_{in}$$

into disjoint closed sets permuted cyclically by f. *Each* Ω_{ij} *is either*

(i) *the set of fixedpoints of* f^{2n} *on an interval where* f^n *is monotone*

or (ii) *a set with a dense* f^{2n} *orbit. In this case, either* $f^n|\Omega_{ij}$ *is topologically mixing or* $f^{2n}|\Omega_{ij}^k$ $(k = 1, 2)$ *is topologically mixing, where* $\Omega_{ij} = \Omega_{ij}^1 \cup \Omega_{ij}^2$ *are sets meeting at a unique point and interchanged under* f.

2. *If there are infinitely many* Ω_i, *then* $\Omega_\infty \neq \phi$ *has a finite decomposition into closed invariant sets*

$$\Omega_\infty = \Omega_{\infty 1} \cup \cdots \cup \Omega_{\infty k}$$

each having a generalized adding machine as a factor, and containing the ω*-limit set of some turning point of* f.

We close this section with a few comments on the relation of (4.17) to results of Jonker-Rand (Jo, JoR 3,5) and Hofbauer (Hof 3-5).

Hofbauer has discovered a similar structure in his study of piecewise monotone maps. He allows f to have jump discontinuities at the "turning" points, and starts with a finite partition which he assumes to be a generator (i.e., itineraries separate points). Note that this excludes the possibility of attractors, non-trivial monotone classes, and "homtervals" (see below). He then moves to the level of symbolic dynamics, and analyzes the structure of the set of itineraries for f.

The announced version of his theorem which I have seen* overlooks the possibility of points in $\Omega(f) \setminus \overline{\mathrm{Per}(f)}$. Hofbauer's primary interest is in the measures which maximize entropy (see 5.8), for which points outside the Birkhoff center are irrelevant.

Jonker and Rand proved the first theorem of this decomposition type. They studied a map $f : I \to I$ which is C^1, has a single turning point, and for which the endpoints of I form an invariant set. These conditions are satisfied by the "quadratic map" $f_a(x) = 4ax(1 - x)$, $0 < a \leq 1$, among others. The work of Jonker-Rand is carried out in the language of the *kneading calculus* originally formulated by Milnor-Thurston (MiT) in a widely circulated but as yet unpublished manuscript, treated in print briefly by Guckenheimer (G 4) and Jonker-Rand (Jo, JoR 5), and in more leisurely fashion by Collet and Eckmann (CE 1). A similar formalism seems to have been discovered independently by Simonov (Si).

The kneading calculus is an elaboration of symbolic dynamics. Suppose $f : I \to I$ is piecewise monotone, with turning points $0 < C_1 < C_2 < \cdots < C_n < 1$. As before, consider the partition induced by turning points and the corresponding itineraries, but with a few changes. First, remove the ambiguity at turning points by introducing some new symbols: thus, set $J_1 = [0, C_1)$, $J_i = (C_{i-1}, C_i)$ for $0 \quad i \leq n$,

*As this paper is being typed, I have received a corrected version of (Hof 5).

$J_{n+1} = (C_n, 1]$, but reserve extra symbols C_i for the turning points themselves. Second, assign to each symbol J_i a sign according to the direction of monotonicity of $f|J_i : \varepsilon(J_i) = +1$ if f is increasing on J_i, $\varepsilon(J_i) = -1$ if f is decreasing on J_i. (Here, assume f increasing on J_1, otherwise reverse the definition.) Finally, to each itinerary $\underline{a} = \{a_i\}_{i=0}^{\infty}$ assign a signed version of $\underline{a}$, called the *invariant coordinate* of $\underline{a}$: $\theta(\underline{a}) = \{\theta_i\}$, where $\theta_0 = +a_0$, and $\theta_i = \varepsilon(a_0) \cdot \ldots \cdot \varepsilon(a_{i-1}) \cdot a_i$ (if $a_j = C_k$ for some $j < i$, set $\theta_i = +a_i$). Thus $\theta(\underline{a})$ is a sequence of symbols $\pm J_i$, $\pm C_i$; note that any two addresses $\underline{a}$, $\underline{b}$ with $a_i = b_i = C_k$ for some i must have $a_j = b_j$ for all $j > i$. We order the invariant coordinates lexicographically, with the understanding that

$$-J_{n+1} < -C_n < -J_n < \cdots < -C_1 < -J_1 < +J_1 < +C_1 < \cdots < +J_{n+1}.$$

The basic observation, then, is that this order on invariant coordinates respects the order of points they represent: if we denote the invariant coordinate of $x \in I$ by $\theta(x)$, then $x \leq y$ iff $\theta(x) \leq \theta(y)$ so that the shift on invariant coordinates

$$\theta(x) = (a_0, \pm a_1, \cdots) \to \theta(f(x)) = \varepsilon(a_0) \cdot (\pm a_1, \cdots)$$

is a representation of the action of f on itineraries which also respects the linear order of points.

In the case of a quadratic-like map as considered by Jonker-Rand, with a single turning point $0 < C < 1$, we have either a maximum or a minimum at C. If we assume a maximum, $f(C) \geq f(x)$ for every $x \in I$, and hence the highest invariant coordinate that can appear is that of $f(C)$, which is called the *kneading invariant* of f, $\nu(f) = \theta(f(C))$. Using the order properties of θ, one can nearly determine the invariant coordinates that occur at all, and it turns out that (if $f(0) = f(1) = 0$) the whole structure is determined by the kneading invariant.

In particular, if one considers the series defined by $\Sigma\, \nu_i t^i$, where $\nu(f) = \nu_0, \nu_1, \cdots$, its radius of convergence, r, if positive, determines a unique map F_r which is piecewise linear with $F_r(0) = F_r(1) = 0$ $C = 1/2$, and slope $\pm 1/r$ on $[0, 1/2]$ and $[1/2, 1]$. In fact, if f is C^1, the map $x \to (r - 1) \sum_{i=0}^{\infty} \theta_i(x)\, r^i$ is a monotone semiconjugacy of f onto F_r.

Jonker-Rand analyze the structure of $\nu(f)$, and find a "decomposition" of the sequence, reflecting the way that the orbit γ of C can be partitioned by intervals whose intersections with γ are permuted. They use this decomposition and the semiconjugacy above to obtain the decomposition we call $\tilde{\Omega}_i$.

Note that if there is only one turning point, then there is a unique set in the decomposition to which (4.12) does not apply. If there exists an attractor, the turning point belongs to its basin of attraction and it is unique. In this case, there are finitely many $\tilde{\Omega}_i$, each equals Ω_i and is described by (4.12). If the turning point belongs to $M_i \setminus M_{i+1}$ for some $i < \infty$, then by (4.5 v) M_{i+1} contains a finite number of pieces Ω_j with $j > i$. Each of these is degenerate or attracting and touches the boundary of M_{i+1}, since the latter contains no nontrivial minimal sets. In the attracting case, or if the turning point falls into the interior of an m-class, $\tilde{\Omega}_i = \Omega_i$ can still be modelled as in 4.12. If the orbit of the turning point is contained in $M_i \setminus M_{i+1}$, the situation is somewhat more delicate, although we can assert that $\Omega(f) \setminus \overline{Per(f)}$ is finite, since it is a subset of the endpoints of M_i.

The most delicate situation, however, is when there are infinitely many distinct pieces $\tilde{\Omega}_i$, so that $\Omega_\infty \neq \phi$. We describe an example which shows that, even with one turning point, it is possible that Ω_∞ contains an entire orbit (which is necessarily infinite) outside the Birkhoff center.

(4.18) <u>Remark:</u> A piecewise-monotone map with $\Omega_\infty = \phi$ *(i.e.,* $\Omega(f)$ *has a finite decomposition) has only finitely many nonwandering points outside the Birkhoff center. On the other hand, there exists an example of* $f : I \to I$ *continuous with one turning point and* $\Omega_\infty \setminus \overline{Per(f)}$ *containing a whole (infinite) forward orbit.*

<u>*Construction of (4.18)*</u>

The example is a variation on the earlier example of a map possessing the periods 2^k, $k = 0, 1, \cdots$ and nothing else. Note that the process we described to create such an example in section 1 yields an infinite set of turning points. But if we modify the recursive step so as to reverse the map before re-scaling (that is, compose with $x \to 1 - x$), then the process yields a sequence $g_i \to g_\infty$ with a single turning point. The graph of $g = g_\infty$ is sketched below:

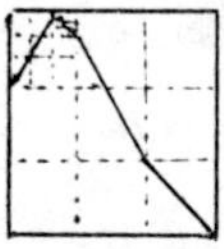

Note the following properties of g:

(i) The turning point $c = 1/3 - 1/9 + 1/27 - \cdots = 1/4$ maps to 1.

(ii) $M_1 = I$ and M_{i+1} is obtained from M_i by deleting the middle third of each component. Thus an endpoint of M_i is also an endpoint of M_j for all $j \geq i$, and these points constitute the images under g of c.

(iii) Each component of $M_i \setminus M_{i+1}$ contains a single periodic point, which is its midpoint and has period 2^{i-1}. It is an orientation-reversing source.

(iv) The map g is linear on each component of $M_i \setminus M_{i+1}$; the slope is ± 1 except on one component, J_i, where it equals $\pm 5/3$. The turning point is interior to M_i for all $i < \infty$.

Thus, M_∞ is precisely the middle-third cantor set, and g is a homeomorphism of M_∞ onto itself. We denote $g^k(c)$ by x_k, $i = 0, 1, 2, \cdots$, and denote by x_{-k}, $k = 1, 2, \cdots$, the unique point in M_∞ with $g^k(x_{-k}) = c$. For $i < \infty$, M_i has 2^{i-1} components and 2^i endpoints: thus by (ii) x_k is an endpoint of M_i whenever $2^i > k > 0$. Suppose M_i is an S_k-neighborhood of x_k and $I \setminus M_i$ is a T_k-neighborhood. By (iii) and (iv) every T_k-neighborhood J_- of x_k has images under g which include a component of some M_j, $j >> i$, and hence by full invariance of M_j, there exist arbitrarily high images of J_- which include c and hence other images which are S_k-neighborhoods of x_k.

Now, consider a perfect set K_∞ whose components are in one-to-one order-preserving correspondence with those of the middle-third cantor set M_∞, such that the component corresponding to x_k is a non-trivial interval J_k and all other components are points. We suppose $0 \in J_2$ and $1 \in J_1$ (remember $x_1 = 1$, $x_2 = 0$). If J_k $(k \in \mathbb{Z})$ lies to the right of J_0, define $f : J_k \to J_{k+1}$ an orientation-reversing affine map, while if J_k lies to the left of J_0, map it to J_{k+1} preserving orientation. Define $f : J_0 \to J_1$ quadratic-like so that both endpoints of J_0 go to the left endpoint of J_1 and the midpoint c' of J_0 goes to 1. Extend f to the complement of these intervals continuously so that K_∞ maps to K_∞, f is strictly increasing to the left of c' and strictly decreasing to the right, and the correspondence with M_∞ is a semi-conjugacy with $g|M_\infty$. Then f is C^0, piecewise monotone, with unique turning point $c' \in J_0$, and there is a semi-conjugacy $h : I \to I$ of f to g $(g \circ h = h \circ f)$ which is one-to-one except that $h(J_k) = x_k$, $k \in \mathbb{Z}$. From this, it is evident that f has a pseudo-filtration given by $\tilde{M}_i = h^{-1}M_i$. Each interval J_k, $k > 0$ has one endpoint $a_k = f^k(c')$ which is an endpoint of $\tilde{M}_i$ for $2^{i-1} > k$ and another, b_k, which is interior to all $\tilde{M}_i$, $i < \infty$. Any T_k-neighborhood J_- of a_k maps under h to a T_k-neighborhood of x_k. Thus, some image of J_- contains c' and hence some high image of J_- is an S_k-neighborhood of a_k. On the other hand, $J_+ = J_k$ remains in $\tilde{M}_i$ and never intersects itself. Thus we have precisely the behavior described in (3.2b), and $a_k \in \Omega(f) \setminus \overline{Per(f)}$ for all $k > 0$. ∎

(4.18) illustrates the fact that the semiconjugacies of (4.17) may really fail to be injective. We have certainly set up things so that on a "nonexceptional" nondegenerate Ω_i, $(i < \infty)$ the coding of K_i by a topological Markov chain separates periodic (and hence eventually periodic) points. However, even in this situation, it is conceivable that some infinite orbit in the topological Markov chain corresponds to a pair of infinite "parallel" orbits. The problem is closely related to the question of whether a partition P including all turning points is a generator - that is, whether itineraries separate points. We have seen, of course, that a degenerate periodic orbit may have a nontrivial monotone class $[(p, S)]$, but this phenomenon is relatively easy to understand.

A more subtle and difficult phenomenon, illustrated by (4.18), is the existence of a *homterval* - defined as a non-trivial interval with disjoint images on which every power of f is a homeomorphism (the term is a fusion of "homeomorphism" and "interval", introduced by Misiurewicz). A trivial way to obtain homtervals is to have a periodic attractor: consider fundamental domains in the local basin of attraction. Thus a *nontrivial homterval* is an interval J satisfying (i) interior $J \neq \phi$, (ii) $f^n|J$ is a homeomorphism for each $n > 0$, (iii) $f^mJ \cap f^nJ = \phi$ for $m \neq n$, and (iv) the ω-limit of J is not a single periodic orbit. A classic C^1 example of a map with nontrivial homtervals is the Denjoy diffeomorphism of the circle (De), which can be adapted (CN) to give a C^1 map $f: I \to I$ with two turning points and exhibiting nontrivial homtervals. Example (4.18) also exhibits homtervals (the intervals J_k, $k > 0$), and it seems likely that a more careful version, employing Denjoy-like estimates, could be made C^1. An outstanding open technical problem in the analytic theory of maps of the interval is:

(4.19) <u>*Homterval problem:*</u> *Are there smoothness conditions which rule out the existence of non-trivial homtervals? In particular, do there exist C^2 maps $f: I \to I$ with nontrivial homtervals?**

There are some partial results on this problem. Jakobson (Ja 1), Szlenk (Sz 1, see also Mi 5), and Misiurewicz and I (see Mi 5) have results that imply that a non-trivial homterval of a C^2 map must contain a critical point in its ω-limit set. Misiurewicz (Mi 5) and Guckenheimer (G 4) have ruled out non-trivial homtervals for C^3 maps $f: I \to I$ satisfying:

(i) f has a single critical point: $Df(c) = 0$

(ii) For $x \neq c$, f has *negative Schwartzion derivative*: $Df(x) \neq 0$ implies

$$2\, Df(x)\, D^3f(x) < 3\, [D^2f(x)]^2.$$

*I have just learned from R. McGehee that R. Hall has constructed a C^∞ map of the circle with homtervals. This suggests that the problem be changed: do there exist such maps with all critical points non-degenerate?

The condition (ii) is equivalent to convexity of $[|Df(x)|]^{-1/2}$, (Mi 5) and holds for any power of f once it holds for the first. It was originally introduced for maps of the interval by D. Singer (Sg) and is related to conditions on cross-ratios studied by Allwright (Al). General consequences of (iii) can be found in (Sg, G 4, Mi 5, Sz 1, CE 1).

(4.20) __*Remark:*__ *If $f : I \to I$ satisfies (2.8), is strictly monotone between turning points, and has no nontrivial homtervals, then $\Omega(f) \setminus \overline{Per(f)}$ is finite, and the semi-conjugacies in (4.12) and (4.16) are conjugacies.*

5. *Topological entropy*

In this section we very briefly review some results on the topological entropy of continuous maps $f : I \to I$.

Given a sequence a_n of positive numbers, define its *growth rate* as

(5.1) $$G(a_n) = \lim_{n\to\infty} \frac{1}{n} \log a_n ,$$

whenever this limit exists. Note that if $a_n \leq CK^n$ for some $C, K > 0$, then

(5.2) $$G(a_n) \leq \log K.$$

The sequence grows roughly like powers of $\exp G(a_n)$, if $G(a_n) > 1$.

The *topological entropy* $h(f)$ can be defined for f a continuous map of a compact metric space X in any of several ways (see, e.g. (DGS, Chap. 14))

$$h(f) = \lim_{\varepsilon\to 0} G(S_n(\varepsilon)) = \lim_{\varepsilon\to 0} G(r_n(\varepsilon)) = \sup_{u} G(C_n(U))$$

where: (i) $S_n(\varepsilon)$ is the largest cardinality of an *n-ε- separated* set, i.e. a set $Y(n,\varepsilon) = \{x_1 \cdots x_m\}$ such that for every $i \neq j$ there exists k, $0 \leq k \leq n$ such that $\mathrm{dist}(f^k(x_i), f^k(x_j)) \geq \varepsilon$; (ii) $r_n(\varepsilon)$ is the smallest cardinality of an *n-ε - dense* set, i.e. $Y(n,\varepsilon) = \{x_1 \cdots x_m\}$ such that for every $x \in X$ there exist $x_i \in Y(n,\varepsilon)$ such that $\mathrm{dist}(f^k(x_i), f^k(x)) < \varepsilon$ for $k = 0, \cdots, n$; and (iii) for any open cover U, $C_n(U)$ is the minimum cardinality of a subcover of $U_n = U \vee f^{-1} U \vee \cdots \vee f^{-(n-1)} U$. A well-known theorem of Goodwyn, Dinaburg and Goodman (see (DGS)) states that $h(f)$ is the supremum of the metric entropy for all f-invariant Borel probability measures.

Misiurewicz and Szlenk (MiS 1, 2) have shown that for $f : I \to I$ satisfying (2.8), $h(f)$ can also be measured by other growth rates:

(5.3) *__Theorem__: (MiS 1,2): If $f : I \to I$ satisfies (2.8), define*

$$t_n(f) = \text{number of turning points of } f^n$$

$$v_n(f) = \text{total variation of } f^n$$

then $h(f) = G(t_n(f)) = G(v_n(f))$.

Furthermore, suppose P *is a partition such that* f *is monotone on each* J_i, *and let* p_n *be the cardinality of* $P \vee f^{-1} P \vee \cdots \vee f^{-(n-1)} P$.

Then $h(f) = G(p_n)$.

The equality $h(f) = G(t_n)$ was also proved by Young (Y 2). It is very plausible, if one notes that given a partition P on which f is monotone and a finite open cover U, (i) there exists a refinement P' of P which refines U, in the sense that every interval of P' is a subset of some single element of U, (so $p' > C(U)$) (ii) there is a subcover U' of U such that each element of P intersects at most 4 elements of U' (so $p < C(U')$), and (iii) the growth rate $G(p_n)$ of any two partitions on which f is monotone is the same, and equals $G(t_n)$. Milnor - Thurston (MiT) have noted that for maps of quadratic type, $G(t_n)$ is the same as $-\log r$, where r is the radius of convergence of the series $\Sigma\, \nu_i\, t^i$ noted at the end of section 4.

A sharp estimate for the topological entropy of any continuous map f was obtained by L. Block et. al. (BGMY) from their proof of Šarkovskiĭ's theorem. This is based on the general fact that the entropy of a factor cannot exceed the entropy of its extensions and the following

(5.4) Proposition (BGMY): Given $n \geq 3$ odd, let S be the topological Markov chain with n states and transitions $S_i \to S_{i+1}$ for each i, $S_1 \to S_1$, and $S_{n-1} \to S_{2k+1}$ for $k = 0, \cdots, (n-3)/2$. Then the entropy of the shift map on S equals $\log \sigma_n$, where σ_n is the largest root of the polynomial

$$P_n(x) = x^n - 2x^{n-2} - 1.$$

This is proved by an ingenious device ("romes") for counting the number of loops of a given length and the fact that the entropy of a topological Markov chain is the growth rate of the number of periodic points of a given period. The graph described above is simply the one appearing in the proof of (1.7). As a consequence of (5.4), the proof of (1.1), and the general fact

(5.5) $h(f^n) = nh(f)$ for $n \geq 1$

one obtains

(5.6) Theorem (BGMY): If $f : I \to I$ is continuous and possesses period $2^k m$, where $m \geq 3$ is odd, then

$$h(f) \geq 2^{-k} \log \sigma_m .$$

In fact, the examples constructed in section 1 have equality in (5.6) so this theorem is the best possible. Earlier estimates of this sort were made by Bowen and Franks (BoF) and Jonker and Rand (JoR 1,2) (this for quadratic-like maps). A corollary of (5.5) is one direction (proved in all the above references) of the following:

(5.7) Theorem: If $f : I \to I$ is continuous, $h(f) = 0$ if and only if f possesses only powers of 2 as periods.

The "only if" part of this follows from (5.6) and the observation that $\sigma_m > 0$ for all $m \geq 3$ odd. For the "if" part, it is fairly easy to see that $h(f) = 0$ if $\Omega(f)$ is the fixedpoint set (using $h(f) = h(f|\Omega(f))$), so that if there are finitely many periods, $h(f) = 0$.

The case of maps possessing each power of 2 and nothing else is more subtle; a proof in this case is given by Misiurewicz (Mi 2). In the piecewise-monotone case, one can obtain this from (4.17) and the Goodwyn-Dinaburg-Goodman theorem, by noting that if $h(f) > 0$, there exists a measure with positive metric entropy, but each piece of $\overline{\mathrm{Per}(f)}$ (which carries any such measure) is either a periodic orbit of period 2^k or an adding machine, both of which have zero topological entropy.

In general, there exist maps (even diffeomorphisms) with no measure that maximizes entropy. However, Hofbauer (Hof 2-4) has shown

(5.8) *Theorem* *(Hof 2-4): If* $f: I \to I$ *satisfies (2.8), and* $h(f) > 0$, *there exists a finite nonzero number of f-invariant ergodic Borel probability measures* μ *such that*

$$h_{\mu}(f) = h(f).$$

One can see this (more or less following Hofbauer's argument) from (4.17) as follows: First, using (5.2) and (5.3), one finds that for any piecewise monotone f with t turning points, $h(f) \leq \log t$. Also, the number of components of M_{ij} (the part of M_i intersecting $M_{\infty j}$), and hence the length of the permutation bringing a single component back to itself goes to ∞ as $i \to \infty$. Using these observations, one can show that $h(f|\Omega_i) \to 0$ as $i \to \infty$. It is also clear that the adding machine has entropy zero. Thus, there are finitely many sets Ω_i for which $h(f)|\Omega_i) = h(f)$. From the structure of these, each carries a unique such measure (which is ergodic) and (5.8) follows.

A final topic in this area is the behavior of entropy under perturbations. We quote the following without proof, which answer questions posed by Block (Bℓ 4):

(5.9) *Theorem* *(Mi 2): The map* $f \to h(f)$ *is lower semi-continuous with respect to the* C^0 *topology, at every continuous* $f: I \to I$.

(5.10) *Theorem* (MiS 2 cf.Bo 3): *If* $f : I \to I$ *is* C^2 *and has only non-degenerate critical points* ($Df(x) = 0$ *implies* $D^2f(x) \neq 0$), *then* $f \to h(f)$ *is continuous at* f *with respect to the* C^2 *topology.*

These results are sharp: upper semi-continuity fails somewhere in the C^r topology for any $r > 0$. Finally, a related result was recently established by Guckenheimer for quadratic-like maps:

(5.11) *Theorem* (G 5): *Suppose* $f_a : I \to I$ *is a family of maps such that* $f_a(x)$ *is jointly* C^1 *in* a *and* x, *and for each* a, f_a *satisfies*

(i) $h(f_a) > 0$

(ii) $f_a(0) = f_a(1) = 0$

(iii) f_a *has a unique critical point, where* $D^2f \neq 0$

(iv) *the Schwartzian derivative is negative:*

$$2\, Df(x)\, D^3f(x) < 3[D^2f(x)]^2 \quad \text{if} \quad Df(x) \neq 0.$$

Then the map $a \to h(f_a)$ *is Hölder continuous of class* α *for some* $\alpha > 0$.

REFERENCES

Ad R. Adler, f-expansions revisited, *Lect. Notes Math.* *318*(1973) 1-5.

Aℓ D. J. Allwright, Hypergraphic functions in recurrence relations, *SIAM J. Applied Math.* *34*(1978) 687-691.

AM R. Adler and M. H. McAndrew, The entropy of Chebyshev polynomials, *Trans. AMS* *121*(1966) 236-241.

Ar V. Arnol'd, Small denominators, I. Mappings of the circumference to itself (Russian) *Izv. Akad. Nauk SSSR* *25*(1961) 21-86 = (English) *Transl. AMS (2)* *46*(1961) 213-284.

AuK J. Auslander and Y. Katznelson, Continuous maps of the circle without periodic points, *Israel J. Math.* *32*(1979) 375-381.

AuY J. Auslander and J. Yorke, Interval maps, factors of maps, and chaos, *Tôhoku J. (2)* *32*(1980) 177-188.

AW R. Adler and B. Weiss, The ergodic infinite measure preserving transformation of Boole, *Israel J. Math.* *16*(1973) 263-278.

B C. Bernhardt, Rotation intervals of a class of endomorphisms of the circle, Preprint, Carbondale, 1981.

BCN L. Block, E. Coven, and Z. Nitecki, Minimizing topological entropy for maps of the circle, *Ergod. Thy. Dyn. Syst.*, to appear.

BGMY L. Block, J. Guckenheimer, M. Misiurewicz and L. Young, Periodic points and topological entropy of one dimensional maps. *Lect. Notes Math. 819* (Springer, 1980) 18-34.

Bℓ1 L. Block, Morse-Smale endomorphisms of the circle, *Proc. AMS 48* (1975) 457-463.

Bℓ2 _______, Diffeomorphisms obtained from endomorphisms, *Trans. AMS 214* (1975) 403-413.

Bℓ3 _______, The periodic points of Morse-Smale endomorphisms of the circle, *Trans. AMS 226* (1977) 77-88.

Bℓ4 _______, An example where topological entropy is continuous, *Trans. AMS 231* (1977) 201-214.

Bℓ5 _______, Topological entropy at an Ω-explosion, *Trans. AMS 235* (1978) 323-330.

Bℓ6 _______, Continuous maps of the interval with finite nonwandering set, *Trans. AMS 240* (1978) 221-230.

Bℓ7 _______, Mappings of the interval with finitely many periodic points have zero entropy, *Proc. AMS 67* (1977) 357-360.

Bℓ8 _______, Homoclinic points of mappings of the interval, *Proc. AMS 72* (1978) 576-580.

Bℓ9 _______, Simple periodic orbits of mappings of the interval, *Trans. AMS 254* (1979) 391-398.

Bℓ10 _______, Periodic orbits of continuous mappings of the circle, *Trans. AMS 260* (1980) 555-562.

Bℓ11 _______, Stability of periodic orbits in the theorem of Šarkovskiĭ, *Proc. AMS 81* (1981) 333-336.

Bℓ12 _______, Periods of periodic points of maps of the circle which have a fixed point, Preprint, Gainesville, 1980

BℓF1 L. Block and J. Franke, A classification of the structurally stable contracting endomorphisms of S^1, *Proc. AMS 36* (1972) 592-602.

BℓF2 _______, Existence of periodic points for maps of S^1, *Invent. math. 22* (1973) 69-73.

Bo1 R. Bowen, Bernoulli maps of the interval, *Israel J. Math. 28* (1977) 161-168.

Bo2 _______, Entropy for maps of the interval, *Topology 16*(1977) 465-467.

Bo3 _______, Invariant measures for Markov maps of the interval, *Comm. Math. Phys. 69*(1979) 1-17.

BoF R. Bowen and J. Franks, The periodic points of maps of the disk and interval, *Topology 15*(1976) 337-342.

Bu L. A. Bunimovič, On a transformation of the circle, (Russian) *Mat. Zametki 8*(1970) 205-216 = (English) *Math. Notes 8*(1970).

By1 A. Boyarsky, Randomness implies order, *J. Math. Anal. Appl. 76* (1980) 483-497.

By2 _______, Approximating the σ-finite measure invariant under a non-expanding map, *J. Math. Anal. Appl. 78*(1980) 222-232.

ByC A. Boyarsky and S. Cooper, Weak continuity of invariant measures for a class of monotonic transformations, *Proc. AMS 80*(1980) 574-576.

ByS A. Boyarsky and M. Scarowsky, On a class of transformations which have unique absolutely continuous invariant measures, *Trans. AMS 255*(1979) 243-262.

CaE M. Campanino and H. Epstein, On the existence of Feigenbaum's fixedpoint, *Comm. Math. Phys. 79*(1981) 261-302.

CE1 P. Collet and J.-P. Eckmann, *Iterated maps on the interval as dynamical systems*, Prog. Phy. 1(Birkhäuser, 1980).

CE2 _______, On the abundance of aperiodic behavior for maps of the interval, *Comm. Math. Phys. 73*(1980) 115-160.

CEL P. Collet, J.-P. Eckmann, and O. Lanford, Universal properties of maps on an interval, *Comm. Math. Phys. 76*(1980) 211-254.

CH1 E. M. Coven and G. A. Hedlund, Continuous maps of the interval whose periodic points form a closed set, *Proc. AMS 79*(1980) 127-133.

CH2 _______, $\overline{P} = \overline{R}$ for maps of the interval, *ibid* 316-318.

CMN E. M. Coven, J. Madden and Z. Nitecki, A note on generic properties of continuous maps, Preprint, Middletown, 1981.

CN E. M. Coven and Z. Nitecki, Non-wandering sets of the powers of maps of the interval, *Ergodic Thy. and Dyn. Syst.,* To appear.

Co J. Coste, Iterations of transformations on the unit interval: approach to a periodic attractor, *J. Stat. Phys. 23*(1980) 521-536.

De A. Denjoy, Sur les courbes définies par les équations differentielles à la surface du tore, *J. de Math. 11*(1932) 42-49.

DGP B. Derrida, A. Gervois, and Y. Pomeau, Universal metric properties of bifurcations of endomorphisms, *J. Phys. A 12*(1979) 269-296.

DGS M. Denker, C. Grillenberger, and K. Sigmund, *Ergodic Theory on Compact Spaces,* Lect. Notes Math. 527 (Springer, 1976).

Dv R. Devaney, Genealogy of periodic points of maps of the interval, *Trans. AMS 265*(1981) 137-146.

Eb E. Eberlein, Toeplitz-Folgen und Gruppentranslationen, *Arch. Math. 22*(1971) 291-301.

Fe1 M. Feigenbaum, Quantitative universality for a class of nonlinear transformations, *J. Stat. Phys. 19*(1978) 25-52.

Fe2 The universal metric properties of nonlinear transformations, *J. Stat. Phys. 21*(1979) 669-706.

Fr J. Franke, Bifurcation of structurally stable contractions on S^1, Preprint, Raleigh, 1978.

G1 J. Guckenheimer, On the bifurcation of maps of the interval, *Invent. math. 39*(1977) 165-178.

G2 _______, The bifurcation of quadratic functions, *Ann. N.Y. Acad. Sci. 316*(1979) 78-85.

G3 _______, Bifurcations of dynamical systems, *Prog. Math. 8* (Birkhäuser, 1980) 115-231.

G4 _______, Sensitive dependence to initial conditions for one-dimensional maps, *Comm. Math. Phys. 70*(1979) 133-160.

G5 _______, The growth of topological entropy for one-dimensional maps, *Lect. Notes Math. 819* (1980) 216-223.

GM1 I. Gumowski and C. Mira, *Recurrences and Discrete Dynamical Systems,* Lect. Notes Math. 809 (Springer, 1980).

GM2 _______, Sur les récurrences, ou transformations ponctuelles, du premier ordre, avec inverse non unique, *C. R. Acad. Sci. Paris 280*(1975) A905-908.

GM3 _______, Accumulations de bifurcations dans une récurrence. *C. R. Acad. Sci. Paris 281*(1975) A45-48.

GoH W. Gottschalk and G. A. Hedlund, *Topological Dynamics,* AMS Colloquium Publ. 36(1955).

GoI J. Guckenheimer, G. Oster, and A. Ipaktchi, Dynamics of density dependent population models, *J. Math. Bio. 4*(1977) 101-147.

He M. Herman, Sur la conjugaison différentiable des difféomorphismes du cercle a des rotations, *Publ. Math. IHES 49*(1979) 5-234.

HK F. Hofbauer and G. Keller, Ergodic properties of invariant measures for piecewise monotonic transformations, Preprint, Vienna, 1981.

HLM M. P. Hassell, J. H. Lawton, and R. M. May, Patterns of dynamic behavior in single-species populations, *J. Animal Ecology 45* (1976) 471-486.

Hn B. Henry, Escape from the unit interval under the transformation $x \to \lambda x(1 - x)$, *Proc. AMS 41*(1973) 146-150.

Hof1 F. Hofbauer, β-shifts have unique maximal measure, *Mh. Math, 85*(1978) 189-198.

Hof2 _______, Maximal measures for piecewise monotonically increasing transformations on [0,1], *Lect. Notes Math. 729*(1979) 66-77.

Hof3 _______, On intrinsic ergodicity of piecewise monotonic transformations with positive entropy, (I, II), *Israel J. Math. 34* (1979) 213-237.

Hof4 _______, On intrinsic ergodicity of piecewise monotone transformations with positive entropy III, Preprint, Vienna, 1978.

Hof5 _______, The structure of piecewise monotonic transformations, Preprint, Vienna, 1979.

Hof6 _______, The topological entropy of the transformation $x \to \alpha x(1 - x)$, *Mh. Math. 90*(1980) 117-141.

Hof7 _______, Maximal measures for simple piecewise monotonic transformations, *Z. Wahrsch. 52*(1980) 289-300.

HoH F. Hoppensteadt and J. Hyman, Periodic solutions of a logistic difference equation, *SIAM J. Appl. Math. 32*(1977) 73-81.

HoM C. Ho and C. Morris, A graph-theoretic proof of Sharkovsky's theorem on the periodic points of continuous functions, Preprint, Edwardsville,1980.

Ja1 M. V. Jakobson, On smooth mappings of the circle into itself, (Russian) *Mat. Sbornik 85*(127) (1971) 163-188 = (English) *Math. USSR Sbornik 14*(1971) 161-185.

Ja2 _______, On the properties of the one-parameter family of dynamical systems $x \to A \cdot x \cdot e^{-x}$ (Russian) *Usp. Mat. Nauk 31* (188) (1976) 239-240.

Ja3 _______, Topological and metric properties of one-dimensional endomorphisms, (Russian) *Dokl. Akad. Nauk SSSR 243*(1978) 866-869 = (English) *Soviet Math. Doklady 19*(1978) 1452-1456.

Ja4 _______, Construction of invariant measures absolutely continuous with respect to dx for some maps of the interval, *Lect. Notes Math. 819*(1980) 246-257.

Ja5 ______, Absolutely continuous invariant measures for one-parameter families of one-dimensional maps, *Comm. Math. Phys.*, to appear.

Ja6 ______, Invariant measures that are absolutely continuous with respect to dx for one-parameter families of one-dimensional mappings, (Russian) *Usp. Nat. Nauk 35*(1980) 215-216.

JM1 M. Jabłonski and J. Malczak, The central limit theorem for expanding mappings of a manifold into itself, Preprint, Krakōw, 1980.

JM2 ______, The rate of convergence of iterates of the Frobenius-Perron operator for piecewise monotonic transformations, Preprint, Krakōw, 1980.

Jo L. Jonker, Periodic points and kneading invariants, *Proc. London Math. Soc. 39*(1979) 428-450.

JoR1 L. Jonker and D. Rand, Une borne inférieure pour l'entropie de certaines applications de l'intervalle dans lui-même, *C. R. Acad. Sci. Paris 287(A)* (1978) 501-502.

JoR2 ______, The periodic orbits and entropy of certain maps of the unit interval, *J. London Math. Soc. (2) 22*(1980) 175-181.

JoR3 ______, The nonwandering set of unimodal maps of the interval, *C. R. Math. Rep. Acad. Sci. Canada 1*(1978/9) 137-140.

JoR4 ______, Bifurcations of unimodal maps of the unit interval, *ibid* 179-181.

JoR5 ______, Bifurcations in one dimension, I: The nonwandering set, *Invent. math., 62*(1981) 347-365.

JoR6 ______, Bifurcations in one dimension, II: A versal model for bifurcations, *Invent. math., 63*(1981) 1-16.

Ka A. B. Katok, Interval exchange transformations and some special flows are not mixing, *Israel J. Math 35*(1980) 301-310.

Kea1 M. Keane, Interval exchange transformations, *Math. Z. 141*(1975) 25-31.

Kea2 ______, Non-ergodic interval exchange transformations, *Israel J. Math. 26*(1977) 188-196.

KeaR M. Keane and G. Rauzy, Stricte ergodicité des échanges d'intervalles, *Math. Z. 174*(1980) 203-212.

Kee J. Keener, Chaotic behavior in piecewise continuous difference equations, *Trans. AMS 261*(1980) 589-604.

Kel G. Keller, Un théorème de la limite centrale pour une class de transformations monotones par morceaux, *C. R. Acad. Sci. Paris 291*(1980) A155-158.

Key H. Keynes and D. Newton, A minimal, non-uniquely ergodic interval exchange transformation, *Math. Z. 148*(1976) 101-105.

Kol R. Kołodziej, An infinite smooth invariant measure for some transformations of a circle, Preprint, Warsaw, 1980.

Kow1 Z. Kowalski, Invariant measures for piecewise monotonic transformations, *Lect. Notes Math. 472*(1975) 77-94.

Kow2 ______, Continuity of invariant measures for piecewise monotonic transformations, *Bull. Acad. Polon. Sci. 23*(1975) 519-524.

Kow3 ______, Some remarks about invariant measures for piecewise monotonic transformations, *Bull, Acad. Polon. Sci. 25*(1977) 7-12.

Kow 4 ______, Invariant measure for piecewise monotonic transformation has a positive lower bound on its support, *Bull. Acad. Polon. Sci. 27*(1979) 53-57.

Kow5 ______, Bernoulli properties of piecewise monotonic transformations, *ibid* 59-61.

Kow6 ______, Piecewise monotonic transformations and their invariant measure, *ibid* 63-69.

La1 A. Lasota, On the existence of invariant measures for Markov processes, *Ann. Polon. Math 28*(1973) 207-211.

La2 ______, Invariant measures and functional equations, *Aeq. Math. 9*(1973) 193-200.

La3 ______, A solution of Ulam's conjecture on the existence of invariant measures and its applications, *Dynamical Systems vol. 2* (Acad. Press, 1976) 47-55.

La4 ______, On mappings isomorphic to r-adic transformations, *Ann. Polon. Math. 35*(1978) 313-322.

La5 ______, Mathematics in the biological sciences, (Polish) *Nauka Polska 11*(1979) 81-88.

La6 ______, Ergodic problems in biology, *Astérisque 50*(1977) 239-250.

LaR A. Lasota and P. Rusek, An application of ergodic theory to the determination of the efficiency of clogged drilling bits, (Polish) *Arch. Gōrnictwa 19*(1974) 281-295.

LaY1 A. Lasota and J. Yorke, On the existence of invariant measures for piecewise monotonic transformations, *Trans. AMS 186*(1973) 481-488.

LaY2 ______, On the existence of invariant measures for transformations with strictly turbulent trajectories, *Bull. Acad. Polon. Sci. 25*(1977) 233-238.

Le F. Ledrappier, Some properties of absolutely continuous measures on an interval, Preprint, Paris 1980.

Li T. Li, Finite approximation for the Frobenius-Perron operator. A solution to Ulam's conjecture, *J. Approx. Thy. 17*(1976) 177-186.

LiMPY T. Li, M. Misiurewicz, G. Pianigiani, and J. Yorke, Odd chaos, To appear.

LiS T. Li and F. Schweiger, The generalized Boole's transformation is ergodic, *Manu. Math. 25*(1978) 161-167.

LiY1 T. Li and J. Yorke, Period three implies chaos, *Am. Math. Monthly 82*(1975) 985-992.

LiY2 _______, Ergodic transformations from an interval to itself, *Trans. AMS 235*(1978) 183-192.

LiY3 _______, Ergodic maps on [0,1] and nonlinear pseudo-random number generators, *Nonlin. Anal. Thy. Meth. Appl. 2*(1978) 473-481.

Lℓ J. Llibre, Continuous maps of the circle with finitely many periodic points, Preprint, Barcelona, 1979.

Lo1 E. Lorenz, Deterministic nonperiodic flow, *J. Atmos. Sci. 20* (1963) 130-141.

Lo2 _______, The problem of deducing the climate from the governing equations, *Tellus 16*(1964) 1-11.

Lo3 _______, On the prevalence of aperiodicity in simple systems, *Lect. Notes Math. 755*(1979) 53-75.

Ma1 R. May, Biological populations with nonoverlapping generations: stable points, stable cycles, and chaos, *Science 186*(1974) 645-647.

Ma2 _______, Simple mathematical models with very complicated dynamics, *Nature 261*(1976) 459-467.

MaO R. May and G. Oster, Bifurcations and dynamic complexity in simple biological models, *Am. Nat. 110*(1976) 573-599.

Mar N. Markley, Homeomorphisms of the circle without periodic points, *Proc. London Math. Soc.(3) 20*(1970) 688-698.

Mas H. Masur, Interval exchange transformations and measured foliations, Preprint, Chicago, 1981.

May D. Mayer, On a ζ function related to the continued fraction transformation, Preprint, Bures-sur-Yvette, 1975.

MeS N. Metropolis, P. Stein, and M. Stein, On finite limit sets for transformations on the unit interval, *J. Comb. Thy. A 15*(1973) 25-44.

Mi1 M. Misiurewicz, On expanding maps of compact manifolds and local homeomorphisms of a circle, *Bull. Acad. Polon. Sci. 18*(1970) 725-735.

Mi2 _______, Horseshoes for mappings of the interval, *Bull. Acad. Polon. Sci. 27*(1979) 167-169.

Mi3 _______, Invariant measures for continuous transformations of [0,1] with zero topological entropy, *Lect. Notes Math. 729* (1980) 144-152.

Mi4 _______, Structure of mappings of an interval with zero entropy, *Publ. Math. IHES*, to appear.

Mi5 _______, Absolutely continuous invariant measures for certain maps of the interval, *Publ. Math. IHES*, to appear.

MiS1 M. Misiurewicz and W. Szlenk, Entropy of piecewise monotone maps, *Astérisque 50*(1977) 299-310.

MiS2 _______, Entropy of piecewise monotone maps, *Studia Math. 67* (1980) 45-63.

MiT J. Milnor and W. Thurston, On iterated maps of the interval. I, The kneading matrix. II, Periodic points, Preprint, Princeton, 1977.

Mr1 C. Mira, Accumulations de bifurcations et "structures boites emboitées" dan les récurrences et transformations ponctuelles, *VII Inter. Konf. über nichtlineare Schwingungen* (Akademie-Verlag, Berlin 1977) 81-93.

Mr2 _______, Structures de bifurcation "boites emboitées" dans les recurrences, ou transformations ponctuelles du premier ordre, dont la fonction présente un seul extrémum. Application à un problème de "chaos" en biologie, *C. R. Acad. Sci. Paris 282*(1976) A219-A222.

Mr3 _______, Etude d'un modèle de croissance d'une population biologique en l'absence de recouvrement de générations, *C. R. Acad. Sci. 282*(1976) A1441-1444.

Mr4 _______, Dynamique complexe engendrée par une récurrence, ou transformation ponctuelle, continue, linéaire par moreaux, du premier ordre, *C. R. Acad. Sci. Paris 285* (1977) A731-734.

Mr5 _______, Systèmes a dynamique complexe et bifurcations de type "boites emboitées", cas des récurrences d'ordre 1 determinées par une fonction a un seul extremum, *RAIRO Automatique/Systems Analysis and Control 12*(1978) 63-94, 171-190.

My1 P. J. Myrberg, Iteration der reellen Polynome zweites Grades. *Ann. Acad. Sci. Fenn. 256A*(1958) 1-10, *268A*(1959) 1-10, *336A* (1963) 1-18.

My2 _______, Sur l'itération des polynomes réels quadratiques, *J. Math. Pures et Appl. 41*(1962) 339-351.

My3 _______, Iteration der Polynome mit reelen Koeffizienten, *Ann. Acad. Sci. Fenn. 374AI*(1965) 1-18.

Na M. Nathanson, Permutations, periodicity, and chaos, *J. Comb. Thy. (A) 22*(1977) 61-68.

Ne S. Newhouse, Hyperbolic limit sets, *Trans. AMS 167*(1972) 125-150.

Ni1 Z. Nitecki, Non-singular endomorphisms of the circle, *Proc. Symp. Pure Math. 14*(1970) 203-220.

Ni2 _______, Factorization of non-singular circle endomorphisms, *Dynamical Systems* (ed. Peixoto) (Acad. Press, 1973) 367-373.

Ni3 _______, Partitions for circle endomorphisms, *ibid,* 375-388.

Ni4 _______, Periodic and limit orbits, and the depth of the center, for piecewise-monotone interval maps, *Proc. AMS 80*(1980) 511-514.

Pa1 W. Parry, On the β-expansion of real numbers, *Acta. Math. Acad. Sci. Hungar. 11*(1960) 401-416.

Pa2 _______, Intrinsic Markov chains, *Trans. AMS 112*(1964) 55-66.

Pa3 _______, Symbolic dynamics and transformations of the unit interval, *Trans. AMS 122*(1966) 368-378.

Pi1 G. Pianigiani, Absolutely continuous invariant measures for the process $x_{n+1} = Ax_n(1 - x_n)$, *Boll. Un. Mat. Ital. 16A*(1979) 374-378.

Pi2 _______, Existence of invariant measures for piecewise continuous transformations, *Ann. Polon. Math.*, to appear.

Pi3 _______, First return map and invariant measures, *Israel J. Math. 35*(1980) 32-48.

R D. Ruelle, Applications conservant une mesure absolument continue par rapport à dx sur [0,1], *Comm. Math. Phys. 55*(1977) 47-51.

RZ H. Rüssman and E. Zehnder, On a normal form for symmetric maps of [0, 1], *Comm. Math. Phys. 72*(1980) 49-53.

Sa A. Šarkovskiĭ, Coexistence of cycles of a continuous map of the line into itself, (Russian) *Ukr. Mat. Z. 16*(1964) 61-71.

SBP M. Scarowsky, A. Boyarsky and H. Proppe, Some properties of piecewise linear expanding maps, *Nonlin. Anal. Thy. Meth. Appl. 4* (1980) 109-121.

Sg D. Singer, Stable orbits and bifurcation of maps of the interval, *SIAM J. Appl. Math. 35*(1978) 260-267.

Si A. A. Simonov, The investigation of piecewise monotone transformations of an interval by the methods of symbolic dynamics, (Russian) *Dokl. Akad. Nauk. SSSR 238*(1978) 1063 = (English) *Soviet Math. Doklady 19*(1978) 185-188.

Sm M. Smorodinsky, β-automorphisms are Bernoulli shifts, *Acta. Math. Acad. Sci. Hungar. 24*(1973) 272-278.

St P. Štefan, A theorem of Šarkovskiĭ on the coexistence of periodic orbits of continuous endomorphisms of the real line, *Comm. Math. Phys. 54*(1977) 237-248.

Str P. Straffin, Periodic points of continuous functions, *Math. Mag. 51*(1978) 99-105.

SW S. Smale and R. F. Williams, The qualitative analysis of a difference equation of population growth, *J. Math. Bio. 3*(1976) 1-4.

Sz W. Szlenk, Some dynamical properties of certain differentiable mappings of an interval, I. *Bol. Soc. Mat. Mex.*, (to appear). II. This volume.

Ta Y. Takahashi, Isomorphism of β-automorphisms to Markov automorphisms, *Osaka J. Math. 10*(1973) 175-184.

Ve W. Veech, Interval exchange transformations, *J. d'Anal. 33*(1978) 222-272. See also work in companion volume.

K E. R. vanKampen, The topological transformations of a simple closed curve into itself, *Am. J. Math. 57*(1935) 142-152.

Wal P. Walters, Invariant measures and equilibrium states for some mappings which expand distances, *Trans. AMS 236*(1978) 121-153.

Wa2 _______, Equilibrium states for β-transformations and related transformations, *Math. Z. 159*(1978) 65-88.

Wg G. Wagner, The ergodic behavior of piecewise monotonic transformations, *Z. Wahrsch. 46*(1979) 317-324.

Wi K. Wilkinson, Ergodic properties of certain linear mod one transformations, *Adv. Math. 14*(1974) 64-72.

WL M. Ważewska-Czyżewska and A. Lasota, Mathematical problems in the dynamics of the red corpuscle system, (Polish) *Mat. Stos. 6*(1976) 23-40.

Wo1 S. Wong, A central limit theorem for piecewise monotonic mappings of the unit interval, *Ann. Prob.* 7(1979) 500-514.

Wo2 _______, Some metric properties of piecewise monotonic mappings of the unit interval, *Trans. AMS 246*(1978) 493-500.

Wo3 Hölder continuous derivatives and ergodic theory, *J. London Math. Soc. (2) 22*(1980) 506-520.

Y1 L. S. Young, A closing lemma on the interval, *Invent. math. 54* (1979) 179-187.

Y2 _______, On the prevalence of horseshoes, *Trans. AMS 263* (1981) 75-88.

Ya K. Yano, Topologically stable homeomorphisms of the circle, *Nagoya Math. J. 79* (1980) 145-149.

Z H. Żołądek, On bifurcations of orientation reversing diffeomorphisms of the circle, *Astérisque 51* (1978) 473-487.

ADDITIONAL REFERENCES

The references below came to my attention between the typing of this paper and its final submission for publication. I give most of them without comment, but wish to point out a few items.

I find further evidence of the neglect of Šarkovskiĭ's work in the West as I do more bibliographic research. One one hand, there appears to have been yet another independent proof of Šarkovskiĭ's theorem [CosE] in in 1977, and an independent proof of the special case (1.9) [Ol] in 1978. On the other, it seems that some of the ideas (but not the main result) in section 4 of this paper were anticipated by Šarkovskiĭ in the mid-1960's [Sa2-6].

The example following (1.8a), which I learned from Misiurewicz, also seems to have been discovered independently by Delahaye [Deℓ 2].

The homterval question (4.19) has had some attention; Hall's example mentioned in my footnote has now appeared on the Xerox circuit [Hℓ]. I have also learned of independent work by J. Harrison [Hr], carrying out a construction like (4.18) in a C^1 setting (and thus giving an example of non-trivial homtervals for a C^1 map different from that in [CN]) and proving further results on the impossibility of non-trivial homtervals in a C^2 setting. This work was carried out a number of years ago, and has recently reached the Xerox circuit; it relates to Harrison's construction of a C^2 counterexample to the Seifert conjecture. Related to the hom-terval problem is McDuff's analytic characterization [McD] of which Cantor sets can be embedded as Denjoy minimal sets.

I have succeeded in using the separation arguments of sections 1 and 2 to extend results of L. Block [Bℓ6] and Coven-Hedlund [CH1], to show that when Per(f) is closed, there are no other non-wandering points. Meanwhile, I have heard third-hand a report from a traveller in China that some results in this direction have been obtained by Xing.

Finally, there seems to be a recent surge of interest in the "applied" literature in chaotic behavior for maps of the interval [CET, Cos2, FY,HZ, KT, MaO2, MH, O, OKY, SK, SMMS, TG, WS]. Much of this work is inspired by, and related to, Feigenbaum's conjecture [Fe1-3]. The Jonker-Rand-Hofbauer theory, and the version in (4.17), seems to offer a geometric explanation of the "band" behavior in the spectrum observed numerically in some of this work.

Aℓu I. C. Alufohai, A class of weak Bernoulli tranformations associated with representations of real numbers, *J. London Math. Soc. (2) 23*(1981) 295-302.

B2 C. Bernhardt, Periodic points of a class of endomorphisms of the circle. Preprint, Carbondale, 1980.

Bℓ13 L. Block, Periodic singularities of one paramenter families of maps of the interval. Preprint, Gainesville, 1981.

By3 A. Boyarsky, Continuity of measures for families of non-expanding maps. Preprint, Montreal 1981.

ByF A. Boyarsky and N. Friedman, Irreducibility and primitivity using Markov maps, *Lin. Alg. Appl. 37*(1981) 103-117.

ByH A. Boyarsky and G. Haddad, All invariant densities of piecewise linear Markov maps are piecewise constant. Preprint, Montreal 1981.

ByP A. Boyarsky and H. Proppe, On the fullness of surjective maps of an interval. Preprint, Montreal 1981.

CET P. Collet, J. P. Eckmann, and L. Thomas, A note on the power spectrum of the iterates of Feigenbaum's function. Preprint, Geneva, 1981.

Cos1 M. Y. Cosnard, On the behavior of successive approximations, *SIAM J. Num. Anal.* *16*(1979) 300-310.

Cos2 _______, Étude du chaos dans ℓ'iteration d'une transformation ponctuelle du premier ordre. Application à des modeles de biologie, *C. R. Acad. Sci. Paris 286*(1978) A639-A642.

CosE M. Y. Cosnard and A. Eberhard, Sur les cycles d'une application continue de la variable réele. *Sem. Anal. Num. 274*, USMG Lab. Math. Appl. Grenoble, 1977.

Deℓ1 J. P. Delahaye, A counterexample concerning iteratively generated sequences, *J. Math. Anal. Appl.* *75*(1980) 236-241.

Deℓ2 _______, Cycles d'ordre 2^i et convergence cyclique de la methode des approximations successives. Preprint, Lille, 1980.

Deℓ3 _______, Cycles des fonctions continues et topologie de $C[0,1]$. Preprint, Lille, 1981.

DK M. Denker and M. Keane, Eine Bemerkung zur topologischen entropie, *Mh. Math.* *85*(1978) 177-183.

Fe3 M. Feigenbaum, Metric universality in nonlinear recurrence, *Lect. Notes Phys.* *93*(1979) 163-166.

FY H. Fujisada and T. Yamada, Theoretical study of time correlation functions in a discrete chaotic process, *Z. Naturforsch.* *33a* (1978) 1455-1460.

Hℓ C. R. Hall, A C^∞ Denjoy counterexample. Preprint, Minneapolis, 1981.

Hr1 J. Harrison, Wandering intervals. Preprint, Oxford, 1981.

Hr2 _______, Smoothing Denjoy diffeomorphisms. Preprint, Berkeley, 1981.

HZ B. A. Huberman and A. B. Zisook, Power spectra of strange attractors, *Phys. Rev. Lett.* *46*(1981) 626-628.

I R. Ito, Rotation sets are closed, *Math. Proc. Comb. Phil. Soc.* *89*(1981) 107-111.

KT T. Kai and K. Tomita, Statistical mechanics of deterministic chaos - the case of one-dimensional discrete processes, *Prog. Theor. Phys.* *64*(1980) 1531-1550.

Ma3 R. M. May, Bifurcations and dynamic complexity in ecological systems, *Ann. N.Y. Acad. Sci.* *316*(1979) 517-529.

MaO2 R. M. May and G. Oster, Period doubling and the onset of turbulence: an analytic estimate of the Feigenbaum ratio, *Phys. Letters 78A*(1980) 1-3.

McD D. McDuff, C^1-minimal subsets of the circle, *Ann. Inst. Fourier, Grenoble 31, 1*(1981) 177-193.

MH C. Mayer-Kress and H. Haken, Intermittent behavior of the logistic system, *Phys. Letters 82A*(1981) 151-155.

Mu I. Mulvey, The Birkhoff center for continuous maps of the circle. Preprint, Middletown, 1981.

Ni5 Z. Nitecki, Maps of the interval with closed periodic set. Preprint, Medford, 1981.

O1 Y. Oono, Period $\neq 2^n$ implies chaos, *Prog. Theor. Phys. 59*(1978) 1028-1030.

O2 _______, A heuristic approach to the Kolmogorov entropy as a disorder parameter, *Prog. Theor. Phys. 60*(1978) 1944-1946.

OKY Y. Oono, T. Kohda, and H. Yamazaki, Disorder parameter for chaos, *J. Phys. Soc. Japan 48*(1980) 738-745.

Pa4 W. Parry, The Lorenz attractor and a related population model, *Lect. Notes Math. 729*(1979) 169-187.

Rh F. Rhodes, Kneading of Lorenz type for intervals and product spaces, *Math. Proc. Camb. Phil. Soc. 89*(1981) 167-179.

Sa2 A. N. Šarkovskiĭ, On the reducibility of a continuous function of a real variable and the structure of the stationary points of the corresponding iterative process, (Russian) *Dokl. ANSSR 139* (1961) 1067-1070 = (English) *Soviet Math. Dokl. 2*(1961) 1062-1064.

Sa3 _______, Attracted and attracting sets. (Russian) *Dokl. ANSSSR 160*(1965) 1036-1038) = (English) *Soviet Math. Dokl. 6*(1965) 268-270.

Sa4 _______, A classification of fixed points. (Ukrainian) *Ukrain. Mat. Ž 17*(1965) *No. 5,* 80-95 = (English) *AMS Transl. (2) 97*(1970) 159-179.

Sa5 _______Behavior of a mapping in the neighborhood of an attracting set. (Ukrainian) *Ukrain. Mat. Ž. 18*(1966) *No. 2,* 60-83 = (English) *AMS Transl. (2) 97*(1970) 227-258.

Sa6 _______, The partially ordered system of attracting sets. (Russian) *Dokl. ANSSSR 170, 6*(1966) 1276-1278 = (English) *Soviet Math. Dokl.* 7(1966) 1384-1386.

Sa7 _______, Characterization of the cosine. (Russian) *Aeq. Math. 9* (1973) 121-128.

SK S. J. Shenker and L. Kadanoff, Band to band hopping in one-dimensional maps, *J. Phys. A 14* (1981) L23-L26.

SMMS A. Shibata, T. Mayuyama, M. Mizutani, and N. Saitô, The nature of chaos in a simple dynamical system, *Z. Naturforsch. 34a* (1979) 1283-1289.

TG1 S. Thomae and S. Grossmann, Invariant distributions and stationary correlation functions of one-dimensional discrete processes, *Z. Naturforsch. 32a* (1977) 1353-1363.

TG2 ________, A scaling property in critical spectra of discrete systems, *Phys. Lett. 83A* (1981) 181-183.

Ve2 W. Veech, Gauss measures for transformations on the space of interval exchange maps, *Ann. Math.*, to appear.

Wo4 S. Wong, Two probabilistic properties of weak-Bernoulli interval maps. Preprint, New York, 1981.

WS A. Wolf and J. Swift, Universal power spectra for the reverse bifurcation sequence, *Phys. Lett. 83A* (1981) 184-187.

Erratum (10/6/81):

The claim in line 9 of the proof of (4.11), that $x \in \Omega(f^N|G_0)$, is unjustified. Nonetheless, one can still find the required periodic point $p \in G_0 \cap \alpha_i$ with x in its unstable set. If $f^N(x) = f^{2N}(x)=p$, then this point is p, and $x \in U(p, f^N, S)$ with G_0 containing an $\mathcal{S}$-neighborhood of p. If $f^N(x) \neq f^{2N}(x)$, we can argue as in the proof of (3.7): let $\{x_0, x_1, x_2\} = \{x, f^N(x), f^{2N}(x)\}$ with $x_0 < x_1 < x_2 \in G_0$. By (3.1) some point y near x_1 satisfies $f^{kN}(y) = x_0$, $f^{(k+\ell)N}(y) = x_2$, and so by (2.5), $x = f^{kN}(y) \in U(p, f^{2N}, \mathcal{S})$ for some $p \in (x_o, x_2) \subset G_0$, $f^{2N}(p) = p$. From here, we proceed as in the text.

SOME DYNAMICAL PROPERTIES OF CERTAIN DIFFERENTIABLE MAPPINGS OF AN INTERVAL

Part II

W. Szlenk

This paper is a continuation of the paper [S]. We present here a sufficient condition for the existence of invariant measure (absolutely continuous with respect to Lebesgue measure) for differentiable mappings of an interval. The condition is equivalent to the one presented in [S] but its formulation is very close to Ruelle's conjecture on absolutely continuous invariant measures for the parabolic mappings:

$$f_r(x) = r\cdot x(1-x) : \langle 0,1\rangle \hookleftarrow, \qquad 0 \le r \le 4. \quad [R].$$

Ruelle conjectured that if the trajectory of the critical point hits a periodic, repulsing orbit, then there exists an invariant measure absolutely continuous with respect to Lebesgue measure. This conjecture was proved in 1979 by Misiurewicz [M] in a more general form.

It seems that the natural extension of the Ruelle's conjecture should be as follows: if a map $f : \langle a,b\rangle \hookleftarrow$ is of class C^2, has a finite number of critical points, all of them non-degenerated the trajectory of each critical point eventually hits a repulsing, periodic orbit, and has no sinks (i.e., no attracting or one-side attracting periodic points), then there exists an f-invariant measure, absolutely continuous with respect to Lebesgue measure.

In the first section we prove a theorem very close to the conjecture formulated above. We assume that the trajectory of every critical point eventually stays in the set where the derivative of the mapping is separated (from below) from 1 (which is slightly more general than the assumption that the trajectory eventually hits a periodic, repulsing orbit) and that there is a uniform hyperbolic structure on the set of all periodic points (see the condition A.5), which is stronger than the assumption that there are no sinks. The conclusion is as in the conjecture.

In the second section some applications of the results of [S] and of this paper are presented. We consider 2 concrete mappings of an interval. Using this technique we show that they have an invariant measure absolutely continuous with respect to Lebesgue measure. All the computations were made on the computer "Helwett-Packard 9830A" in IHES.

The author is indebted to A. Katok for very helpful suggestions.

1. Let $f : \langle 0,1 \rangle \hookleftarrow$ be a differentiable mapping. Set $C_n^0 = \{x : f^{n'}(x) = 0\}$, $n = 1,2,\ldots$, $C_n = C_n^0 \cup \{0,1\}$. If Card $C_1^0 < +\infty$, then by the chain rule Card $C_n^0 < +\infty$ for every $n = 1,2,\ldots$. Let $C_n = \{c_{n,i}\}_{i=0}^{r_n}$:

$$0 = c_{n,0} < c_{n,1} < \cdots < c_{n,r_n} = 1.$$

Denote by $\Delta_{n,i} = (c_{n,i-1}, c_{n,i})$. By chain rule we see that $C_{n+1} \supset C_n$ for every n.

We shall assume that the mapping f satisfies the following conditions:

A.1. $f \in C^2$

A.2. Card $C_1 < +\infty$

A.3. $f''\big|_{C_1^0} \neq 0$

A.4. There exists an integer m_0 and a number $\lambda_0 > 1$ such that

$$R \overset{df}{=} \bigcup_{n=m_0}^{\infty} f^n(C_1) \subset \{x : |f'(x)| > \lambda_0\} \overset{df}{=} V_0.$$

This means that every point $c \in C_1$ eventually stays

in the set V_0, where we have uniform expansion.

A.5. There exist two constant numbers $\varkappa > 1$ and $\gamma > 0$ such that for every periodic point $x : f^p(x) = x$

$$|f^{p'}(x)| \geq \gamma\varkappa^p$$

(p is not necessarily the prime period). This condition we could call the uniform hyperbolic structure on set at all periodic points.

Replacing f by an iterate f^m we may assume $\gamma = 1$. Indeed, if $\tilde{f} = f^m$, where $\varkappa^m \cdot \gamma \overset{df}{=} \varkappa_1 > 1$, then for every x such that $\tilde{f}^p(x) = x$ we have

$$|\tilde{f}^{p'}(x)| = |f^{pm'}(x)| \geq \gamma\varkappa^{pm} > \varkappa_1^p.$$

Therefore without loss of generality we shall assume that for every periodic point $x : f^p(x) = x$ we have

$\bar{A}$.5 $$|f^{p'}(x)| > \varkappa^p,$$

where $\varkappa > 1$.

Remark 1. The condition A.5 implies immediately that there are no sinks. So the condition A.5 from [S] is fulfilled. Also replacing f by one of its iterates we may assume that m_0 in the assumption A.4 is equal to 1. The proof is trivial in the case where $f^k(C_1^0) \cap C_1^0 = \emptyset$ for every k (we proceed as in the Lemma 3.1 in [M]). It requires some slight changes if for some k $f^k(C_1^0) \cap C_1^0 \neq \emptyset$. But in fact all the results of the paper [S] are true if we replace A.4 in [S] by A.4 formulated above. So we have

Remark 2. The condition A.4 is equivalent to the following one:

$\bar{A}$.4. There exists an integer m such that for $\tilde{f} = f^m$ the following condition holds:

$$\bigcup_{n=1}^{\infty} \tilde{f}^n(\tilde{C}_1) \subset \{x : |\tilde{f}'(x)| \geq \tilde{\lambda}_0\} \overset{df}{=} \tilde{V}_0,$$

where $\tilde{\lambda}_0 > 1$, and $\tilde{C}_1 = \{x : |\tilde{f}'(x)| = 0\} \cup \{0,1\}$.

Without loss of generality we shall assume that the assumption A.4 is fulfilled with $m_0 = 1$.

Set $V_1 = \{x : |f'(x)| > \lambda_1\}$ where $1 < \lambda_1 < \lambda_0$; clearly $V_1 \supset \bar{V}_0$ (the set V_1 is the same set as in [S]). Denote by A.6 the following condition:

<u>A.6</u>. There exist: $\tau_1 > 1$, $\tau_2 > 1$, $n_0 \in Z^+$ such that if $D = \{x : |f'(x)| < \tau_1\}$, $f^n(x) \in D$ for $n \geq n_0$, then

$$|f^{n'}(x)| \geq \tau_2.$$

This is exactly the same condition as A.6 in [S].

Let $\Delta_{n,i} = (c_{n,i-1}, c_{n,i})$. By definition of the set C_n there exist two integer numbers $k \leq l \leq n-1$ such that $f^k(c_{n,i-1})$, $f^l(c_{n,i}) \in C_1$; without loss of generality we may assume $l = n$ (see Remark 5 in [S]).

<u>Proposition</u>. There exists a number $\gamma_0 > 0$ such that for every $m \geq n$ and for every $\Delta_{n,i}$ $|f^m(\Delta_{n,i})| \geq \gamma_0$.

<u>Proof</u>. Notice that $|f^n(\Delta_{n,i})| \geq \min\{ \min_{1 \leq i \leq r^1} |c_{1,i-1} - c_{1,i}|,$ $\operatorname{dist}(R, V_1^c)\} \overset{df}{=} \lambda_1$. By A.3 there exists a number $\rho_1 > 0$ such that for every interval $I \subset \langle 0,1 \rangle$ we have (see Lemma 7 in [S]).

$$|f(I)| \geq \rho_1 |I|^2.$$

If both end points of $f^{n+j}(\Delta_{n,i})$ belong to the same component of V_1 for $1 \leq j \leq s$, then obviously

$$|f^{n+j}(\Delta_{n,i})| \geq \lambda_1^j |f^n(\Delta_{n,i})| > |f^n(\Delta_{n,i})|$$

for all $1 \leq j \leq s$. If for a k the end points of

$f^{n+k}(\Delta_{n,i})$ belong to different components of V_1, then in view of the fact that they belong to $V_0 \subset \overline{V}_0 \subset V_1$ we have

$$|f^{n+k}(\Delta_{n,i})| \geq \operatorname{dist}(\overline{V}_0, V_1^c) \overset{df}{=} \gamma_2 .$$

Thus

$$|f^{n+j}(\Delta_{n,i})| \geq \rho\gamma_2^2 \overset{df}{=} \gamma_0$$

for any $j \geq 0$.

Theorem 1. If the assumptions A.1 - A.4 are satisfied, then A.5 and A.6 are equivalent.

Proof of A.6 $\Longrightarrow$ A.5. This implication is easy to prove. Let x_0 be a periodic point: $f^p(x_0) = x_0$. Choose the period p so that $p \geq n_0$ (of course p is not necessarily the prime period). Consider the sequence $|f'(x_0)|, \ldots, |f'(x_{p-1})|$, where $x_i = f^k(x_0)$, $i = 0, \ldots, p-1$. If for every $x_i : x_i \notin D$, then

$$|f'(x_i)| \geq \tau_2$$

which implies

$$|f^{p'}(x_0)| \geq \tau_2^p .$$

Assume now that there exists an x_{i_0} such that $x_{i_0} \in D$. Consider the sequence $x_{i_0+1}, \ldots, x_{p-1}, x_0, \ldots, x_{i_0}$. We have $f^p(x_{i_0+1}) = x_{i_0} \in D$, $p \geq n_0$, so in view of Lemma 6 from [S]

$$|f^{p'}(x_{i_0+1})| = \prod_{i=1}^{p-1} |f'(x_i)| \geq \lambda_8^p$$

where $\lambda_8 > 1$ is a constant number. Therefore for any period $p \geq n_0$ we have

$$|f^{p'}(x_0)| \geq \tau_3^p$$

where $\tau_3 = \min(\tau_2, \lambda_8) > 1$.

Suppose now that $p < n_0$. Let k be an integer such that $kp \geq n_0$ Then

$$|f^{p'}(x_0)|^k = |f^{kp'}(x)| \geq \tau_3^{kp}$$

which implies

$$|f^{p'}(x_0)| \geq \tau_3^p.$$

Let $D = \{x : |f'(x)| < \tau_1\}$ where $1 < \tau_1 < \lambda_1$, where λ_1 is from [S] (also see the definition of the set V_1). To prove the converse implication we need several lemmas:

Lemma 1. Assume that A.1 - A.5 hold. Then there exist two numbers b_1, $K > 0$ such that for every periodic point $a_0 \in D$, $f^p(a_0) = a_0$, there exist two intervals $I' = \langle a_0, \beta' \rangle$, $I'' = \langle \beta'', a_0 \rangle$ such that $|f^p(I')| \geq b_1$, $|f^p(I'')| \geq b_1$ and

$$\left| \frac{f^{p'}(x)}{f^{p'}(y)} \right| \leq K$$

for any $x, y \in I'$ or I''.

Proof. Let $I' = I = \langle a_0, \beta \rangle$. Assume $I_i = f^i(I)$ are mutually disjoint for $i = 0, 1, \ldots, p-1$ and that they are small enough: this means that

1°. $|I_i| < \delta_1$ for $i = 0, \ldots, p$, where $\delta_1 > 0$ is a number such that if $I_i \cap U_j^c \neq \emptyset$ then $\inf_{x \in I_i} |f'(x)| \overset{df}{=} \delta_2 > 0$; the set U_δ is the same set as in Lemma 2a in [S].

2°. If $I_i \subset U_\delta$ and $I_i = \langle a_i, \beta_i \rangle$, $a_i < \beta_i < c$, $c \in C_1^0$, then

$$\frac{|I_1|}{|\alpha_{i-c}|} < \frac{1}{2}$$

where $\vartheta_2 = \inf_{x \in U_\delta} |f''(x)|$.

By standard estimations we have

$$\frac{|f^{p'}(x)|}{|f^{p'}(y)|} = \prod_{i=0}^{p-1} \left|\frac{f'(x_i)}{f'(y_i)}\right| \leq \prod_{i=0}^{p-1} \left[1 + \frac{|f''(\xi_i)||x_i - y_i|}{|f'(y_i)|}\right]$$

$$\leq \prod_{i=0}^{p-1} \left[1 + \frac{\vartheta}{f'(y_i)} |x_i - y_i|\right] \leq \exp\left\{\vartheta \sum_{i=0}^{p-1} \frac{|x_i - y_i|}{|f'(y_i)|}\right\};$$

$$\vartheta = \max_{x \in <0,1} |f''(x)|.$$

There are two possibilities: either $I_i \cap U_\delta^c \neq \emptyset$ and then $|f'(y_i)| \geq \delta_2$, or $I_k \subset U_\delta$ and then by Lemma 2b [S] there exists an integer $k(i)$ such that

$$(1) \qquad |I_{i+k(i)}| \geq d_1 \cdot \frac{|I_i|}{\max_{x \in I_i} |f'(x)|};$$

moreover, for $i_1 \neq i_2 : i_1 + k(i_1) \neq i_2 + k(i_2)$. Suppose $I_i = <a_i, \beta_1>$, $a_1 < \beta_i < c$, $c \in C_1^0$. By the assumption 2° we have

$$(2) \qquad \frac{|I_i|}{\max_{x \in I_i} |f'(x)|} = \frac{|I_i|}{|f'(a_i)|} = \frac{|I_i|}{|f'(c) + f''(\xi)(a_i - c)|}$$

$$\leq \frac{|I_i|}{\vartheta_2 |a_i - c|} > \frac{1}{2}$$

and therefore by Remark 4 from [S] we have

$$\frac{|I_i|}{\max_{x \in I_i} |f'(x)|} \geq \frac{1}{2} \frac{|I_i|}{\min_{x \in I_i} |f'(x)|}$$

which give us

$$\frac{|x_i - y_i|}{|f'(y_i)|} \geq \begin{cases} \dfrac{|I_i|}{\delta_2} & \text{if } I_i \cap U_\delta^c \neq \emptyset \\ \\ \dfrac{2}{d_1} |I_{i+k(i)}| & \text{if } I_i \subset U_\delta \end{cases}$$

and $I_{i_0+k(i_0)}$ is contained in V_1. The intervals I_i are pairwise disjoint: if $I_i \cap I_j \neq \emptyset$, then there must be a point $\bar{x} \in f^p(I_i \cup I_j)$ such that $f^{p'}(\bar{x}) = 0$ (otherwise there would be a sink), which contradicts the assumption 2°. Since the point $x_0 \in D$, and $D \cap V_1 = \emptyset$, then $i_0 + k(i_0) \leq p-1$. Thus $\sum_{i_0} |I_{i_0+k(i_0)}| \leq 1$. Thus in view $i_1 + k(i_1) \neq I_2 + k(i_2)$ for $i_1 \neq i_2$ we have

$$\sum_{i=0}^{p-1} \frac{|x_i - y_i|}{|f'(y_i)|} \leq \frac{1}{\delta_2} \sum_{I_i \cap U_j \neq \emptyset} |I_i| + \frac{2}{d_1} \sum_{U_\delta \supset I_i} |I_{i+k(i)}|$$

$$\leq \frac{1}{\delta_2} + \frac{2}{d_1} .$$

Therefore it is enough to set $K = \exp\{\vartheta(\frac{1}{\delta_2} + \frac{1}{d_1})\}$.

Now we shall define the number b_1 (independent of the point x_0). We start to enlarge the length of the interval I while ensuring that the condition 2° is preserved. There are two possibilities: 1) before we get the equality in 2° for some i the length of one of the intervals $I_0, \ldots I_{p-1}$ is greater than δ_1; 2) the lengths of all I_i are smaller than δ_1 and for some i_0 we have

$$\frac{|I_{i_0}|}{|a_{i_0} - c|} = \frac{1}{2} .$$

Suppose $a_{i_0} \leq \beta_{i_0} < c$, $c \in C_1^0$. Thus $\max_{x \in I_i} |f'(x)| = |f'(a_i)| =$

$= |f'(c) + f''(\xi)(a_i - c)| = |f''(\xi)(a_i - c)| \leq \vartheta|a_i - c|$. By Lemma 2b from [S] there exists an integer $k(i_0)$ such that

$$|I_{i_0+k(i_0)}| \geq d_1 \frac{|I_{i_0}|}{\max\limits_{I_{i_0}} |f'(x)|} \geq d_1 \frac{|I_{i_0}|}{|a_{i_o} - c|} = \frac{d_1}{2\vartheta}.$$

Therefore we can find an interval I such that the intervals I_i, $i = 0,\dots,p-1$, are pairwise disjoint and one of them is of length greater than δ_1 or $\frac{d_1}{2\vartheta}$. Let m be an integer such that

$$\max_{1\leq i\leq r_m} |\Delta_{m,i}| < \frac{1}{2}\min(\delta_1, \frac{d_1}{2\vartheta}).$$

Such m exists in view of Theorem 2 from [S]. Then the interval I_{i_0} contains an interval $\Delta_{m,i}$. Therefore by Remark 1 we have

$$|I_p| \geq \min\{\min_{\substack{1\leq i\leq r_m\\ 0\leq j\leq m}} |f^j(\Delta_{m,i})|, \min_{j\geq m}|f^j(\Delta_{m,i})|\} \stackrel{df}{=} b_1.$$

Corollary 1. For every $x \in I$ we have

$$\frac{1}{K}|f^{p'}(a)| \leq |f^{p'}(x)| \leq K\cdot|f^{p'}(a)|.$$

Thus in view of A.5 for every $x \in I$

$$|f^{p'}(x)| \geq \frac{1}{K}\varkappa^p.$$

Lemma 2. There exists a number $d_3 > 0$ such that for every $\Delta_{n,i}$ the following inequality holds:

$$\sum_{s=0}^{n} |f^s(\Delta_{n,i})| \leq d_3.$$

Proof. Let $\Delta_{n,i} = (\alpha,\beta)$. By definition of $\Delta_{n,i}$ there exists two integers $k \le l \le n$ such that $f^k(\alpha), f^l(\beta) \in C_1$; without loss of generality we may assume $l = n-1$ (see Remark 5, [S]). We consider $f^s(\Delta_{n,i})$ separately for $s \le k$ and for $s > k$.

Assume $s \le k$. Since every $f^s(\Delta_{n,i})$ is an interval of the family $\{\Delta_{n-s,j}\}$, every two intervals $f^r(\Delta_{n,i}), f^s(\Delta_{n,i})$ either are disjoint, or one contains the other, $r \le s \le k$. Let s_0 be a number such that for every two $t_1 < s_0$, $t_2 \le k$ $f^{t_1}(\Delta_{n,i}) \cap f^{t_2}(\Delta_{n,i}) = \emptyset$. Thus

$$(3) \qquad \sum_{s=0}^{s_0} |f^s(\Delta_{n,i})| \le 1.$$

Let p be the smallest integer such that $f^{s_0+p}(\Delta_{n,i}) \cap f^{s_0}(\Delta_{n,i}) \ne \emptyset$, i.e., $f^{s_0+p}(\Delta_{n,i}) \supset f^{s_0}(\Delta_{n,i})$. Thus there exists a periodic point $a_0 \in f^{s_0}(\Delta_{n,i})$, $f^p(a_0) = a_0$. Let s_1 be an integer such that for $s_0 \le s < s_1$

$$f^s(\Delta_{n,i}) \subset I_j$$

where I_j are some intervals which have the following properties: 1) $a_j \in I_j$; 2) if $I_j = (\alpha,\beta) : \alpha < a_j < \beta$, then $|f^p((a_j,\beta))| = \frac{b_1}{2}$, $|f^p((\alpha,a_j))| = \frac{b_1}{2}$; 3) all of them are pairwise disjoint. In view of Lemma 1 such intervals exist. Moreover, $|f^{p'}|\big|_{I_j} \ge \varkappa^p K^{-1}$. We assume s_1 to be of the form: $s_1 = s_0 + rp$. It is easy to see that

$$(4) \qquad \sum_{s=s_0}^{s_1-1} |f^s(\Delta_{n,i})|$$

$$\le K \sum_{s=s_0+(r-1)p}^{s_1-1} |f^s(\Delta_{n,i})|\left(1 + \frac{1}{\varkappa^p} + \frac{1}{\varkappa^{2p}} + \cdots + \frac{1}{\varkappa^{(r-2)p}}\right) \le$$

$$\le K \cdot \frac{1}{1-\frac{1}{\varkappa^p}} \le K \frac{1}{1-\frac{1}{\varkappa}} = \frac{K\varkappa}{\varkappa-1}.$$

In the sequence of intervals $(f^s(\Delta_{n,i}))_{s=s_1}^{s_1+p}$ there exists an interval $f^{\bar{s}}(\Delta_{n,i})$ such that

$$f^{\bar{s}}(\Delta_{n,i}) \not\subset I_{\bar{s}-s_1}.$$

In view of the property 2) we have $|f^p(f^{\bar{s}}(\Delta_{n,i}))| \ge \frac{b_1}{2}$. Set $s_1 = \bar{s}-1$ and consider $f^s(\Delta_{n,i})$ for $s_1 \le s \le s_1+p$. Since every two intervals $f^s(\Delta_{n,i})$, $f^t(\Delta_{n,i})$ are either disjoint or one is contained in the other, we have

$$\bigcup_{s=s_1}^{s_1+p} f^s(\Delta_{n,i}) = L_1 \cup \cdots \cup L_w$$

where $L_1,\ldots,L_k$ are pairwise disjoint intervals (they are of course of the form $f^s(\Delta_{n,i})$). Take $L_1 = f^{s_1+r_1}(\Delta_{n,i})$. This interval covers some of the intervals $f^s(\Delta_{n,i})$, $s_1 \le s \le s_1+p$. But if it covers for instance an interval $f^{s_1+j}(\Delta_{n,i})$, then there exists a periodic point $x_0 \in f^{s_1+j}(\Delta_{n,i})$ of period $r_1-j : f^{r_1-j}(x_0) = x_0$. Since $|L_1| < \frac{b_1}{2}$, the estimate (6) is valid, or there exists an $s_2 < k$ such that $f^{s_2}(\Delta_{n,i})$ is not contained in the corresponding I_j. Then using (6) and (7) we get

$$(8) \qquad \sum_{s=0}^{n} |f^s(\Delta_{n,i})| \le d_4 + d_5.$$

Now we have only to estimate the sum $\sum_{s=k}^{n} |f^s(\Delta_{n,i})|$ in the first possibility. Since $f^2(\alpha) \in R \subset V_0$ for every $s > k$, the intervals $f^s(\Delta_{n,i})$ stay in V_1 for $s > k$ for some s. But $|f'(x)| \ge \lambda_1 > 1$ for $x \in V_1$, so that

$$\sum_{s=k+1}^{j} |f^s(\Delta_{n,i})| \le |f^j(\Delta_{n,i})|(1 + \frac{1}{\lambda_1} + \cdots + \frac{1}{\lambda_1^{j-k}})$$

if $f^s(\Delta_{n,i}) \subset V_1$ for $s \le j$. Therefore there exists a j_0 such that $f^{j_0}(\beta) \notin V_1$ (and $f^{j_0}(\alpha) \in R$), so that

$$\sum_{s=k+1}^{j_0} |f^s(\Delta_{n,i})| \le |f^{j_0}(\Delta_{n,i})| \sum_{s=0}^{\infty} \frac{1}{\lambda_1^s} .$$

But in this case $|f^{j_0}(\Delta_{n,i})| \ge \mathrm{dist}(R,V_1^c) = b$, so

$$(9) \qquad \sum_{s=k+1}^{j_0} |f^s(\Delta_{n,i})| \le \frac{b\lambda_1}{\lambda_1 - 1} \overset{\mathrm{df}}{=} d_6 .$$

In view of Theorem 2 [S] there exists an m_2 such that $n - j_0 \le m_2$. Thus

$$(10) \quad \sum_{s=j_0+1}^{n} |f^s(\Delta_{n,i})| \le \max_{1\le j\le r_{m_2}} \sum_{s=0}^{m_2} |f^s(\Delta_{m_2,j})| \overset{\mathrm{df}}{=} d_7.$$

In view of (8), (9) and (10) we get finally that

$$\sum_{s=0}^{n} |f^s(\Delta_{n,i})| \le d_4 + d_5 + d_6 + d_7 \overset{\mathrm{df}}{=} d_3.$$

Now let $\Delta_{n,i} = (\alpha,\beta)$ be arbitrary. Set $B_s = (\alpha_s,\beta_s) = f^s(\Delta_{n,i})$, $s = 0,\dots,n$. In view of the proposition, always $|B_n| \ge \gamma$. Let $L_n^1 = (\alpha_n,a_n^1)$. $L_n^2 = (a_n^2,\beta_n)$ be two intervals such that $|L_n^1| \geq \frac{\gamma}{3}$, $|L_n^2| < \frac{\gamma}{3}$. Set $K_n = B_n - (L_n^1 \cup L_n^2)$.

Lemma 3. There exists a number $u > 0$ such that for every $x,y \in \boldsymbol{f}^{-n}(K_n) \cap \Delta_{n,i}$ the following inequality holds:

$$\frac{|f^{n'}(x)|}{|f^{n'}(y)|} \leq u.$$

Proof. Let $f^k(\alpha)$, $f^1(\beta) \in C_1$; without loss of generality we can assume that $k \leq 1 = n - 1$. In view of A.4 we have $\mathrm{dist}(\alpha_n, D)$, $\mathrm{dist}(\beta_n, D) \geq \mathrm{dist}(D,R)$. Assume $|L_n^1| = |L_n^2| \overset{\mathrm{df}}{=} d_8$ where $d_8 < \min(\frac{1}{3}\gamma, \mathrm{dist}(D,R))$. By Lemma 7 in [S] we have

$$(11) \qquad |L_{n-1}^1|, |L_{n-1}^2| \geq \frac{1}{\sqrt{\rho_1}} \cdot \sqrt{d_8} \overset{\mathrm{df}}{=} d_9,$$

where $L_{n-1}^1 = f_{B_{n-1}}^{-1}(L_n^1)$, $L_{n-1}^2 = f_{B_{n-1}}^{-1}(L_n^2)$; in this Lemma we consider only preimages contained in B_s, i.e. $f_{B_{n-1}}^{-1}$ denotes the inverse mapping to the map $f : B_{n-1} \to B_n$. In the sequel we shall drop the sub-index B_s, $s = 0,\dots,n-1$. In view of (11) we have

$$(12) \qquad \frac{|L_{n-1}^1|}{|B_{n-1}|}, \frac{|L_{n-1}^2|}{|B_{n-1}|} \geq d_9.$$

Now, we see that for $s = 1,2$ we have

$$(13) \qquad \frac{|L_{k+1}^s|}{|B_{k+1}|} = \frac{|f^{-(n-k-2)}(L_{n-1}^s)|}{|f^{-(n-k-2)}(B_{n-1})|} = \frac{\int_{L_{n=1}^s} |f^{-(n-k-2)'}(y)|\,dy}{\int_{B_{n-1}} |f^{-(n-k-2)'}(y)|\,dy} \geq$$

$$\geq \frac{|L^s_{n-1}| \min\limits_{y\in B^s_{n-1}} |f^{-(n-k-2)'}(y)|}{|B_{n-1}| \max\limits_{y\in B_{n-1}} |f^{-(n-k-2)'}(y)|} .$$

In view of Lemma 10 of [S]

$$\frac{|f^{-(n-k-2)'}(y)|}{|f^{-(n-k-2)'}(\bar{y})|} = \frac{|f^{(n-k-2)'}(\bar{x})|}{|f^{(n-k-2)'}(x)|} \geq u_2^{-1}$$

for every $y,\bar{y} \in B_{n-1}$; $\bar{y} = f^{(n-k-2)}(\bar{x})$, $y = f^{(n-k-2)}(x)$, $x,\bar{x} \in B_{k+1}$. By (12) and (13) we get

$$\frac{|L^s_{k+1}|}{|B_{k+1}|} \geq d_9u_2^{-1}, \qquad s = 1,2.$$

Hence

$$\frac{|K_{k+1}|}{|B_{k+1}|} \leq 1 - \frac{|L^1_{k+1}|}{|B_{k+1}|} - \frac{|L^2_{k+1}|}{|B_{k+1}|} \leq 1 - 2d_9u_2^{-1}.$$

Therefore

$$\frac{|K_{k+1}|}{|L^1_{k+1}|} = \frac{|K_{k+1}|}{|B_{k+1}|} \cdot \frac{|B_{k+1}|}{|L^1_{k+1}|} \leq 1 - 2d_9u_2^{-1}.$$

Let $x_{k+1}, y_{k+1} \in K_{k+1}$. Then

$$(14) \qquad \frac{|x_{k+1}-\alpha_{k+1}|}{|y_{k+1}-\alpha_{k+1}|} \leq \frac{|K_{k+1}|+|L^1_{k+1}|}{|L^1_{k+1}|} \leq 1 + \frac{|K_{k+1}|}{|L^1_{k+1}|}$$

$$\leq 2 - 2d_9u_2^{-1}.$$

Notice that $B_k = (\alpha_k, \beta_k)$ where $\alpha_k \in C^0_1$. Now there are two possibilities: either 1° $|B_k| < \delta_1$ and $B_k \subset U_\delta$ (see the proof of Lemma 1); or 2° $|B_k| \geq \delta_1$ or $|B_k| < \delta_1$ and $B_k \cap U_\delta^c \neq \emptyset$ which implies $|f'(x)| \geq \delta_2$ for any $x \in B_k$.

Assume that 1° holds. Then for any $x_k, y_k \in K_k$ we have by Taylor's Formula:

$$\frac{|f'(x_k)|}{|f'(y_k)|} = \frac{|f'(x_k)-f'(\alpha_k)|}{|f'(y_k)-f'(\alpha_k)|} = \frac{|f''(\xi)|\cdot|x_k-\alpha_k|}{|f''(\eta)|\cdot|y_k-\alpha_k|} \leq \frac{\vartheta}{\vartheta_2}\,\frac{|x_k-\alpha_k|}{|y_k-\alpha_k|} .$$

On the other hand (once again we apply the Taylor's Formula)

$$(15)\qquad \frac{|x_{k+1}-\alpha_{k+1}|}{|y_{k+1}-\alpha_{k+1}|} = \frac{\frac{1}{2}|f''(\xi')|\,|x_k-\alpha_k|^2}{\frac{1}{2}\,f''(\eta')|\,|y_k-\alpha_k|^2} \geq \frac{\vartheta_2}{\vartheta}\,\frac{|x_k-\alpha_k|^2}{|y_k-\alpha_k|^2} .$$

We conclude from (14) and (15) that

$$\frac{|x_k-\alpha_k|}{|y_k-\alpha_k|} \leq \sqrt{\frac{2\vartheta}{\vartheta_2}(1-d_9u_2^{-1})} .$$

Thus

$$(16)\qquad \frac{|f'(x_k)|}{|f'(y_k)|} \leq \sqrt{\frac{2\vartheta^3}{\vartheta_2^3}(1-d_9u_2^{-1})} .$$

Assume now that 2° holds. If $|B_k| \geq \delta_1$, then $|B_{k+1}| \geq \rho\delta_1^2$ which implies $|L_{k+1}^1| \geq d_9u_2^{-1}\cdot\rho_1\delta_1^2$. Thus $\rho_1|L_k^1|^2 \geq |L_{k+1}^1|$ implies

$$|L_k^1| \geq \sqrt{d_9u_2^{-1}\delta_1^2}$$

which means that there exists a number $\delta_4 > 0$ such that $|f'(x)| > \delta_4$ if $x \in K_k$. The same happens if $B_k \cap U_\delta^c \neq \emptyset$ and $|B_k| < \delta_1$. The arguments above show that there exists a number $u_3 > 0$ such that

$$\frac{|f'(x_k)|}{|f'(y_k)|} \le u_3 \qquad \text{if} \quad x_k, y_k \in K_k.$$

The same holds for $x_{n-1}, y_{n-1} \in K_{n-1}$:

$$\left|\frac{f'(x_{n-1})}{f'(x_{n-1})}\right| \le u_4$$

for some number u_4 since K_{n-1} is separated from C_1^0. Therefore by Lemma 10 of [S] we have

$$\frac{|f^{n'}(x)|}{|f^{n'}(y)|} = \prod_{i=0}^{n-1} \frac{|f'(x_i)|}{|f'(y_i)|} = \prod_{i=0}^{k} \frac{|f'(x_i)|}{|f'(y_i)|} \cdot \frac{|f'(x_k)|}{|f'(y_k)|}$$

$$\cdot \prod_{i=k+2}^{n-2} \frac{f'(x_i)}{f'(y_i)} \cdot \frac{f'(x_{n-1})}{f'(y_{n-1})}$$

$$\le u_1 \cdot u_3 \cdot u_2 \cdot u_4 \overset{\text{df}}{=} u$$

which completes the proof.

Proof of the implication A.5 $\Longrightarrow$ A.6. Let n_0 be a number such that for every $n \ge n_0$ $\max_{1 \le i \le r_n} |\Delta_{n,i}| \le \frac{1}{u} 6\gamma$, where γ is from Proposition and u is from Lemma 3. Suppose that $f^n(x) \in D$, $n \ge n_0$. Let $x \in \overline{\Delta}_{n,i}$ for some i. Set $F_n = B_n - (L_n^1 \cup L_n^2)$, where $B_n = f^n(\Delta_{n,i})$, L_n^1, L_n^2 are as in Lemma 3. Let $F = f^{-n}(F_n) \cap \Delta_{n,i}$. Obviously $x \in F$. Since

$$\frac{|F_n|}{|F|} \ge \frac{|B_n| - |L_n^1| - |L_n^2|}{|\Delta_{n,i}|} \ge \frac{\frac{1}{3}\gamma}{\frac{1}{u}\cdot 6\gamma} = 2u,$$

there exists a point $y \in F$ such that $|f^{n'}(y)| \ge 2u$. Thus by Lemma 3

$$\left|\frac{f^{n'}(y)}{f^{n'}(x)}\right| \leq u$$

which implies

$$|f^{n'}(x)| \geq \frac{1}{u}|f^{n'}(y)| \geq 2.$$

In view of Theorem 4 in [S] we have the following

Corollary 2. If a mapping $f:\langle 0,1\rangle \hookleftarrow$ satisfies the assumptions A.1 - A.5 (or A.6), then there exists an f-invariant measure absolutely continuous with respect to Lebesgue measure.

It follows from the Misiurewicz's results [M] that if a mapping $f:\langle 0,1\rangle \hookleftarrow$ satisfies A.1, A.2, A.3, if moreover $Sf \leq 0$ $\left(Sf = \frac{f''}{f'} - \frac{3}{2}\left(\frac{f''}{f'}\right)^2\right)$, and f has no sinks, then the condition A.4 implies the following stronger condition for an iterate of f:

Â.4. There exists a neighbourhood U of C_1^0 such that

$$\bigcup_{n=1}^{\infty} f^n(C_1^0) \cap U = \emptyset.$$

More precisely: if f satisfies A.4, then there exists an iterate $f = f^m$ such that f satisfies the condition Â.4. ([M], Theorem 1.3 and Lemma 3.1). The proof in [M] works in the case that f satisfies A.1, A.2, A.3, A.6 (it is not necessary to assume $Sf \leq 0$). So we have the following:

Theorem 2. If $f:\langle 0,1\rangle \hookleftarrow$ satisfies A.1, A.2, A.3, Â.4, A.6, then there exists an f-invariant measure absolutely continuous with respect to Lebesgue measure.

2. The condition A.6 is checkable. Suppose that a mapping f satisfies A.1 - A.4. If a point x is close enough to a critical point, then for its first iterate $f^n(x)$ such that $f^n(x) \in D$ holds $|f^{n'}(x)| > 1$. Indeed, by Lemma 2a of [S] we see that if $x \approx c$, $c \in C_1^0$, then there exists an

integer k such that

$$|f^{(k+1)'}(x)| \geq \frac{d_0}{|f'(x)|}$$

and $f^j(x) \in V_1 = \{x : |f'(x)| \geq \lambda_1\}$, $\lambda_1 > 1$, for $j = 1,\dots,k$. Hence if $|f'(x)| < d_0$, and $f^n(x)$ is the first iterate such that $f^n(x) \in D$, then $|f^{n'}(x)| > 1$. So we have to deal only with the x such that $d_0 \leq |f'(x)| \leq \tau_1$. It is more difficult to check the condition A.4 (or Â.4). Practically it is possible if the trajectory of every critical points hits a periodic repulsing orbit.

Now we shall show that some mappings satisfies the conditions A.1, A.2, A.3, A.4 and A.6, so that they have an invariant measure absolutely continuous with respect to Lebesgue measure.

<u>Example 1</u>. Let $f_\varepsilon(x) = (\beta+1)x^5 = \varepsilon x^3 - (\beta-\varepsilon)x$; assume that $f_\varepsilon : <-1,1> \hookleftarrow$. The number β is chosen in this way that the images of the critical points (there are two of them) are -1 and 1 respectively. (Fig. 1)

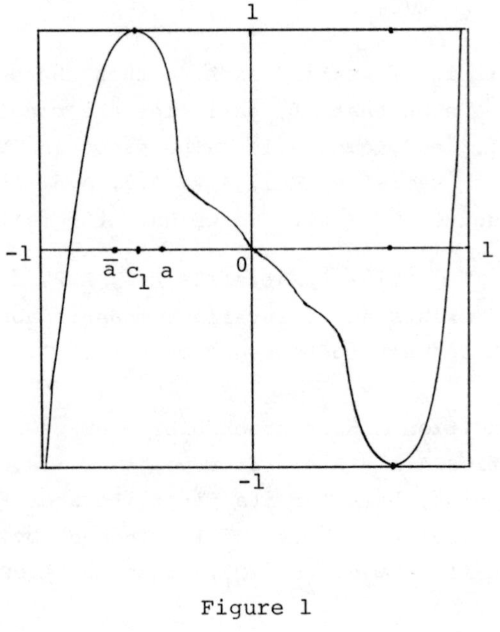

Figure 1

Set $\varepsilon = 0.1$. Then $\beta \approx 2.1364$. Notice that the derivative at ± 1 is larger than 1. The critical points are $c_1 \approx -0.6083151$ and $c_2 = -c_1$. We set $U_\delta = \{x : |f'(x)| < 1\}$ and D a set a little bit larger than U_δ. Let $a, \bar{a}$ be such that $f'(\bar{a}) = 1$, $f'(a) = -1$, $\bar{a}, a < 0$. The images $a_1 = f(a)$, $\bar{a}_1 = f(\bar{a})$ are bigger than 0.95. We set $V_1 = \{x : 0.95 < |x| \leq 1\}$. Then $f(D) \subset V_1$. By computations we find that $\lambda_1 \approx 10.465938$ and $d_0 \approx 0.05343 > 0.05$. Let $F = \{x : 0.05 \leq |f'(x)| < 0,1\}$. It turns out that $f(F)$, $f^2(F)$ is contained in V_1.

We shall show that the condition A.6 holds. We have to check it only in the case $0.05 \leq |f'(x)| \leq 1$. Suppose first that $0.1 \leq |f'(x)| \leq 1$. Then

$$|f^{2'}(x)| = |f'(x)| \cdot |f'(x_0)| \geq 0.1 \cdot \lambda_1 > 1.$$

If $0.05 \leq |f'(x)| < 0.1$, then

$$|f^{3'}(x)| = |f'(x)| \cdot |f'(x_1)| \cdot |f'(x_2)| > 0.05 \cdot \lambda_1^2 > 5.$$

Thus there exists an invariant measure absolutely continuous with respect to Lebesgue measure. Notice that for this mapping the condition $Sf \leq 0$ does not hold. Indeed, we have $f'(0) = -(\beta - 0.1) < -2$, $f''(0) = 0$, $f''(0) = -0.6$, so that $Sf(0) = \frac{f''(0)}{f'(0)} - \frac{3}{2}\left(\frac{f''(0)}{f'(0)}\right)^2 = 0.3$. Therefore the exixtence of the measure is not implied by [M].

In a similar way we check that for $\varepsilon = 0$ the condition A.6 holds, with all estimates "sharp" (equalities excluded). So there exists an $\varepsilon_0 > 0$ such that for every $\varepsilon \in \langle 0, \varepsilon_0 \rangle$ there exists a $\beta = \beta(\varepsilon)$ such that the mapping $f_\varepsilon(x) : \langle -1, 1 \rangle \hookleftarrow$ has the property: the images of the critical points are $-1, 1$ respectively, $f_\varepsilon(-1) = -1$, $f_\varepsilon(1) = 1$, $f'_\varepsilon(-1) = f'_\varepsilon(1) > 1$, and A.6 holds. Therefore for each f_ε there exists an invariant measure μ_ε absolutely continuous with respect to Lebesgue measure. Notice that no two of them are smoothly conjugate (although they are topologically conjugate): if for two f_β and $f_{\overline{\beta}}$ we have $f'(1) = f'(1)$ and $f'(0) = f'(0)$, then $\beta = \overline{\beta}$.

Example 2. Let $f_\beta(x) = 2x - \frac{2}{\pi^2} + \beta \sin^3 x$. Assume that f_β maps the interval $<0,\pi>$ onto itself, i.e. that the maximum of f over $<0,\pi>$ is equal to π (Fig. 2)

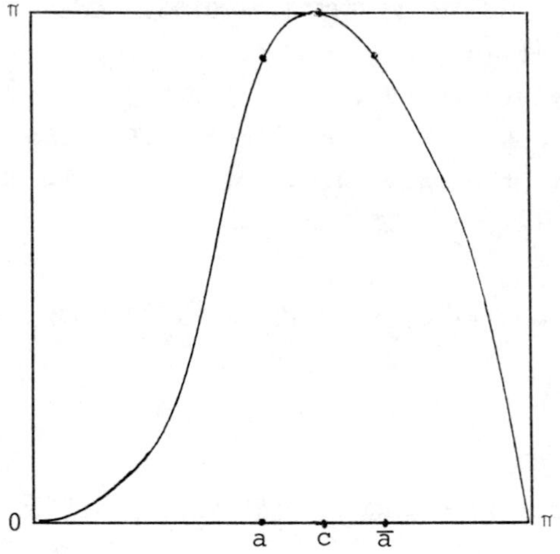

Figure 2

There exists exactly one value of β_0 for which it occurs: $\beta_0 \approx 0.75568$. The mapping has one critical point $c \approx 1.695$. For this mapping the assumptions of Corollary 2 are satisfied: the conditions A.1 - A.4 are apparently fulfilled, we have only to check the condition A.6. We set $D = <a,\overline{a}>$ where $a = 1.44$, $\overline{a} = 1.95$, $U_\delta = \{x : |f'(x)| < 1\}$, $V_1 = <0;0.53>$. It turns out that $f^2(D) \subset V_1$, $\lambda_1 = 2$, $d_0 \approx 0.20605$. In the same way as in the previous example we show that the condition A.6 holds. Notice that the Schwartzian derivative Sf is positive at $x = 0$.

The existence of an invariant measure absolutely continuous with respect to Lebesgue measure for the mappings in Examples 1 and 2 follows also of the Ognev's result [0].

REFERENCES

[M] M. Misiurewicz, Absolutely continuous measures for certain maps of an interval, Preprint IHES/M/79/293.

[E] D. Ruelle, Applications conservant une measure absolument continue par rapport à dx sur $<0,1>$, Comm. Math. Phys. vol. 55 (1977), 47-51.

[S] W. Szlenk, Some dynamical properties of certain differentiable mappings of an interval, Part I. Bol. Soc. Mat. Mex., to appear.

[O] A. Ognev, Metric Properties of a class of Maps of the Interval, Mat. Zametki (1981) (to appear).

Warsaw Agricultural University
Institute of Applied Mathematics
Warsaw

A NOTE ON GENERIC PROPERTIES OF CONTINUOUS MAPS

E. M. Coven, J. Madden and Z. Nitecki

Let M be a compact manifold, with or without boundary. The genericity theorem of J. Palis, C. Pugh, M. Shub and D. Sullivan [PPSS] asserts that, among others, the property $\Omega = \overline{P}$ (the set of non-wandering points is the closure of the set of periodic points) is C^0-generic, i.e., holds for all homeomorphisms in some residual subset of the space Homeo(M) of all homeomorphisms of M to itself. This note points out and corrects a technical error in their proof, and extends the result to the space $C^0(M,M)$ of all continuous maps of M to itself.

Our proof mimics Pugh's proof of the General Density Theorem [P]. His proof can be formulated as follows. Let $\mathcal{X}$ denote the appropriate complete metric space of maps, in this case Homeo(M) or $C^0(M,M)$. One establishes a <u>weak closing lemma</u>: $\Omega(f) \subset \limsup_{g\to f} \overline{P(g)}$ for all $f \in \mathcal{X}$, and a <u>semi-continuity lemma</u>: $\overline{P(f)} \subset \liminf_{g\to f} \overline{P(g)}$ for all g in some residual subset $\mathcal{X}'$ or $\mathcal{X}$, i.e., the mapping $f \to \overline{P(f)}$ (of $\mathcal{X}$ to the space of compact subsets of M, with the Hausdorff metric) is lower semicontinuous on $\mathcal{X}'$. Since $\mathcal{X}'$ is a Baire space, it follows from the semi-continuity lemma that this mapping has a residual (in $\mathcal{X}'$ and hence in $\mathcal{X}$) set $\mathcal{X}''$ of points of continuity. The weak closing lemma then implies that $\Omega(f) = \overline{P(f)}$ for all $f \in \mathcal{X}''$.

The weak closing lemma follows immediately from the standard C^0 closing lemma: if $f \in \mathcal{X}$, $x \in \Omega(f)$ and $\varepsilon > 0$, then $x \in P(g)$ for some g ε-close to f. For $\mathcal{X} = \text{Homeo}(M)$, this is a well-known result of Folk. We prove it for $\mathcal{X} = C^0(M,M)$.

Choose $\delta > 0$ so that if y is δ-close to x, then $f(y)$ is ε-close to $f(x)$. Since $x \in \Omega(f)$, there exists y δ-close to x and $n > 1$ such that $f^n(y)$ is ε-close to x. We may assume that $f(x), y, f(y), \ldots, f^n(y)$ are distinct. Then there is a continuous map $h : M \to M$, ε-close to the identity map, such that $h(f(x)) = f(y)$, $h(f^i(y)) = f^i(y)$ for $i \leq n-1$, and $h(f^n(y)) = x$. Let $g = h \circ f$. □

The proof of the semi-continuity lemma is based on the idea [PPSS] of a <u>permanent periodic point</u>: $x \in P(f)$ is permanent, denoted $x \in \mathrm{Perm}(f)$, if for every $\varepsilon > 0$ there exists $\delta > 0$, such that any map δ-close to f has a periodic point ε-close to x. The mapping $f \to \overline{P(f)}$ is lower semi-continuous at f whenever $P(f) = \mathrm{Perm}(f)$.

Palis, et. al. erroneously claim [PPSS, p. 244] that the mapping $f \to \overline{\mathrm{Perm}(f)}$ is everywhere lower semi-continuous. To see that this is not the case, consider the following example, defined on $[-1,1]$. For $n \geq 3$, let

$$f_n(x) = \begin{cases} -1 & \text{if } \quad -1 \leq x \leq -1/2 \\ x & \text{if } \quad -1/n \leq x \leq 1/n \\ 1 & \text{if } \quad 1/2 \leq x \leq 1 \end{cases}$$

and extend f_n linearly to the rest of $[-1,1]$. Then $f_n \to f$ where

$$f(x) = \begin{cases} -1 & \text{if } \quad -1 \leq x \leq -1/2 \\ 2x & \text{if } \quad -1/2 \leq x \leq 1/2 \\ 1 & \text{if } \quad 1/2 \leq x \leq 1. \end{cases}$$

Here 0 is in $\mathrm{Perm}(f)$ but not $\overline{\mathrm{Perm}(f_n)}$ for any n.

The following result implies the semi-continuity lemma.

<u>Permanence Lemma</u>. The property $P = \mathrm{Perm}$ is C^0-generic.

The proof of this lemma uses the notion of fixed point index (see [GP]. Let X be either $\mathrm{Homeo}(M)$ or $C^0(M,M)$ and let $f \in X$. Let U be an open ball in M whose boundary ∂U is an embedded sphere. Suppose further that

(1) f has no fixed points in ∂U.

(2) U is <u>sufficiently small</u> for f in the sense that either

(a) $\overline{U} \cap \overline{f(U)} = \phi$, or

(b) $\bar{U} \cup \overline{f(U)}$ is contained in a single coordinate patch of M.

Note that given U, (1) and (2) hold for an open subset of X, and that given f, every sufficiently small U is sufficiently small for f.

Assuming that (1) and (2) hold, the <u>fixed point index</u> $\iota_f(U)$ is defined in the usual way: if (2a) holds, then $\iota_f(U) = 0$; if (2b) holds, then $\iota_f(U) = \deg(\gamma)$, where $\gamma : \partial U \simeq S^{n-1} \to S^{n-1}$ is defined from local coordinates by $\gamma(x) = [f(x)-x]/\|f(x)-x\|$, $n = \dim(M)$ and $\deg(\ )$ denotes degree in the sense of Hopf. This definition is consistent (when (2a) and (2b) both hold) and is independent of the choice of coordinates. It satisfies (see [GP])

(3) If $\iota_f(U)$ is defined, then there exists a neighborhood N of f in X such that $\iota_g(U) = \iota_f(U)$ for every $g \in N$.

(4) If $\iota_f(U) \neq 0$, then f has a fixed point in U.

(5) If f is C^1, has exactly one fixed point in U and that fixed point is non-degenerate, then $\iota_f(U) \neq 0$.

In the following proof, we assume that M has no boundary, omitting the details necessary to extend the argument to manifolds with boundary.

<u>Proof of the Permanence Lemma</u>. Let $\{U_i\}$ be a countable base for the topology of M, consisting of open balls whose boundaries are embedded spheres. Define

$$A_i = \{f \in X \mid f(x) \neq x \text{ for all } x \in \bar{U}_i\},$$

$$B_i' = \{f \in X \mid f(x) \neq x \text{ for all } x \in \partial U_i \text{ and } \iota_f(U_i) \neq 0\},$$

$$B_i = \cup\{B_j' \mid \bar{U}_j \subset U_i\}.$$

Any C^1 map with no degenerate fixed points belongs to every $A_i \cup B_i$. Hence the set of Kupka-Smale maps in X is contained in every

$$\mathcal{D}_{n,i} = \{f \in \mathcal{X} | f^n \in \mathcal{A}_i \cup \mathcal{B}_i\}.$$

Since the set of Kupka-Smale maps is C^1-residual [S1], it and hence every $\mathcal{D}_{n,i}$ is dense in $\mathcal{X}$. Since $\mathcal{A}_i$ and $\mathcal{B}_i$ are open and the mapping $f \to f^n$ is continuous, every $\mathcal{D}_{n,i}$ is open and dense. Thus $\cap \mathcal{D}_{n,i}$ is residual in $\mathcal{X}$.

We claim that $P(f) = \text{Perm}(f)$ for all $f \in \cap\mathcal{D}_{n,i}$. Suppose $f \in \cap\mathcal{D}_{n,i}$ and $f^n(x) = x$. Then for every U_i containing x, there exists U_j such that $\overline{U}_j \subset U_i$ and $\iota_{f^n}(U_j) \neq 0$. It follows from (3) and (4) that $x \in \text{Perm}(f)$. □

<u>Remarks</u>. If M is the interval or the circle, thr Permanence Lemma can be proved without explicitly using the notion of fixed point index. For the interval, a fixed point x of f is permanent if and only if the graph of f crosses the diagonal at (x,x). Thus for the interval, we set

$$\mathcal{A}_i = \{f | f(x) \neq x \text{ for all } x \in \overline{U}_i\},$$

$$\mathcal{B}_i = \{f | f(x)-x \text{ takes on both positive and negative values in } U_i\}$$

and proceed as in the proof.

The proof of the closing lemma for continuous maps easily extends to the chain-recurrent points (see [S2], denoted CR: if $x \in CR(f)$ and $\varepsilon > 0$, then $x \in P(g)$ for some g ε-close to f. (This result also holds for homeomorphism.) Since $\Omega \subset CR$, the genericity theorem can be extended to state that $CR = \overline{P}$ holds generically in both Homeo(M) and $C^0(M,M)$.

One proof of the genericity theorem shows that the property of being a point of continuity of the mappings $f \to \Omega(f)$ and $f \to CR(f)$ is generic in both Homeo(M) and $C^0(M,M)$. Thus so is (1) f has no C^0 Ω-explsions, hence also (2) f has a fine sequence of filtrations (for Homeo(M), see [SS] and [NS], or [S2]), and as in [PPSS] (3) f has no fine filtration. For further generic properties, see [PPSS].

References

[GP] V. Guillemin and A. Pollack, Differential Topology, Prentice-Hall, Englewood Cliffs, N.J., 1974.

[NS] Z. Nitecki and M. Shub, Filtrations, decompositions and explosions, Amer. J. Math. 97 (1976), 1029-1047.

[PPSS] J. Palis, C. Pugh, M. Shub and D. Sullivan, Genericity theorems in topological dynamics, Dynamical Systems - Warwick 1974, pp. 241-250. Lectures Notes in Math., vol. 468, Springer, Berlin, 1975.

[P] G. Pugh, An improved closing lemma and a general density theorem, Amer. J. Math. 89 (1967), 1010-1021.

[S1] M. Shub, Endomorphisms of compact differentiable manifolds, Amer. J. Math. 91 (1969), 175-199.

[S2] M. Shub, Stabilité globale des systèmes dynamiques, Astérisque, No. 56, Soc. Math. France, Paris, 1978.

[SS] M. Shub and S. Smale, Beyond hyperbolicity, Ann. of Math. (2) 96 (1972), 587-591.

Wesleyan University
Middletown, Conn. 06457

and

Tufts University
Medford, Mass. 02155

CROSS SECTION MAPS FOR GEODESIC FLOWS, I
(The Modular Surface)

Roy L. Adler
and
Leopold Flatto

1. Introduction

In this paper we investigate the relationship between two topics which at first sight seem unrelated. The first deals with ergodic properties of geodesic flows on two-dimensional surfaces of constant negative curvature, a rather active area in the thirties studied by many well known mathematicians. For a detailed survey of the work during that period see [H2]. The second one deals with ergodic properties of noninvertible mappings of the unit interval, a current popular subject and one also with an interesting history going back to Gauss (See [B]). We shall show how each of these subjects sheds light on the other. Ergodic properties of interval maps can be used to prove ergodicity of the flows and conversely. Furthermore, explicit formulas for invariant measures of interval maps can be derived from the invariance of hyperbolic measure for the flows. (Actually we could go a step further and trace a connection of these formulas to Liouville's theorem for Hamiltonian Systems.) This fact is particularly interesting as there is a paucity of explicit formulas for invariant measures of interval maps and we have here a method of deriving a class of these. In particular we shall show how Gauss's formula for the invariant measure associated with continued fractions, which seems to have been produced ad hoc, can be derived anew.

The connection between geodesic flows and noninvertible maps of the interval is achieved by a series of reductions. The first one, attributed to Poincaré, reduces the study of a flow to that of a cross section map. We mention some examples where a cross section map has been successfully used to study flows.

(i) Flow on the 2-torus. For this we have the classical

work of Poincaré-Denjoy in which the cross-section of a flow is a circle and the cross section map induced by the flow is an orientation preserving homeomorphism. Generically, under a suitable coordinatization of the circle the homeomorphism becomes a rotation (see Chapter 17 [CL]).

(ii) Billiards is an ellipse. In [Bi) this motion is described by means of a cross section map. The same method can also be applied to study the geodesic flow on an ellipsoid, a surface of positive curvature.

However, as far as the previous work on 2-dimensional surfaces of constant negative curvature is concerned this natural idea, though implicit in the works of Morse, has not been fully developed.

In the geodesic flows that we are considering, the motion takes place in a 3-dimensional manifold—namely the unit tangent bundle of a 2-dimensional surface.

The first reduction yields a cross section map T_C on a 2-dimensional region C. If the measure of C is infinite, an intermediate reduction, called inducing, can be made in order to replace C by a subset of finite measure.

A suitable coordinatization of C shows that a second reduction is possible—namely the existence of a one-dimensional factor map whose natural extension is T_C.

As is well known, geodesics can be given symbolic descriptions [M,N]. We show how such descriptions are related to f-expansions, a symbolism associated with maps of the interval [R].

All the aforementioned notions are standard ones in ergodic theory and have been given general formulations by various mathematicians. An abstract treatment of cross sections was given by Ambrose and Kakutani [AK]. They showed that every measurable flow can be represented by a special flow built under a function and over an individual transformation which plays the role of a cross section map.

The concepts of factor map and natural extension were studied by Rochlin [Ro]. The notion of induced transformations, which is the discrete time analogue of cross section maps for continuous time flows, was developed for invertible transformations by Kakutani [K] and for non-invertible ones by Adler and Weiss [AW,S]. Finally the existence of a symbolism with simple Markovian rules was established for geodesic flows on negative curvature surfaces in [O,OW]. Indeed all steps in our reduction scheme are known to exist abstractly from the above quoted works. However, in the present work all the above concepts take on concrete forms and have simple geometrical descriptions.

In this paper we restrict the discussion to one particular cross section for the geodesic flow on the modular surface. We have chosen here one of the simplest examples to illustrate our ideas. The geometrical constructions associated with other cross sections and other Fuchsian groups get more complex and we hope to present these in subsequent papers. The example that we have chosen is also interesting because it deals with a cross section map which is the natural extension of the so called continued fraction transformation. We shall see how the invariant measure guessed by Gauss can be derived from our recipe. The reversibility property of the Gauss measure (Theorem 9.2) can ultimately be traced to the fact that reflection about the y-axis commutes with the modular flow.

We shall attempt to make our presentation as graphic and elementary as possible. For instance, we shall forego the elegant formulation in which each tangent vector of the hyperbolic plane is represented as a pair of real unimodular matrices $\pm\begin{pmatrix} a & b \\ c & d \end{pmatrix}$ and the action of the geodesic flow as right multiplication by $\begin{pmatrix} e^{t/2} & 0 \\ 0 & e^{-t/2} \end{pmatrix}$. All our arguments are based on very simple geometrical ideas.

Lest the reader be put off by the discrepancy between the promise of simplicity and the frightful detail which confronts him, we wish to make the following statement. There is one basic simple discovery from which all else follows: namely, "bulges fit into corners" (figure 6.2). The reason for all the tedious and messy details is due to the fact that our purpose is to account for all geodesics and to give a complete description of a symbolic dynamical system representing a cross section map. No set of measure zero is discarded. If we were to do so, certain complications could easily be eliminated, but then the complete symbolic descriptions of §8 would be lost One of the intriguing aspects of our approach is that it is basically solving a puzzle that miraculously fits together. To appreciate this places a heavy burden on the reader (and writer); so to lighten the load we recommend that a reader at first ignore all boundary considerations in §§4, 8 and discard for himself the appropriate invariant set of measure zero from the flow. Indeed he should concentrate on appropriate diagrams and dispense with formal definitions of various sets appearing in these. Also he should skip §5 which has been included for the sake of completion but unnecessary for the remainder of the paper. We have also prepared a shorter paper written according to these recommendations [AF].

Finally we wish to acknowledge the source of the present ideas:

First, Artin [A] who originally used continued fractions to exhibit geodesics which are everywhere dense on the modular surface, and second, Rufus Bowen and Caroline Series [BS] who pointed out a relation between more general f-expansions and Fuchsian groups.

2. The Geodesic Flow

Let $\mathbb{H} = \{x+iy : y > 0\}$ be the upper half plane endowed with the metric $ds^2 = \frac{dx^2+dy^2}{y^2}$. This surface is called the hyperbolic plane and has constant negative curvature -1. The geodesics of $\mathbb{H}$ are half circles and straight lines orthogonal to the x-axis. Let $\mathbb{U}$ denote the bundle of unit tangent vectors emanating from each point of $\mathbb{H}$. Each element $u \in \mathbb{U}$ can be given coordinates $u = u(x,y,\theta)$ where (x,y) are coordinates of the base point of u and θ the angle* measured, say, in the counter clockwise direction from the positive direction from the positive x-axis around to the

---

*(Hopf [Ho] specifies directions by another angular parameter χ, the difference $\chi-\theta$ being a function of x and y.)

direction of u. Throughout this paper we shall find it convenient to ignore semantics and identify an object with its coordinates - e.g. we shall write (x,y,θ) instead of $u(x,y,\theta)$. The spaces $\mathbb{H}$ and $\mathbb{U}$ are endowed with the respective <u>hyperbolic</u> <u>measures</u> $dA = \frac{dxdy}{y^2}$ and $dm = dA \cdot d\theta$.

To each element $u \in \mathbb{U}$ there is a unique geodesic passing tangentially through its base point. The geodesic flow is a group G_t, $t \in R$, of homeomorphisms of $\mathbb{U}$ defined by

$$G_t : u = (x,y,\theta) \rightarrow u' = (x',y',\theta')$$

where u and u' are unit vectors tangent to the initial and terminal points of a geodesic segment of hyperbolic length t (see figure 2.1). The flow G_t is better described in another set of coordinates. In the second coordinatization each $u \in \mathbb{U}$ is specified by (ξ,η,s) where ξ and η are the points of intersection of the geodesic determined by u with the x-axis, ξ being the one in the forward direction, and s is the hyperbolic arc length parameter. For vertical lines one of the coordinates ξ,η takes on the value ∞. The (ξ,η)-space consists of the Cartesian product of the one point compactification of the real line with itself minus the diagonal. The origin of the arc length parameter s on a half circle can be chosen to be its midpoint, but for vertical lines some other convention must be adopted.

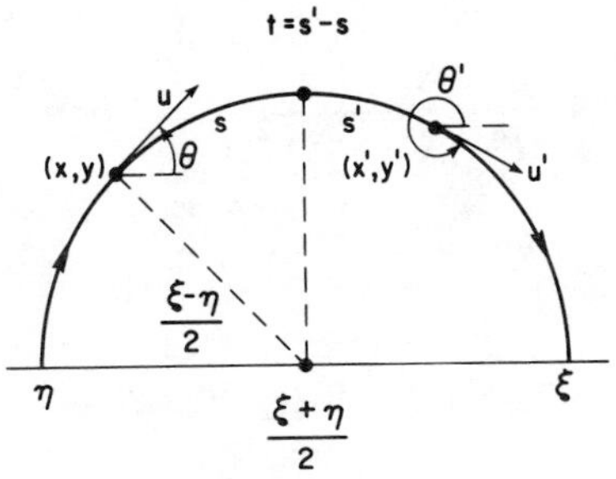

Figure 2.1

In these coordinates the flow becomes

$$G_t : (\xi,\eta,s) \rightarrow (\xi,\eta,s+t).$$

To express the measure dm in these new coordinates we compute the Jacobian $J = \frac{\partial(x,y,\theta)}{\partial(\xi,\eta,s)}$. In computing J we follow Figure 2.1 covering the case $\xi > \eta$. For $\xi < \eta$ similar computations lead to the same formula for J. From Figure 1 we have the relations

$$y = \frac{(\xi+\eta)}{2} - \frac{(\xi-n)}{2} \sin\theta$$

$$y = \frac{(\xi-\eta)}{2} \cos\theta.$$

A simple way of calculating J is to treat the change of variables as a composition of two maps

$$(x,y,\theta) \rightarrow (\xi,\eta,\theta) \rightarrow (\xi,\eta,s)$$

where $J_1 = \frac{\partial(x,y,\theta)}{\partial(\xi,\eta,\theta)} = \frac{\partial(x,y)}{\partial(\xi,\eta)} = -\frac{1}{2}\cos\theta$ is the Jacobian of the first map and

$$J_2 = \frac{\partial(\xi,\eta,\theta)}{\partial(\xi,\eta,s)} = \frac{\partial\theta}{\partial s}$$

is the Jacobian of the second. In this instance $\frac{\partial\theta}{\partial s} = 1/\frac{\partial s}{\partial\theta}$ so that

$$J_2 = \frac{-y}{\sqrt{(\frac{\partial x}{\partial\theta})^2 + (\frac{\partial y}{\partial\theta})^2}} = -\cos\theta$$

whereupon

$$J = J_1 J_2 = \frac{1}{2}\cos^2\theta.$$

Thus

$$dm = \frac{dxdyd\theta}{y^2} = \frac{|J|d\xi d\eta ds}{(1/4)(\xi-\eta)^2\cos^2\theta} = \frac{2d\xi d\eta ds}{(\xi-\eta)^2}.$$

Expressing dm in the variables (ξ,η,s) puts into evidence the fact that this measure if G_t-invariant.

We introduce another group of homeomorphisms of $\mathbb{U}$ whose action commutes with that of G_t. This action is induced by the group of fractional linear transformations on $\mathbb{H}$

$$\tau : z \to \frac{az+b}{cz+d}$$

$a,b,c,d \in R$ and $ad-bc = 1$. A well known fact about these transformations is that they are isometries of $\mathbb{H}$ with respect to ds. This can be readily seen by writing

$$w = \frac{az+b}{cz+d} = \frac{(az+b)(c\bar{z}+d)}{|cz+d|^2}$$

whence

$$\mathrm{Im}\, w = \frac{ad-bc}{|cz+d|^2}, \ \mathrm{Im}\, z = \frac{\mathrm{Im}\, z}{|cz+d|^2}.$$

Since

$$\frac{dw}{dz} = \frac{1}{(cz+d)^2},$$

we obtain

$$\frac{|dz|}{\mathrm{Im}\, z} = \frac{|dw|}{\mathrm{Im}\, w}.$$

Because they are isometries the transformations τ preserve the measure dA.

Each τ induces a map $\bar{\tau}$ on $\mathbb{U}$ specified by

$$\bar{\tau} : (z,\theta) \to (\tau(z), \theta+\arg\, \tau'(z)).$$

We see at once that the transformations $\bar{\tau}$ act as a shear (skew product) on the space $\mathbb{U}$ and preserve the measure $dm = dA \cdot d\phi$. Another way to see the invariance of dm is to express $\bar{\pi}$ in the (ξ,η,s)-coordinates. Because τ is an isometry it follows that

$$\bar{\tau}(\xi,\eta,s) = (\tau\xi,\tau\eta,s+s_0(\xi,\eta))$$

where $s_0(\xi,\eta)$ is defined by

$$\bar{\tau}(\xi,\eta,0) = (\tau\xi,\tau\eta,s_0(\xi,\eta)).$$

It is then a pleasant exercise to compute the Jacobian of the map $\bar{\tau} : (\xi,\eta,s) \to (\xi',\eta',s')$ to show

$$\frac{d\xi' d\eta' ds'}{(\xi'-\eta')^2} = \frac{d\xi d\eta ds}{(\xi-\eta)^2}.$$

Finally it is evident by the geometry and even more so by the (ξ,η,s)-coordinates that

$$\bar{\tau}G_t = G_t\bar{\tau}.$$

3. The Modular Surface

Let Γ be the modular group - ie., the group of all fractional linear transformations $\tau: z \to \frac{az+b}{cz+d}$, $ad-bc = 1$, $a,b,c,d \in Z$ (see [L] for standards facts about the modular group).

As is well known Γ is generated by the two transformations $\alpha : z \to z + 1$, $\beta : z \to - 1/z$ which satisfy the relations

$$\beta^2 = (\beta\alpha)^3 = \text{identity}.$$

These relations will play an important role in §6.

Since Γ is a subgroup of the group of all fractional linear transformations acting on $\mathbb{H}$, we have from §2 that Γ induces a group $\bar{\Gamma}$ acting on $\mathbb{U}$. Accordingly, we let $\mathbb{M}$ and M denote the spaces of Γ-orbits of $\mathbb{H}$ and $\bar{\Gamma}$ -orbits of

$\mathbb{U}$ resp. -i.e., $\{\mathbb{M} = \Gamma z : z \in \mathbb{H}\}$, $M = \{\bar{\Gamma} u : u \in \mathbb{U}\}$ where $\Gamma z = \{\tau z : \tau \in \Gamma\}$ and $\bar{\Gamma} u = \{\bar{\tau} u : \tau \in \Gamma\}$. Let π and $\bar{\pi}$ be the projection maps from $\mathbb{H}$ to $\mathbb{M}$ to M resp. - i.e.,

$$\pi(z) = \Gamma z, \quad z \in \mathbb{H} \quad \text{and} \quad \bar{\pi}(u) = \bar{\Gamma} u, \quad u \in \mathbb{U}.$$

One can obtain a concrete realization of $\mathbb{M}$ and M in the following manner. As is well known the set

$$F = \{z = x+iy : |z| > 1, -\tfrac{1}{2} \le x < \tfrac{1}{2}\} \cup \{z = x+iy : |z| = 1, -\tfrac{1}{2} \le x < 0\}$$

is a <u>fundamental</u> <u>set</u> for Γ -i.e., the following holds:

1. $\tau_1 F \cap \tau_2 F = \emptyset, \quad \tau_1 \neq \tau_2, \quad \tau_1, \tau_2 \in \Gamma,$

2. $\bigcup_{\tau \in \Gamma} \tau F = \mathbb{H}$.

Thus $\mathbb{H}$ is tesselated with images of F under Γ. (See Figure 3.1.)

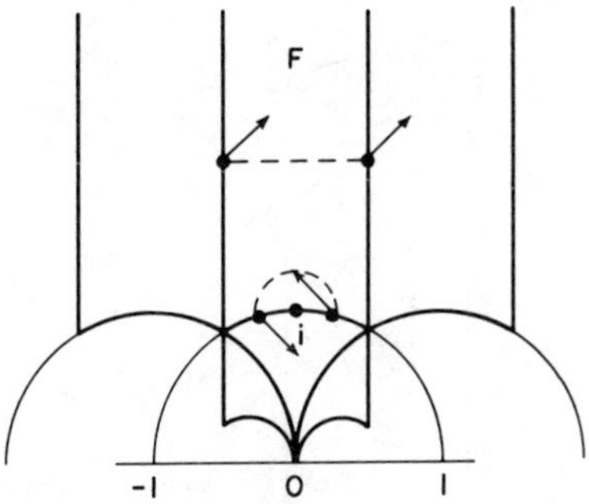

Figure 3.1

Opposite vertical boundary lines of F are identified under α, and the left half of the bottom boundary with the right under β. Consequently $\mathbb{M}$ can be thought of as the closure of F with the above identifications. Similarly, unit vectors with base points on the boundary of F can be also identified under $\bar{\alpha}$ and $\bar{\beta}$, and so the space M can be thought of as unit vectors emanating from points of the closure of F modulo these identifications (see Figure 3.1). Projections by π and $\bar{\pi}$ of neighborhoods of $\mathbb{H}$ and $\mathbb{U}$ form a basis of neighborhoods for $\mathbb{M}$ and M resp. Topologically $\mathbb{M}$ is a punctured sphere (open disk), and M is an open solid torus. With the exception of Γ-orbits of the points i and $\frac{1}{2}+\frac{\sqrt{3}}{2}i$, and the $\bar{\Gamma}$-orbits of unit vectors based at i and $\frac{1}{2}+\frac{\sqrt{3}}{2}i$ the projection π and $\bar{\pi}$ are locally 1-1; hence x,y or ξ,η provide local coordinates for $\mathbb{M}-\{\pi(i),\pi(\frac{1}{2}+\frac{\sqrt{3}}{2}i)\}$, and x,y,θ or ξ,η,s provide local coordinates for $M-\{\pi(0,1,\theta),\bar{\pi}(\frac{1}{2},\frac{\sqrt{3}}{2},\theta) : 0 \le \theta \le 2\pi\}$. If we avoid the exceptional points all formulas of the previous section go over verbatim.

As we saw geodesics in $\mathbb{H}$ are quite simple to describe. In $\mathbb{M}$ they are piecewise the same as in $\mathbb{H}$ but globally quite complicated (see Figure 3.2).

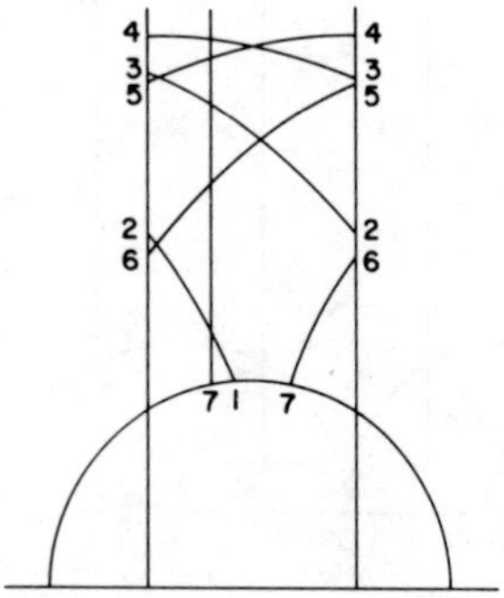

Figure 3.2

However, as we shall see this complication can be rendered manageable by means of continued fractions and other special symbolic expansions. Artin used continued functions for the same purpose, but his method does not keep track of successive segments of a geodesic across F while ours does.

To summarize, $\mathbb{M}$ and M inherit measures from $\mathbb{H}$ and $\mathbb{U}$ via π and $\bar{\pi}$. Because G_t commutes with maps on $\mathbb{U}$ induced by Γ, we have that M inherits a geodesic flow $\bar{G}_t = \bar{\pi} G_t$ from $\mathbb{U}$ and the inherited measure for M is invariant under the inherited flow.

Finally, denoting the inherited measure on M by $\bar{m} = m\bar{\pi}^{-1}$ we have

$$\bar{m}(M) = \int_F = \int_0^{2\pi}\int_{-1/2}^{1/2}\int_{\sqrt{1-x^2}}^{\infty} \frac{dy\,dx\,d\theta}{y^2} = \frac{2}{3}\pi^2.$$

In order to normalize the measure so that $\bar{m}(\mathbb{M}) = 1$ we set for the rest of the paper

$$d\bar{m} = \left(\frac{3}{2\pi^2}\right)\frac{dx\,dy\,d\theta}{y^2} = \frac{3}{\pi^2}\frac{d\xi\,d\eta\,ds}{(\xi-\eta)^2}.$$

4. Cross Section

Roughly speaking a cross section is a subset which every orbit hits again and again, and the correspondence between successive points of return to this set serves to define a cross section map. Generally this map preserves a measure which the cross section inherits from an invariant measure on the whole space. We shall discuss this further at the end of the section.

The cross section which we propose for the geodesic flow on the modular surface essentially consists of projections into M of vectors of $\mathbb{U}$ emanating from the boundary of F and pointing to its exterior. We say essentially because we are at once confronted with a difficulty. There are orbits which do not visit the proposed cross section infinitely often both past and future. These are the orbits which are $\bar{\pi}$ projections of vertical orbits of $\mathbb{U}$. They are described by $\bar{\pi}(\xi,\eta,s), -\infty < s < \infty$ with at least one of ξ,η taking on a rational value or ∞. Thus for some elements lying in our proposed cross section, the cross section map would remain undefined. A simple remedy, a standard one in ergodic theory, would be to remove these orbits from the flow and their points of intersection from the proposed cross section. The totality of removed orbits is a set of measure zero, and the same holds for the removed points from the proposed cross section. However, since we wish to keep track of as much as possible, we shall add a set of measure zero to our proposed cross section rather than remove one, and, as a consequence, shall be involved in unpleasant details.

First, it is convenient to remove from the flow and treat separately the two orbits, one being the time reversal of the other, that are projections of vectors in $\mathbb{U}$ that run tangentially along the boundary of F.

We now give the formal definition of our cross section C. The set C is defined in terms of four disjoint subsets

$$C = C_1 \cup C_2 \cup C_3 \cup C_4.$$

Each C_i is further decomposed as

$$C_i = C_i^m \cup C_i^u \cup C_i^d \cup C_i^v \cup C_i^{1/4} \cup C_i^{-1/4}$$

where the superscripts have the following connotation: m for main part, u and d for vertical vectors pointing respectively up and down, v for ones associated with a vertex, and $\pm 1/4$ for ones based on the lines $x = \pm 1/4$. Only the main parts will turn out to be sets of nonzero measure. The geometric content of the definition of each part of C_i will be made evident by an accompanying diagram.

$$C_1^m = \{\bar{\pi}(x,y,\theta) : x = \tfrac{1}{2},\ y > \tfrac{\sqrt{3}}{2},\ -\pi/2 < \theta < \pi/2\}$$

$$C_2^m = \{\bar{\pi}(x,y,\theta) = \bar{\pi}(\xi,\eta,s) : x^2 + y^2 = 1,\ -\tfrac{1}{2} < x < \tfrac{1}{2},\ x < \xi < 1\}$$

C_4^m is obtained from C_1^m by replacing x, θ in the conditions by $-x$, $\theta+\pi$. Similarly, C_3^m is obtained from C_2^m by replacing x, ξ by $-x$, $-\xi$.

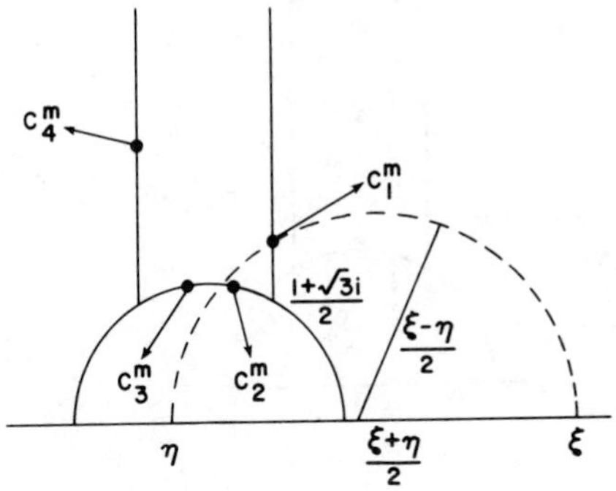

Figure 4.1

$$C_1^u = \{\bar{\pi}(x,y,\theta) : -\tfrac{1}{2} < x < 0, \quad y = 2,3,\ldots, \quad \theta = \tfrac{\pi}{2}\}$$

$$C_1^d = \{\bar{\pi}(x,y,\theta) : 0 \le x < \tfrac{1}{2}, \quad y = 2,3,\ldots, \quad \theta = -\tfrac{\pi}{2}\}$$

$$C_2^d = \{\bar{\pi}(x,y,\theta) : 0 \le x < \tfrac{1}{2}, \quad y = +\sqrt{1-x^2}, \quad \theta = -\tfrac{\pi}{2}\}$$

C_4^u and C_4^d are obtained from C_1^d and C_1^u by replacing θ by $-\theta$. C_3^d is obtained from C_2^d by replacing $0 \le x < \frac{1}{2}$ by $-\frac{1}{2} < x < 0$. $C_2^u = C_3^u = \emptyset$.

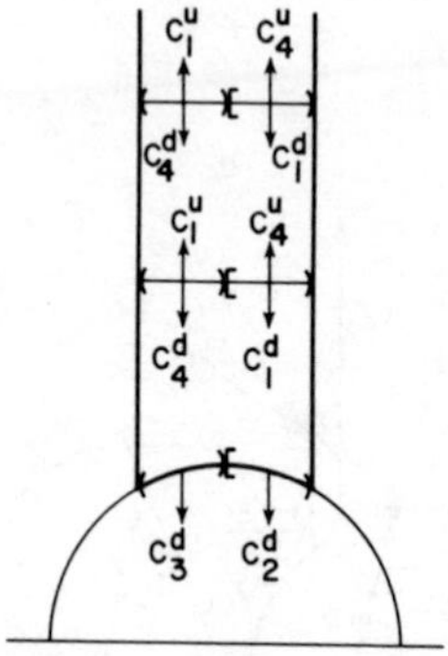

Figure 4.2

$$C_1^v = \{\overline{\pi}(x,y,\theta) = \overline{\pi}(\xi,\eta,s) : x = \tfrac{1}{2},\ y = \tfrac{\sqrt{3}}{2},\ \tfrac{1}{2} < \xi < 1\}$$

C_4^v is obtained from C_1^v by replacing x, ξ by $-x$, $-\xi$. $C_2^v = C_3^v = \emptyset$.

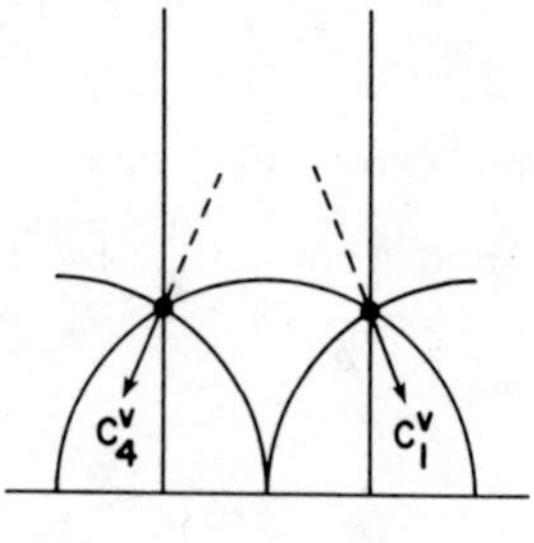

Figure 4.3

Consider now a preliminary choice of cross section C^p defined by

$$C^p = \bigcup_{i=1}^{4} [C_i^m \cup C_i^d \cup C_i^v \cup C_i^u].$$

$\bar{\pi}$ maps outward vectors based on ∂F in a one-to-one manner into M except for vectors at the vertices where it is three-to-one. In any case, for every outward vector based on ∂F there is a unique inward one which has the same $\bar{\pi}$ projection. Furthermore, nonvertical geodesics in $\mathbb{H}$ passing through the interior of F meet the boundary in two points while vertical ones meet the bottom boundary and each of the horizontal lines $y = 2,3,\ldots$ in unique points. These remarks make it clear that the set C^p satisfies the requirements demanded of a cross section—namely, each orbit hits it again and again both past and future.

In order to obtain a simple coordinate description of a cross section map we augment C^p by adding sets $C_i^{\pm 1/4}$ defined by

$$C_1^{\frac{1}{4}} = \{\bar{\pi}(u) : u = (x,y,\theta) \text{ is a tangent to a geodesic through } \tfrac{-1}{2} + \tfrac{\sqrt{3}}{2}\, i,$$
$$x = \tfrac{1}{4},\ y > +\sqrt{1-x^2}\ \}.$$

$C_2^{-1/4}$ is obtained from $C_1^{1/4}$ by replacing x by $-x$. $C_3^{1/4}$, $C_4^{-1/4}$ are obtained from $C_1^{1/4}$, $C_2^{-1/4}$ by replacing $-\frac{1}{2}+\frac{\sqrt{3}}{2}i$ by $\frac{1}{2}+\frac{\sqrt{3}}{2}i$. $C_1^{-1/4} = C_2^{1/4} = C_3^{-1/4} = C_4^{1/4} = \emptyset$.

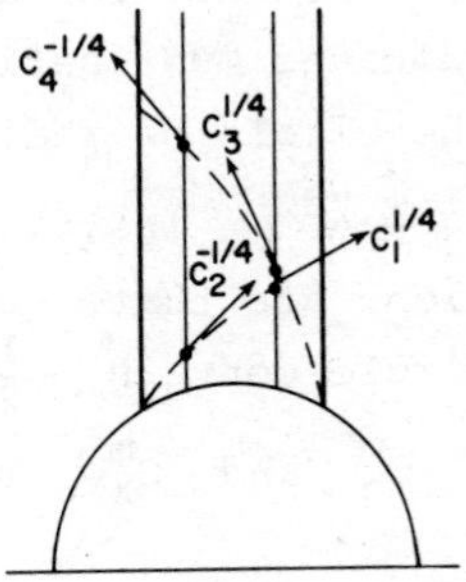

Figure 4.4

Orbits which pass through a vertex will next cross the lines $x = \pm\frac{1}{4}$ before crossing the boundary of F again. The set C also satisfies the requirements of a cross section and the correspondence between successive visits of orbits to C defines a one-to-one cross section map T_C to C onto itself.

We now make a unique assignment of coordinates (ξ,η) to every member of C. Before the (ξ,η)-coordinate space was a subset of the torus, but for current purposes it is convenient to select (ξ,η) from a slightly different extended plane. Our <u>extended plane</u> is the Cartesian product $E \times E$ of an <u>extended line</u> where $E = [-\infty,-0] \cup [+0,+\infty]$ with -0, $-\infty$ distinct from $+0$, $+\infty$ respectively. Introducing signed zeros and infinities seems artificial at this stage but proves to be useful in discussing symbolic dynamics in §8. We adopt the following conventions regarding zeros and infinities. For $\xi > 0$, $\xi - \xi = +0$, $-\xi + \xi = -0$. $1/\pm 0 = \pm\infty$; $1/\pm\infty = \pm 0$; $-(+0) = -0$; $-(-0) = +0$. We refer to this coordinatization of C as <u>curvilinear coordinates</u>, the reason for this term being explained later. The coordinates assigned to C lie in a certain subset of $E \times E$ called the <u>curvilinear domain</u>. With a slight abuse of notation we use the same letters that denoted the various parts of C to label the corresponding parts of the curvilinear domain.

To each element $v \in \bigcup_{i=1}^{4} C_i^m$, we assign the coordinates (ξ,η) where $u = (\xi,\eta,s)$ is the unique vector in $\mathbb{U}$ emanating from the boundary of F and pointing out such that $\bar{\pi}(u) = v$. It is a nice exercise in analytic geometry to express C_i^m in these coordinates. In order for an element to be in C_1 its curvilinear coordinates must satisfy the conditions that $\xi > \eta \neq +0$, and the circle of radius $\frac{\xi-\eta}{2}$ centered at $\frac{\xi+\eta}{2}$ contain the point $\frac{1}{2} + \frac{\sqrt{3}}{2}i$ in its interior (see Figure 4.4). For C_2^m the conditions are that $-0 \neq \xi > \eta \pm -\infty$ and the aforementioned circle contain $-\frac{1}{2} + \frac{\sqrt{3}}{2}i$ but not $\frac{1}{2} + \frac{\sqrt{3}}{2}i$, and so on for C_3^m and C_4^m. The result is

$$C_1^m = \{(\xi,\eta) : (\xi-\tfrac{1}{2})(\eta-\tfrac{1}{2}) < \tfrac{3}{4}, \quad \xi > \eta \neq +0\}$$

$$C_2^m = \{(\xi,\eta) : (\xi+\tfrac{1}{2})(\eta+\tfrac{1}{2}) < -\tfrac{3}{4} < (\xi-\tfrac{1}{2})(\eta-\tfrac{1}{2}), - 0 \neq \xi > \eta\}$$

C_3^m, C_4^m are obtained from C_2^m, C_1^m by replacing (ξ,η) by $(-\xi, -\eta)$ (See Figure 4.6a).

To each $v \in C_1^v$ we assign the coordinates (ξ,η) where $u = (\xi,\eta,s) = (x,y,\theta)$ is the unique vector in $\mathbb{U}$ with $x = \frac{1}{2}$, $y = \frac{\sqrt{3}}{2}$, $\frac{1}{2} < \xi < 1$, such that $\overline{\pi}(u) = v$. Likewise, to each vector $v \in C_4^v$ we assign the coordinates (ξ,η) where $u = (\xi,\eta,s) = (x,y,\theta)$ with $x = -\frac{1}{2}$, $y = \frac{\sqrt{3}}{2}$, $-1 < \xi < -\frac{1}{2}$, such that $\overline{\pi}(u) = v$. In curvilinear coordinates

$$C_1^v = \{(\xi,\eta) : (\xi-\tfrac{1}{2})(\eta-\tfrac{1}{2}) = -\tfrac{3}{4}, \quad \tfrac{1}{2} < \xi < 1\},$$

C_4^v being obtained from C_1^v by replacing ξ, η by $-\xi$, $-\eta$ (see darkened left side of C_1 and right side of C_4 in Figure 4.6a).

To each $v \in C_1^{1/4}$, $C_3^{1/4}$ we assign respectively the coordinates $(\xi+1, \eta+1)$, $(-\frac{1}{\xi-1}, -\frac{1}{\eta-1})$, where $u = (x,y,\theta) = (\xi,\eta,s)$ is the unique vector in $\mathbb{U}$ ith $x = \frac{1}{4}$ such that $\overline{\pi}(u) = v$. Similarly, to each $v \in C_4^{-1/4}$, $C_2^{-1/4}$ we assign respectively the coordinates $(\xi-1, \eta-1)$, $(-\frac{1}{\xi+1}, -\frac{1}{\eta+1})$ where $u = (x,y,\theta) = (\xi,\eta,s)$ is the unique vector $x = -\frac{1}{4}$ such that $\overline{\pi}(u) = v$.

The above coordinate assignments are related to those of C_i^v in the following fashion. Given a vector $u_1 = (\xi,\eta,s)$, $\frac{1}{2} < \xi < 1$, based at $\frac{1}{2} + \frac{\sqrt{3}}{2}i$, there is a unique vector $u_1' = (-\frac{1}{\xi-1} - 1, -\frac{1}{\eta-1} - 1, s')$, based at $-\frac{1}{2} + \frac{\sqrt{3}}{2}i$ pointing into the interior of F, such that $\overline{\pi}(u_1) = \overline{\pi}(u_1')$ (see Figure 4.5). Our assignment gives the respective coordinates $(\xi-1, \eta-1)$, $(-\frac{1}{\xi-1}, \frac{1}{\eta-1})$ to $\pi(u_2) \in C_2^{-1/4}$, $\pi(u_3) \in C_1^{1/4}$, where u_2, u_3 are based in the lines $x = -\frac{1}{4}$, $x = \frac{1}{4}$ and tangent to the geodesic determined by u_1'. We conclude that in curvilinear coordinates

$$C_1^{1/4} = \{(\xi,\eta) : (\xi-\tfrac{1}{2})(\eta-\tfrac{1}{2}) = -\tfrac{3}{4}, \quad 2 < \xi < \infty\}$$

$$C_2^{-1/4} = \{(\xi,\eta) : (\xi+\tfrac{1}{2})(\eta+\tfrac{1}{2}) = -\tfrac{3}{4}, \quad -\tfrac{1}{2} < \xi < 0\}.$$

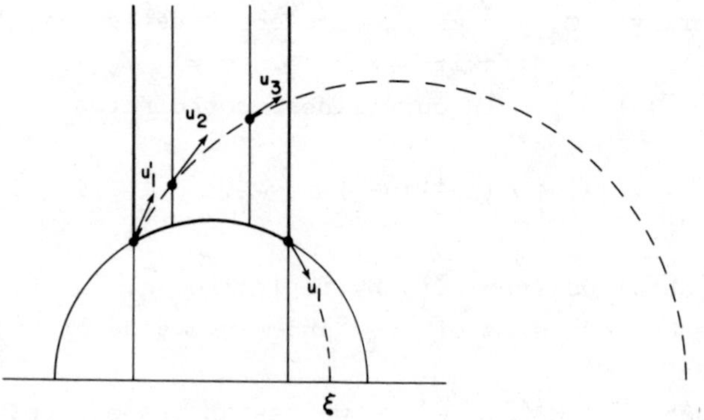

Figure 4.5

Similarly, one shows that the curvilinear coordinate description of $C_4^{-1/4}$, $C_3^{1/4}$ are obtained from those of $C_1^{1/4}$, $C_2^{-1/4}$ by replacing ξ, η by $-\xi$, $-\eta$.

Finally, we assign coordinated to elements of C_2^u, C_2^d according to the following table.

Set	curvilinear coordinates of $\tilde{\pi}(x,y,\theta) \in$ set
C_1^u	$(+\infty, x-y+2)$
C_1^d	$(x+y-1, -\infty)$
C_4^u	$(-\infty, x+y-2)$
C_4^d	$(x-y+1, +\infty)$
C_2^d	$(x, -\infty)$
C_3^d	$(x, +\infty)$

To express C_2^d, C_2^u in (ξ,η) coordinates we introduce the following sets which will be useful later on.

$$U_{-k} = \{(+\infty,\eta) : -k - \tfrac{1}{2} < \eta < -k\}$$

$$U_{+k} = \{(-\infty,\eta) : k \le \eta < k + \tfrac{1}{2}\}$$

$$D_{-k} = \{(-\xi,+\infty) : -k - \tfrac{1}{2} < \xi < -k\}$$

$$D_{+k} = \{(\xi,-\infty) : k \le \xi < \tfrac{1}{2}\}$$

$$k = 0,1,2,\ldots$$

Then

$$C_2^d = D_{+0}$$

$$C_1^d = \bigcup_{k=1}^{\infty} D_{+k}$$

$$C_1^u = \bigcup_{k=0}^{\infty} U_{-k}$$

C_3^d, C_4^d, C_4^u can be obtained from C_2^d, C_1^d, C_1^u by replacing D_k, U_{-k} by D_{-k}, U_{+k} respectively. In Figure 4.6 the sets D_k, U_k are depicted by horizontal and vertical segments along the boundary.

It is convenient to partition C_2 and C_3 further:

$$C_{2+} = \{(\xi,\eta) \in C_2 : \xi \ge +0\}$$

$$C_{2-} = \{(\xi,\eta) \in C_2 : \xi < -0\}$$

$$C_{3+} = \{(\xi,\eta) \in C_3 : \xi > +0\}$$

$$C_{3-} = \{(\xi,\eta) \in C_3 : \xi \le -0\}.$$

In the following figure we write i for C_i and i' for the image of C_i. We shade boundaries to indicate the set they belong to—e.g. the left boundary of 1 belongs to 1 and not 2+.

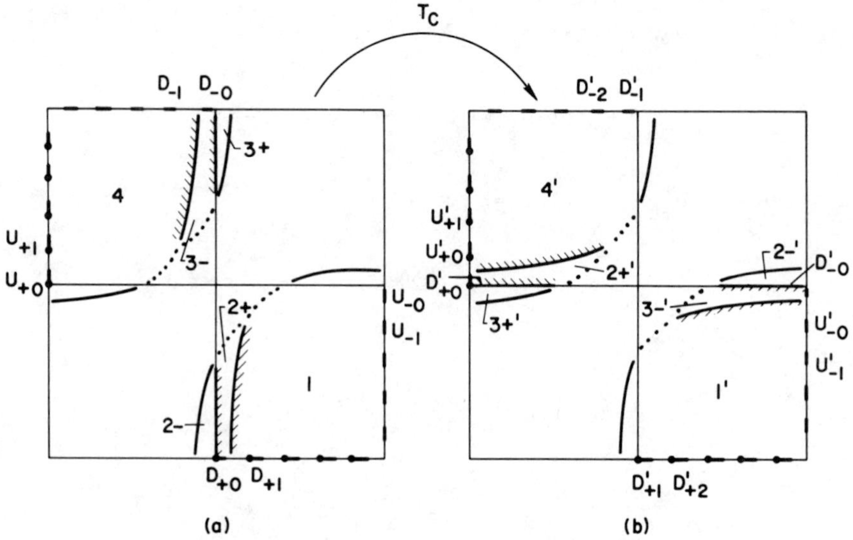

Figure 4.6

In curvilinear coordinates the cross section map, which will be also referred to as the <u>curvilinear map</u>, is expressed as follows:

$$T_C(\xi,\eta) = \begin{cases} (\xi-1,\ \eta-1) & \text{on } C_1 \\ (-1/\xi,\ -1/\eta) & \text{on } C_2 \cup C_3 \\ (\xi+1,\ \eta+1) & \text{on } C_4. \end{cases}$$

We leave it to the reader to check these formulas. The following remark will help clarify matters. A geodesic leaving F from the right vertical wall at (ξ,η,s) not a vertex is identified under α^{-1} with a geodesic entering F on the left vertical wall at $(\xi-1,\ \eta-1,s)$. This geodesic leaves F at some point $(\xi-1, \eta-1, s')$. Thus the next return to C from an element $(\xi,\eta) \in C_1^m$ is the element with coordinates $(\xi-1, \eta-1)$ be it either in C_1 or C_2.

Finally, we return to a point made at the beginning of this section, that the $\overline{G}_t$-invariant $\overline{m}$ induces a T_C-invariant measure, denoted m_C, on a cross section. The measure m_C is defined as follows.

$$m_C(B) = \lim_{\Delta s \to 0} \frac{1}{\Delta s} \overline{m}(\{\overline{G}_t u : u \in B, \quad 0 \le t \le \Delta s\})$$

for a measurable subset $B \subseteq C$ (see Figure 4.7).

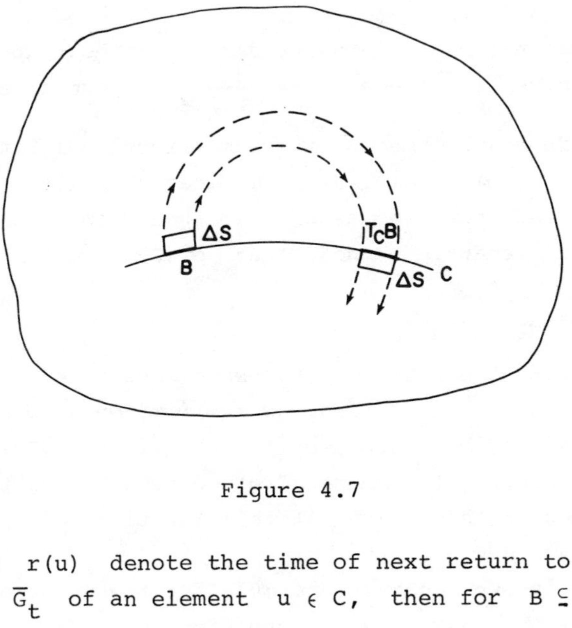

Figure 4.7

If we let $r(u)$ denote the time of next return to C under the flow $\overline{G}_t$ of an element $u \in C$, then for $B \subseteq C$

$$T_C B = \{\overline{G}_{r(u)} u : u \in B\};$$

so

$$\overline{m}\{\overline{G}_t u : u \in T_C B, \ 0 \ge t \le \Delta s\} = \overline{m}\{\overline{G}_t u : u \in B, \ r(u) \le t \le r(u) + \Delta s\}$$

$$= \overline{m}\{\overline{G}_t u : \ u \in B, \ 0 \le t \le \Delta s\}$$

The first equality follows by definition. Under the assumption that $r(u)$ is constant the second follows from the $\bar{G}_t$-invariance of $\bar{m}$. For nonconstant $r(u)$ this equality is derived from the constant case by a standard approximation argument. Thus

$$m_C(B) = m_C(T_C B).$$

In curvilinear coordinates dm_C is obtained from $d\bar{m} = (\frac{3}{\pi^2}) \frac{d\xi d\eta ds}{(\xi-\eta)^2}$ by dropping ds; thus

$$dm_C = (\frac{3}{\pi^2}) \frac{d\xi d\eta}{(\xi-\eta)^2}.$$

The T_C-invariance of m_C can be derived without appealing to the above argument. The measure $\frac{d\xi d\eta}{(\xi-\eta)^2}$ is preserved whenever ξ and η are transformed by the same fractional linear transformation (a Jacobian computation indicated earlier) and T_C is piecewise defined by means of just such transformations.

One final remark. We note that $m_C(C) = \infty$.

5. Return Time Function

The return time function h, sometimes referred to as the height function, is defined as the time on an orbit (in this case the length of a geodesic segment) from a given point on the cross section to the next return to it. For the sake of completeness we shall exhibit this function for the cross-section in §4.

To do this, we require a formula for the hyperbolic distance $d(z_1,z_2)$, $z_1,z_2 \in \mathbb{H}$, involving $x_1 = \text{Re } z_1$, $x_2 = \text{Re } z_2$, Let γ be the geodesic from η_0 to π_0, z_1 preceding z_2 on γ. Let $w(z) = \frac{z-\eta_0}{(\eta_0-\xi_0)(z-\xi_0)}$, $w(x_j) = u_j$, $w(z_j) = iv_j$, $j = 1,2$. w maps $\mathbb{H}$ onto $\mathbb{H}$, γ onto the positive y-axis, and the two parallel lines $\text{Re } z = x_j$, $j =$

1,2, onto the two geodesics γ_j passing respectively through u_j, iv_j, $\frac{1}{\eta_0-\xi_0}$.

Let $\{z_2,z_1,\xi_0,\eta_0\}$ denote the cross ratio $\frac{\xi_0-z_1}{\xi_0-z_2} / \frac{\eta_0-z_1}{\eta_0-z_2}$. Since $w(z)$ preserves both cross ratios and hyperbolic distances, we have

$$\{x_2,x_1,\xi_0,\eta_0\} = \{u_2,u_1,0,\infty\} = \frac{u_2}{u_1}$$

$$(5.1) \qquad \{z_2,z_1,\xi_0,\eta_0\} = \{i\,v_2,\, i\,v_1,0,\infty\} = \frac{v_2}{v_1}$$

$$d(z_2,z_1) = d(i\,v_2,\, i\,v_1) = \int_{v_1}^{v_2} \frac{dv}{v} = \log \frac{v_2}{v_1} .$$

Applying elementary geometry to the circles γ_j, we get

$$(5.2) \qquad v_j^2 = \frac{u_j}{\eta_0-\xi_0}, \qquad j = 1,2.$$

From (5.1), (5.2) we obtain the desired formula

$$(5.3) \qquad d(z_1,z_2) = \frac{1}{2} \log\{x_2,x_1,\xi_0,\eta_0\}.$$

In order to compute h we define more subsets of C_i^m, $i = 1,4$:

$$C_{1a}^m = C_1^m \cap T_C^{-1}C_1$$

$$C_{1b}^m = C_1^m \cap T_C^{-1}C_2$$

$$C_{4a}^m = C_4^m \cap T_C^{-1}C_4$$

$$C_{4b}^m = C_4^m \cap T_C^{-1}C_3$$

$$R_2^{\ell} = \{(\xi,\eta) \in C_2 : \xi = +0\}$$

$$R_3^r = \{(\xi,\eta) \in C_3 : \xi = -0\}$$

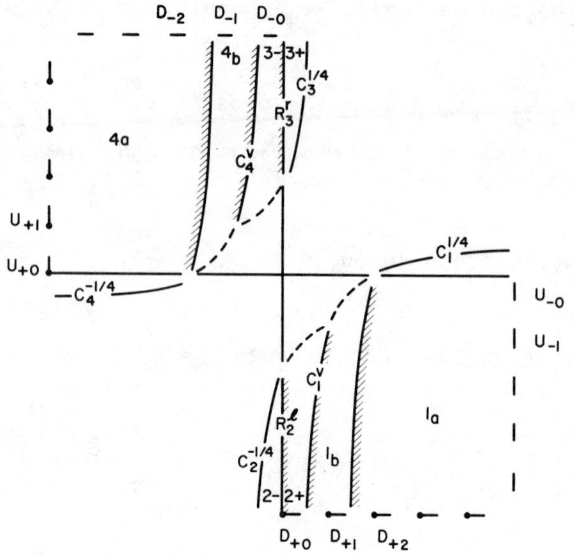

Figure 5.1

To compute h on C^m_{1a} we observe that orbits leaving the cross section through elements of C^m_{1a} traverse F from the left wall to the right; therefore we substitute $x_1 = -\frac{1}{2}$, $x^2 = \frac{1}{2}$, $\xi_0 = \xi - 1$, $\eta_0 = \eta - 1$ in (5.3) to find the length of such segments. The other regions are handled similarly, but we use formula (2) on C^u_2, C^d_i $i = 1,4$. The computations are somewhat tedious but straightforward analytic geometry. We summarize the results in three tables, a main one and two dealing with boundary sets.

Region	$h(\xi,\eta)$
C_{1a}^{m}	$\frac{1}{2}\log\left[\frac{\xi-\frac{1}{2}}{\xi-\frac{1}{2}} / \frac{\eta-\frac{1}{2}}{\eta-\frac{3}{2}}\right]$
C_{1b}^{m}	$\frac{1}{2}\log\left[\frac{\xi-\frac{1}{2}}{\xi(\xi-2)} / \frac{\eta-\frac{1}{2}}{\eta(\eta-2)}\right]$
$C_{2+}-R_2^{\ell}$	$\frac{1}{2}\log\left[\frac{\xi^2-1}{\xi(\xi-2)} / \frac{\eta^2-1}{\eta(\eta-2)}\right]$

On $C_{3+}-C_3^{1/4}$ the same expression appear for h as the one on $C_{2+}-R_2^{\ell}$. On C_{4a}^{m}, C_{4b}^{m}, $C_{2-}-C_2^{1/4}$, $C_{3-}-R_3^{r}$ repleace ξ, η by $-\xi$, $-\eta$ in the expressions for h on C_{1a}^{m}, C_{1b}^{m}, $C_{3+}-C_3^{1/4}$, $C_{2-}-R_2^{\ell}$ resp. On D_{+0} (left end point deleted), D_{-0}, the same expressions appearing in $C_{2+}-R_2^{\ell}$, $C_{3-}-R_2^{r}$ are used with $\eta = \infty$.

Region	$h(\xi,\eta)$
C_1^{v}	$\frac{1}{2}\log \frac{\xi-1}{3\xi+1} / \frac{\eta-1}{3\eta+1}$
$C_1^{1/4}$	$\frac{1}{2}\log\left[\frac{4\xi-5}{2\xi-3}\right]$
$C_2^{-1/4}$	$\frac{1}{2}\log\left[\frac{3\xi+4}{5\xi+4} / \frac{3\eta+4}{5\eta+4}\right]$
R_2^{ℓ}	$\frac{1}{2}\log\left[\frac{4\eta^2}{\eta^2-1}\right]$

On C_4^{v}, $C^{-1/4}$, $C_3^{1/4}$, R_3^{r} replace ξ, η by $-\xi$, $-\eta$ in the expressions for h on C_1^{v}, $C_1^{1/4}$, $C_2^{-1/4}$, R_2^{ℓ} respectively.

Region	$h(\xi,\eta)$
$U_k, \forall k$	$\log \frac{\lvert k\rvert+1}{\lvert k\rvert}$
$D_k, \lvert k\rvert \geq 2$	$\log \frac{\lvert k\rvert}{\lvert k\rvert-1}$
D_{+1}	$\frac{1}{2} \log \frac{4}{\xi(2-\xi)}$

On D_{-1} replace ξ by $-\xi$ in the expression appearing in D_{+1}.

If the reader has been perplexed by the fact that $m_C(C) = \infty$ and $\overline{m}(M) = 1$, let us remark here that the paradox is resolved by the integrability of h. We have

$$\overline{m}(M) = \frac{3}{\pi^2} \int_C \frac{h(\xi,\eta)}{(\xi-\eta)^2} d\xi d\eta = 1.$$

6. Conjugacy

We construct a map T_R conjugate to T_C, the purpose of which will be discussed once it has been defined.

Let us introduce the subset R of our extended plane in terms of our disjoint subsets

$$R = R_1 \cup R_2 \cup R_3 \cup R_4,$$

each R_i being further decomposed as

$$R_i = R_i^m \cup R_i^\ell \cup R_i^r \cup R_i^t \cup R_i^b$$

where the superscripts have the following connotation: m for main part, ℓ, r, t, b respectively for left, right, top and bottom. We define the various parts of R_i which are depicted in Figure 6.1.

$$R_1^m = \{(\bar{\xi},\bar{\eta}) : 1 < \bar{\xi} < \infty, \ -\infty < \bar{\eta} < -0\}$$

$$R_2^m = \{ \quad " \quad : +0 < \bar{\xi} < 1, \ -\infty < \bar{\eta} < -1\}.$$

R_3^m, R_4^m are gotten from R_2^m, R_1^m by replacing $\bar{\xi}$, $\bar{\eta}$ by $-\bar{\xi}$, $-\bar{\eta}$. As in C_i the only subsets of R_i which have non zero measure are R_i^m.

$$R_1^\ell = \{(\bar{\xi},\bar{\eta}) : \bar{\xi} = 1, \ -\infty < \eta < -1\}$$

$$R_1^r = \{ \quad " \quad : \bar{\xi} = +\infty, \ -k - \frac{1}{2} < \bar{\eta} < -k, \ k = +0,1,2,\ldots\}$$

$$R_1^t = \{ \quad " \quad : 1 < \bar{\xi} < +\infty, \ \bar{\eta} = -0\}$$

$$R_1^b = \{ \quad " \quad : k \le \xi < k + \frac{1}{2}, \ \eta = -\infty, \ k = 1,2,\ldots\}$$

$$R_2^b = \{ \quad " \quad : +0 \le \xi < \frac{1}{2}, \ \eta = -\infty\}$$

Let $\alpha(\bar{\xi},\bar{\eta}) = (\bar{\xi}-1,\bar{\eta}-1)$. Then

$$R_2^\ell = \alpha R_1^\ell, \ R_4^r = -R_1^\ell, \ R_4^b = -R_1^t, \ R_3^r = -R_2^\ell.$$

R_4^ℓ, R_4^t are obtained from αR_1^b, αR_1^r by interchanging $\bar{\xi}$, $\bar{\eta}$. $R_3^t = -R_2^b$ with $(-0,+\infty)$ deleted. Finally $R_2^r = R_2^t = R_3^\ell = R_3^b = \phi$.

We define the mapping T_R of R onto itself by

$$T_R(-\bar{\xi},\bar{\eta}) = \begin{cases} (\bar{\xi}-1, \ \bar{\eta}-1) & \text{on } R_1 \\ (-\frac{1}{\bar{\xi}}, \ -\frac{1}{\bar{\eta}}) & \text{on } R_2 \cup R_3 \\ (\bar{\xi}+1, \ \bar{\eta}+1) & \text{on } R_4. \end{cases}$$

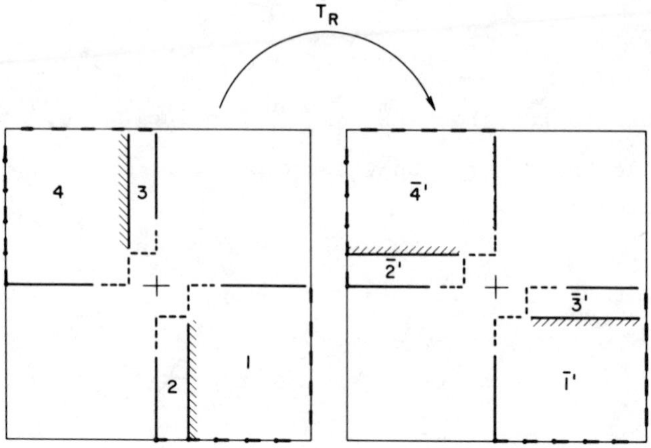

Figure 6.1

The sets R_i are straightened out versions of the sets C_i in §4. For this reason we call the set R the <u>rectilinear domain</u>, and the map T_R the <u>rectilinear map</u>. This is the rationale behind the terminology "curvilinear." For emphasis we use the notation $(\bar{\xi},\bar{\eta})$ in this section and call these variables the <u>rectilinear coordinates</u>. Because the rectilinear map is defined by piecewise transforming the variables by the same fractional linear transformation just like in the curvilinear case, it preserves the same measure—namely

$$dm_c = \left(\frac{3}{\pi^2}\right) \frac{d\bar{\xi}d\bar{\eta}}{(\bar{\xi}-\bar{\eta})^2} .$$

The reason for introducing the rectilinear map is due to the fact that it has a feature which the curvilinear one does not—namely T_R maps vertical lines in R into vertical lines and T_R^{-1} maps horizontal lines into horizontal ones. Thus we can write

$$T_R(\bar{\xi},\bar{\eta}) = (f_E(\bar{\xi}),\cdot)$$

f_E given by

$$\text{(6.1)}\quad f_E(\bar{\xi}) = \begin{cases} \bar{\xi}-1, & 1 \le \bar{\xi} \le +\infty \\ -1/\bar{\xi}, & -1 < \bar{\xi} \le -0, \quad +0 \le \bar{\xi} < 1 \\ \bar{\xi}+1, & -\infty \le \bar{\xi} \le -1 . \end{cases}$$

The map f_E is called a <u>factor</u> of T_R and T_R an extension of f_E. Remarkably T_R^{-1} can be written as

$$T_R^{-1}(\bar{\xi},\bar{\eta}) = (\cdot, f_E(\bar{\eta}))$$

with the same function f_E.

We shall make use of these properties in §8.

Our aim is to set up a conjugacy between T_C and T_R. We construct a one-to-one map Φ from C onto R satisfying

$$\text{(6.2)}\qquad T_R \circ \Phi = \Phi \circ T_C$$

$$\text{(6.3)}\qquad \Phi = \text{identity on } C \cap R.$$

We shall show that this serves to determine Φ: indeed (6.2) and (6.3) force Φ to map the four pieces of $C - R = U_1 \cup U_2 \cup V_1 \cup V_2$ respectively onto the four pieces of $R - C = \bar{U}_1 \cup \bar{U}_2 \cup \bar{V}_1 \cup \bar{V}_2$ defined below and depicted in Figure 6.2.

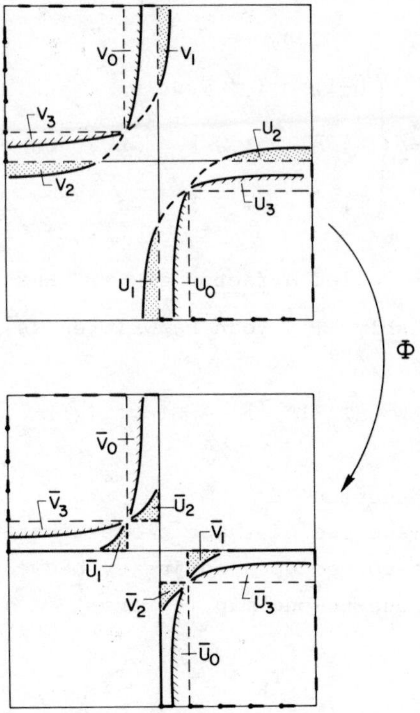

Figure 6.2.

"Bulges into Corners"

$$U_1 = C_2 - R \cap C$$
$$U_2 = C_1 - R \cap C$$
$$V_1 = C - R \cap C$$
$$V_2 = C_4 - R \cap C$$

$$\overline{U}_1 = R_4 - R \cap C$$
$$\overline{U}_2 = R_3 - R \cap C$$
$$\overline{V}_1 = R_1 - R \cap C$$
$$\overline{V}_2 = R_2 - R \cap C$$

In Figure 6.2 the first four sets are referred to as "bulges" and the last four as "corners."

To show that Φ is fixed by (6.2) and (6.3) we introduce the following four sets in $R \cap C$

$$\begin{aligned} U_0 &= \overline{U}_0 = T_C^{-1} U_1 \\ U_3 &= \overline{U}_3 = T_C U_2 \\ V_0 &= \overline{V}_0 = T_C^{-1} V_1 \\ V_3 &= \overline{V}_3 = T_C V_2 \, . \end{aligned}$$

Recalling that $\alpha z = z+1$, $\beta z = -1/z$ we define with a slight abuse of notation the mappings $\alpha(\xi,\eta) = (\alpha\xi,\alpha\eta)$ and $\beta(\xi,\eta) = (\beta\xi,\beta\eta)$. In these terms

$$T_C(\xi,\eta) = \begin{cases} \alpha^{-1}(\xi,\eta) & \text{on } C_1 \\ \beta(\xi,\eta) & \text{on } C_2 \cup C_3 \\ \alpha(\xi,\eta) & \text{on } C_4 \end{cases}$$

and

$$T_R(\overline{\xi},\overline{\eta}) = \begin{cases} \alpha^{-1}(\overline{\xi},\overline{\eta}) & \text{on } R_1 \\ \beta(\overline{\xi},\overline{\eta}) & \text{on } R_3 \cup R_2 \\ \alpha(\overline{\xi},\overline{\eta}) & \text{on } R_4 \, . \end{cases}$$

Verifying the nontrivial part of the conjugacy relation $\Phi \circ T_C = T_R \circ \Phi$ reduces to checking commutativity in the following diagrams.

$$\begin{array}{ccccccc} U_0 & \xrightarrow{T_C = \alpha^{-1}} & U_1 & \xrightarrow{T_C = \beta} & U_2 & \xrightarrow{T_C = \alpha^{-1}} & U_3 \\ \downarrow \Phi = I & & \downarrow \Phi & & \downarrow \Phi & & \downarrow \Phi = I \\ \overline{U}_0 & \xrightarrow{T_R = \beta} & \overline{U}_1 & \xrightarrow{T_R = \alpha} & \overline{U}_2 & \xrightarrow{T_R = \beta} & \overline{U}_3 \end{array}$$

$$\begin{array}{ccccccc}
V_0 & \xrightarrow{T_C=\alpha} & V_1 & \xrightarrow{T_C=\beta} & V_2 & \xrightarrow{T_C=\alpha} & V_3 \\
\downarrow{\scriptstyle \Phi=I} & & \downarrow{\scriptstyle \Phi} & & \downarrow{\scriptstyle \Phi} & & \downarrow{\scriptstyle \Phi=I} \\
\overline{V}_0 & \xrightarrow{T_R=\beta} & \overline{V}_1 & \xrightarrow{T_R=\alpha^{-1}} & \overline{V}_2 & \xrightarrow{T_R=\beta} & \overline{V}_3
\end{array}$$

The commutativity forces Φ to satisfy

$$\Phi = \begin{cases} \beta\alpha & \text{on } U_1 \\ (\alpha\beta)^2 & \text{on } U_2 \\ \beta\alpha^{-1} & \text{on } V_1 \\ (\alpha^{-1}\beta)^2 & \text{on } V_2 \\ (\beta\alpha)^3 & \text{on } U_3 \\ (\beta\alpha^{-1})^3 & \text{on } V_3 \,. \end{cases}$$

Observe that the group relations yield $(\beta\alpha)^3 = (\beta\alpha^{-1})^3 =$ identity, which is consistent with condition (6.3) because $U_3, V_3 \subseteq R \cap C$.

Finally, we abbreviate the above relation for Φ as follows:

$$(6.4) \qquad (\overline{\xi},\overline{\eta}) = \Phi(\xi,\eta) = \begin{cases} (\xi,\eta) & \text{on } C \cap R \\ \left(-\frac{1}{\xi+1}, -\frac{1}{\eta+1}\right) & \text{on } U_1 \cup V_2 \\ \left(-\frac{1}{\xi-1}, -\frac{1}{\eta-1}\right) & \text{on } U_2 \cup V_1 . \end{cases}$$

In Figure 6.3 the sets U_i, V_i $i = 1,2$ are depicted as wedges at a typical point of ∂F. Projection of vectors in these wedges are given rectilinear coordinates $\overline{\xi}$, $\overline{\eta}$ which are related to ξ, η by (6.4).

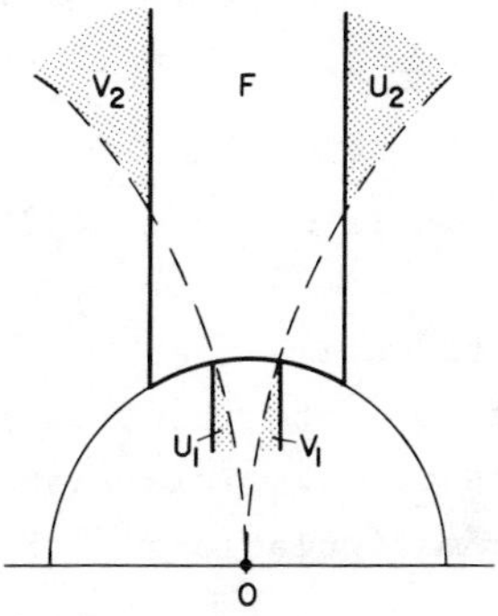

Figure 6.3

7. Inducing

Ergodic theory of factors and extensions was developed by Rohlin [Ro] for transformations on finite measure spaces. In order to use standard results in this area we must overcome the technicality that T_R acts on $\mathbb{R}$ where $m_c(\mathbb{R}) = \infty$. This is handled by introducing a related map T_Q, called the <u>induced rectilinear map</u>, which acts on a subset of R of finite measure. Let

$$Q = R_2 \cup R_3 \cup R_1^b \cup R_1^r \cup R_4^t \cup R_4^\ell ,$$

which we call the <u>induced rectilinear domain</u>. We have

$$m_c(Q) = \frac{3}{\pi^2}\int_{-1}^{0} d\xi \int_{1}^{\infty} \frac{d\bar{\eta}}{(\xi-\bar{\eta})^2} + \frac{3}{\pi^2}\int_{0}^{1} d\xi \int_{-\infty}^{-1} \frac{d\bar{\eta}}{(\bar{\xi}-\bar{\eta})^2} = \frac{6 \log 2}{\pi^2} < \infty .$$

Also

$$(7.1) \qquad R = \bigcup_{n=1}^{\infty} T_R^{-n} Q = \bigcup_{n=1}^{\infty} T_R^{n} Q .$$

Define

$$T_Q(\bar{\xi},\bar{\eta}) = T_R^{n(\bar{\xi},\bar{\eta})}(\bar{\xi},\bar{\eta}), \qquad (\bar{\xi},\bar{\eta}) \in Q$$

where

$$n(\bar{\xi},\bar{\eta}) = \inf\{n : n \geq 1, \ T_R^n(\bar{\xi},\bar{\eta}) \in Q\}$$

From (7.1) it is easy to verify that T_Q is well defined and is a one-to-one map of Q onto itself. T_Q preserves the measure m_C on subsets of Q. This last fact follows from (7.1) and standard set manipulations. It is easy to verify that

$$T_Q(\bar{\xi},\bar{\eta}) = \begin{cases} (-(1/\bar{\xi}), -1/\bar{\eta} + [1/\bar{\xi}]) & \text{on } R_2 - R_2^{\ell} \\ -T_Q(-\bar{\xi},-\bar{\eta}) & \text{on } R_3 - R_3^{r} \\ T_R(\bar{\xi},\bar{\eta}) & \text{elsewhere on } Q \end{cases}$$

where $(\bar{\xi})$, $[\bar{\xi}]$ denote respectively the fractional and integral part of the real number $\bar{\xi}$.

The first coordinate of $T_Q(\bar{\xi},\bar{\eta})$ depends only on $\bar{\xi}$, like that of T_R, but the second coordinate of $T_Q^{-1}(\bar{\xi},\bar{\eta})$, $\bar{\xi} \neq \pm\infty$, is not the same as that of $T_Q^{-1}(\pm\infty,\bar{\eta})$. So in the spirit of this work, when an absent property is desired, we perform a conjugacy to get it. For this we introduce a <u>modified extended line</u> $\tilde{E}$ with a countable number of "infinites"—i.e. $\tilde{E} = (-\infty,-0] \cup [+0,\infty) \cup \{\cdots\infty_{-2},\infty_{-1},\infty_1,\infty_2,\ldots\}$—and the <u>modified extended plane</u> $\tilde{E} \times \tilde{E}$. We shall find it convenient to adopt the convention, $-\infty_k = \infty_{-k}$. We refer to elements $(\tilde{\xi},\tilde{\eta}) \in \tilde{E} \times \tilde{E}$ as modified rectilinear coordinates. We define a one-to-one mapping Ψ of $Q \subset E \times E$ into $\tilde{E} \times \tilde{E}$ by:

$$(\tilde{\xi},\tilde{\eta}) = \Psi(\bar{\xi},\bar{\eta}) = \begin{cases} (\bar{\xi},-1/\bar{\eta}) & \text{on } R_2 \cup R_3 \\ (\bar{\xi},\infty_k) & \text{on } D_k, |k| \geq 1 \\ (\infty_{k-1},\eta-1) & \text{on } U_k, \ k \leq -0 \\ (\theta_{k+1},\eta+1) & \text{on } U_k, \ k \geq +0 . \end{cases}$$

We call $P = \Psi Q$ the <u>modified induced rectilinear domain</u> and $T_P = \Psi T_Q \Psi^{-1}$ the <u>modified induced rectilinear map</u>. In order to express T_P in modified rectilinear coordinates we define the following partition of P into subsets (see Figure 7.1).

$$P_k = \begin{cases} \{(\tilde{\xi},\tilde{\eta}) \in P : \frac{1}{k+1} < \tilde{\xi} \le 1/k, \quad k \ge 2\} \\ \\ \{(\tilde{\xi},\tilde{\eta}) \in P : \frac{1}{k} \le \tilde{\xi} < \frac{1}{k+1}, \quad k \le -2\} \end{cases}$$

$$P_1 = \{(\tilde{\xi},\tilde{\eta}) \in P : \tfrac{1}{2} < \tilde{\xi} < 1\}$$

$$P_{-1} = \{(\tilde{\xi},\tilde{\eta}) \in P : -1 < \tilde{\xi} < -\tfrac{1}{2}\}$$

$$P_{+0} = \Psi R_2^{\ell} \cup \{(+0,+0)\}$$

$$P_{-0} = \Psi R_3^{r}$$

$$P_{d_k} = \Psi D_k, \quad |k| \ge 1$$

$$P_{u_k} = \begin{cases} \Psi U_{k+1}, & k \le -1 \\ \Psi U_{k-1}, & k \ge +1 . \end{cases}$$

We then have

$$T_P(\tilde{\xi},\tilde{\eta}) = \begin{cases} (-(1/\tilde{\xi}), -\frac{1}{\tilde{\eta}+[1/\tilde{\xi}]}) & \text{on } \bigcup_{k\ge 1} P_k \\ (\infty_1, \tilde{\eta}+1) & \text{on } P_{+0} \\ (\infty_{k+1}, \tilde{\eta}+1) & \text{on } P_{u_k}, \ k \ge 1 \\ (\tilde{\xi}-1, \infty_{k-1}) & \text{on } P_{d_k}, \ k \ge 2 \\ (\tilde{\xi}-1, +0) & \text{on } P_{d_1} \\ -T_P(-\tilde{\xi},-\tilde{\eta}) & \text{elsewhere on } P \end{cases}$$

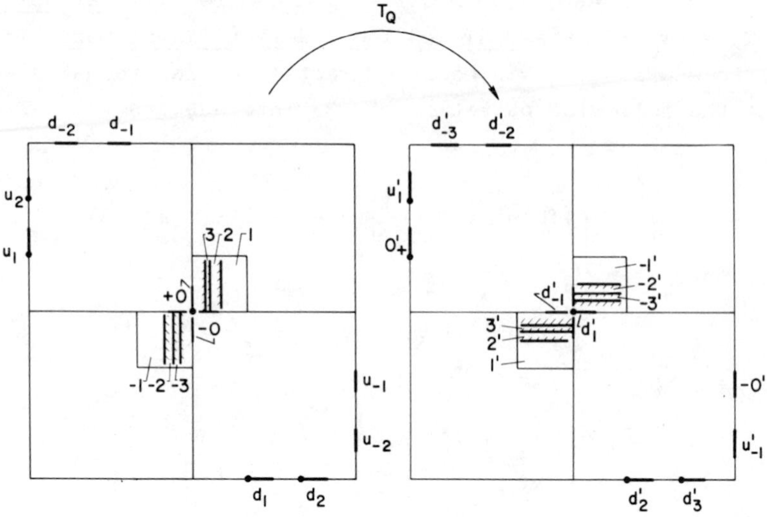

Figure 7.1

$$T_P(\tilde{\xi},\tilde{\eta}) = (f_{\tilde{I}}(\tilde{\xi})) \quad \text{where} \quad f_{\tilde{I}} \text{ is a mapping of}$$

$$\tilde{I} = (-1,-0] \cup [+0,1) \cup \bigcup_{k\geq 1}^{\infty} [k,k+\tfrac{1}{2}) \cup -k-\tfrac{1}{2},-k] \cup \{\infty_k,\infty_{-k}\}$$

onto itself satisfying

$$f_{\tilde{I}}(\tilde{\xi}) = \begin{cases} -(1/\tilde{\xi}), & 0 < \tilde{\xi} < 1 \\ \infty_1, & \tilde{\xi} = +0 \\ \tilde{\xi}-1, & k \leq \tilde{\xi} < k+\frac{1}{2},\ 1 \leq k \\ \infty_{-(k+1)}, & \xi = \infty_{-k},\ k \geq 1 \\ -f_{\tilde{E}}(-\tilde{\xi}), & \text{elsewhere on } \tilde{E} \end{cases}$$

Figure 7.1 hints at what a case by case analysis confirms:

if $(\tilde{\xi}',\tilde{\eta}') = T_P(\tilde{\xi},\tilde{\eta})$, then $(\tilde{\eta},\tilde{\xi}) = T_P(\overline{\xi}',\overline{\eta}')$. It follows that $T_P^{-1}(\tilde{\xi},\tilde{\eta}) = (\cdot, f_{\tilde{I}}(\tilde{\eta}))$.

We have a T_P —invariant measure defined by $m_P = m_C\psi^{-1}$ which can be expressed in modified rectilinear coordinates by

$$dm_P = \frac{3}{\pi^2}\frac{d\tilde{\xi}d\tilde{\eta}}{(1+\tilde{\xi}\tilde{\eta})^2}.$$

Finally, we remark that T_P itself is conjugate to a cross section map—namely, if we set

$$V = \Phi^{-1}\Psi^{-1}P$$

and define

$$T_B = (\Psi\Phi)^{-1}T_P\,\Psi\Phi ,$$

then T_B is the cross section map induced by G_t on the cross section B. The main part of B is depicted in Figure 7.2.

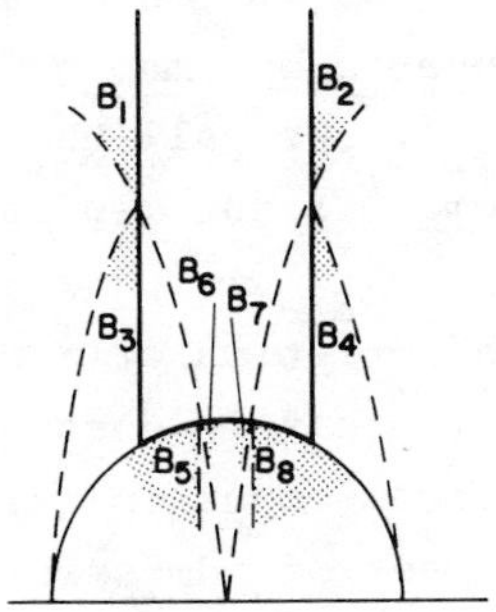

Figure 7.2

The projection of vectors in the various wedges are given modified rectilinear coordinates $(\tilde{\xi},\tilde{\eta})$ which are related to curvilinear ξ, η by

$$(\tilde{\xi},\tilde{\eta}) = \begin{cases} (-\frac{1}{\xi-1},\eta-1 & \text{on } B_1 \\ (-\frac{1}{\xi+1},\eta+1) & \text{on } B_2 \\ (\xi,-\frac{1}{\eta}) & \text{on } \bigcup_{i=3}^{8} B_i. \end{cases}$$

8. Symbolic Dynamics

Given an abstract dynamical system (X,T) —i.e. a space X and a mapping T of X onto itself, a finite or countable alphabet A of symbols, and a partition $P = \{X_a : a \in A\}$ of X into disjoint subsets, we can associate with each point x a sequence $\{a_n\}$ of symbols $a_n \in A$ according as $T^n x \in X_{a_n}$. The sequences describe the history of orbits through the partition. They are bilateral, $\{a_n\}, -\infty < n < \infty$, or unilateral $\{a_n\}$, $0 \le n < \infty$, depending on whether T is invertible or not. In specific instances T will indicate invertible maps and f noninvertible. In the latter case a sequence $\{a_n\}$, $0 \le n < \infty$, is called an f-expansion of a point x. Let $\Omega(T)$ denote the space of the above sequences. We call the definition just given the orbit history description of $\Omega(T)$. Let ϕ denote the mapping of X onto $\Omega(T)$ defined by $\phi x = \{a_n\}$ and σ the one-to-one map of $\Omega(T)$ onto itself defined by $\sigma\{a_n\} = \{a_{n+1}\}$. We call the pair $(\Omega(T),\sigma)$ a symbolic dynamical system. If the map is invertible, we have the conjugacy $T = \phi^{-1}\sigma\phi$.

The orbit history description of a symbolic system is inadequate as it stands in that it does not give a procedure for deciding which sequences occur in it. What is needed is another description by a set of admissibility rules expressible by a finite number of sentences. Our admissibility rules will be of two kinds: a set of Markovian transition rules T imposed on the members of A which require $a_n \to a_{n+1}$ for all relevant n, and a list L of omitted sequences specified by a given pattern. The sequence space defined by admissibility rules will be denoted by $\Omega_a(T)$.

In order that the two descriptions specify the same space of sequences, i.e. $\Omega_a(T) = \Omega(T)$, we must show that $\psi\{a_n\} =$

$\cap T^{-n}X_{a_n} \neq \emptyset$ iff $\{a_n\} \in \Omega_a(T)$. For invertibility we must prove that $\psi\{a_n\}$ consists of a single point.

In the present section we show that T_R, T_P, their factors f_E, $f_{\tilde{I}}$, and T_C are conjugate to shifts on corresponding sequeces spaces $\Omega(T_R)$, $\Omega(T_P)$, $\Omega(f_E)$, $\Omega(f_{\tilde{I}})$, and $\Omega(T_C)$. A sixth one, $\Omega(f_I)$, is introduced in order to facilitate the proof of conjugacy between f_E and σ on $\Omega(f_E)$. All the symbolic spaces except $\Omega(T_C)$ have descriptions by admissibility rules. For $\Omega(T_C)$ we must settle for merely the orbit history description.

For economy of notation we drop from now on bars and tildas from variables ξ, η unless otherwise reintroduced. Also we introduce here projections $p_\xi(\xi,\eta) = \xi$ and $p_\eta(\xi,\eta) = \eta$.

We proceed to list the various spaces $\Omega(T)$ and $\Omega_a(T)$, $\Omega(T)$ being specified by X, T, A, L and $\Omega_a(T)$ by T, L. Whenever any of these items are self understood it will be omitted form the specification.

I. $\underline{\Omega(f_I)}$: $I = (-1,-0] \cup [+0,1) \cup \{\pm\infty\}$ and f_I is the transformation induced on I by f_E —i.e.

$$f_I(\xi) = \begin{cases} -(1/\xi), & +0 < \xi < 1 \\ (-1/\xi), & -1 < \xi < -0 \\ -\infty, & \xi = +0,-\infty \\ +\infty, & \xi = -0,+\infty \end{cases}$$

$$A = \{-\infty,\ldots,-1,-0,+0,1,\ldots,+\infty\}$$

$$P = \{I_a : a \in A\} \text{ where } I_{+0} = \{+0\},\ I_{+\infty} = \{+\infty\}, I_1 = (\tfrac{1}{2}, 1),$$

$$I_n = (\tfrac{1}{n+1}, \tfrac{1}{n}),\ 2 \le n < \infty,\ I_{-n} = I_n,\ +0 \le n \le +\infty.$$

$\Omega_a(f_I)$:

$$T: \begin{array}{l} 1 \to -1,\ldots,-n,\ldots \\ k \to -0,-1,\ldots,-n,\ldots, \quad 2 \le k < \infty \\ +0 \to -\infty \\ +\infty \to +\infty \end{array}$$

To these add the rules obtained by replacing each symbol by its negative.

II. $\Omega(f_E)$:

$A = \{1,2,3,4\}$

$P = \{E_a : a \in A\}$ where $E_1 = [1,+\infty]$, $E_2 = [+0,1]$,

$E_3 = (-1,-0]$, $E_4 = [-\infty,-1]$, i.e. $E_i = p_\xi R_i$, $1 \le i \le 4$,

$\Omega_a(f_E)$:

$$T: \begin{array}{l} 1 \to 1,2 \\ 2 \to 4 \\ 3 \to 1 \\ 4 \to 3,4 \end{array}$$

L : ...2431...1..., ...3124...4...

III. $\Omega(T_R)$:

$A = \{1,2,3,4\}$

$P = \{R_1,R_2,R_3,R_4\}$

$\Omega_a(T_R)$:

T : Same as for $\Omega(f_E)$.

$$
L : \begin{array}{ll}
\ldots 1 \ldots 1 \ldots, & \ldots 4 \ldots 4 \ldots \\
\ldots 2431 \ldots 1 \ldots, & \ldots 3124 \ldots 4 \ldots \\
\ldots 1 \ldots 1243 \ldots, & \ldots 4 \ldots 4312 \ldots \\
\ldots 1 \ldots 124431 \ldots 1 \ldots, & \ldots 4 \ldots 431124 \ldots 4 \ldots \\
\ldots 4 \ldots 431 \ldots 1 \ldots &
\end{array}
$$

All items in the above list are paired except the last, which is due to the fact that R is not symmetric about the origin.

IV. $\underline{\Omega(f_{\tilde{I}})}$:

$$A = \{k, -k, d_{k+1}, d_{-(k+1)}, u_{k+1}, u_{-(k+1)} : +0 \le k < \infty\}$$

$$P = \{\tilde{I}_a : a \in A\} \text{ where } \tilde{I}_a = p_\xi P_a$$

$\underline{\Omega_a(f_{\tilde{I}})}$:

$$
T : \begin{array}{ll}
1 \to -1, \ldots, -n, \ldots & \\
k \to -0, -1, \ldots, -n, \ldots, & 2 \le k < \infty \\
+0 \to u_1 & \\
u_k \to u_{k+1}, & 1 \le k < \infty \\
d_{k+1} \to d_k, & 1 \le k < \infty \\
d_1 \to +0, 2, \ldots, n, \ldots & \\
d_{-1} \to -1, \ldots, -n, \ldots &
\end{array}
$$

To these add the rules obtained from the first five by replacing k, u_k, d_k by $-k, u_{-k}, d_{-k}$.

$$
L : \begin{array}{l}
\ldots d_{+0}, +2, -0, \ldots \\
\ldots d_{-0}, -2, +0, \ldots
\end{array}
$$

V. $\underline{\Omega(T_P)}$:

A = Same as for $\Omega(f_{\tilde{I}})$.

$$P = \{P_a : a \in A\}$$

$\underline{\Omega_a(T_p)}$:

T : Same as for $\Omega_a(f_{\tilde{I}})$.

L : "

VI. $\Omega(T_C)$:

$A = \{1,2,3,4\}$

$P = \{C_1, C_2, C_3, C_4\}$.

We prove a series of theorems to the effect that, in each of the cases I-IV, $\Omega(T) = \Omega_a(T)$ and the given transformation T is conjugate to the action of σ on $\Omega_a(T)$. This amounts to proving that, in each of these cases, $\psi\{a_n\} = \cap T^{-n}X_{a_n}$ = single point in X whenever $\{a_n\} \in \Omega_a(X)$ and $\psi\{a_n\}$ maps $\Omega_a(T)$ onto X.

We use the notation $[a_0,\ldots,a_n]$ as an abbreviation for the continued fraction

$$\cfrac{1}{a_0+\cfrac{1}{a_1+\ddots+\cfrac{1}{a_n}}}$$

and $[a_0,\ldots,a_n\ldots]$ for the corresponding infinite continued fraction.

Theorem 8.1. For $\{a_n\} \in \Omega_a(f_I)$ we have

i) If $a_0 = +\infty, -\infty$, then respectively $\psi\{a_n\} = +\infty, -\infty$

ii) If $a_0 = +0, -0$, then respectively $\psi\{a_n\} = +0, -0$

iii) If $a_n \neq \pm 0, \pm\infty$ for $0 \le n \le N$, where $0 \le N < \infty$ and $a_{N+1} = \pm 0$, then $\psi\{a_n\} = \operatorname{sgn} a_0 \cdot [|a_0|, \ldots, |a_N|]$

iv) If $a_n \neq \pm 0, \pm\infty$ $\forall n$, then $\psi\{a_n\} = a_0 \cdot [\ a_0, \ldots |a_N|, \ldots]$.

In case iii) the transition rules T imply that $|a_N| \ge 2$. Since the rational numbers in $(0,1)$ are in 1-1 correspondence with the finite continued fractions $[a_0, \ldots, a_N]$, $\forall a_n \in Z^+$ and $a_N \ge 2$, and the irrational numbers in $(0,1)$ are in 1-1 correspondence with the infinite continued fractions $[a_0, \ldots, a_n, \ldots]$ $\forall a_n \in Z^+$, we conclude that $\psi\{a_n\}$ consists of a single point and $\psi\{a_n\}$ maps $\Omega_a(f_I)$ onto I. Thus we have $\Omega(f_I) = \Omega_a(f_I)$ and the conjugacy $f_I = \phi^{-1} \circ \sigma \circ \phi$.

Proof. i) If $a_0 = +\infty$, then $a_n = +\infty$ $\forall n$. Since $f_I^{-n}(I_{+\infty}) = \{+\infty\}$ $\forall n$, $\psi\{a_n\} = +\infty$. Similarly, $\psi\{a_n\} = -\infty$ when $a_0 = -\infty$.

ii) If $a_0 = +0$, then $a_n = -\infty$, $n \ge 1$. $I_{+0} = \{+0\}$ and $+0 \in f_I^{-n}(-\infty)$, $n \ge 1$. Hence $\psi\{a_n\} = +0$ when $a_0 = +0$. Similarly, $\psi\{a_n\} = 0$ when $a_0 = -0$.

iii) The condition $\xi \in \psi\{a_n\}$ means that $\operatorname{sgn} \xi = \operatorname{sgn} a_0$ and $\dfrac{1}{f_I^n(|\xi|)} = |a_n| + f_I^{n+1}(|\xi|)$, $0 \le n \le N$, $f_I^{N+1}(|\xi|) = 0$. Solving for ξ, we obtain $\psi\{a_n\} = \operatorname{sgn} a_0 \cdot [|a_0|, \ldots, |a_N|]$.

iv) The condition $\xi \in \psi\{a_n\}$ means that $\operatorname{sgn} \xi = \operatorname{sgn} a_0$ and $\dfrac{1}{f_I^n(|\xi|)} = |a_n| + f_I^{n+1}(|\xi|)$, $0 \le n < \infty$. This is equivalent to $|\xi| = [|a_0|, \ldots, |a_n|, \ldots]$, [HW; p. 139]. Hence $\psi\{a_n\} = \operatorname{sgn} a_0 \cdot [|a_0|, \ldots, |a_n|, \ldots]$.

We obtain next a similar result for $\Omega(f_E)$. We use the following terminology. Let $\{a_n\}$ be a sequence of $\Omega(f_E)$ containing an infinite number of 1's and 4's. Call these sequences non-terminating and the remaining one terminating. Then:

either $\{a_n\} = \overbrace{1\ldots1}^{\ell_{-1}}\ 2\ \overbrace{4\ldots4}^{\ell_0}\ 3\ \overbrace{1\ldots1}^{\ell_1}\ 2\ldots$

or $\{a_n\} = \overbrace{4\ldots4}^{\ell_{-1}}\ 3\ \overbrace{1\ldots1}^{\ell_0}\ 2\ \overbrace{4\ldots4}^{\ell_1}\ 3\ldots$

where ℓ_{-1} is an arbitrary non-negative integer and ℓ_n, $0 \le n < \infty$, are arbitrary positive integers. For the terminating sequences, i.e. those for which a_n is identically 1 or 4 from some n on, we obtain a finite number of block lengths $\ell_{-1},\ldots,\ell_N$. The restrictions on the ℓ_n's are the same as before except for ℓ_{N-1}, ℓ_N which now satisfy $2 \le \ell_{N-1} < \infty$, $\ell_N = \infty$. The restriction $\ell_{N-1} \ge 2$ is due to the fact that the sequences ...2431...1...,...3124...4... are omitted from $\Omega(f_E)$.

<u>Theorem 8.2</u>. For $\{a_n\} \in \Omega_a(f_E)$ and $a_0 = 1,2$ we have

i) If $\ell_{-1} = \infty$, then $\psi\{a_n\} = +\infty$

ii) If $\ell_{-1} < \infty$, $\ell_0 = \infty$, then $\psi\{a_n\} = \ell_{-1}$

iii) If $\ell_n < \infty$, $-1 \le n \le N-1$, $\ell_N = \infty (N \ge 1)$, then $\psi\{a_n\} = \ell_{-1} + [\ell_0,\ldots,\ell_{N-1}]$

iv) If $\forall \ell_n < \infty$, then $\psi\{a_n\} = \ell_{-1} + [\ell_0,\ldots,\ell_n,\ldots]$

If $\{a_n\} \in \Omega_a(f_E)$ and $a_0 = 3,4$ then the above values for $\psi\{a_n\}$ are to be replaced by their negatives.

Thus $\psi\{a_n\}$ consists of a single point and $\psi\{a_n\}$ maps $\Omega_a(f_E)$ onto E. We conclude that $\Omega(f_E) = \Omega_a(f_E)$ and $f_E = \phi^{-1}\circ\sigma\circ\phi$.

<u>Proof</u>. We assume that $a_0 = 1,2$, the proofs for $a_0 = 3,4$ being identical.

i) $\ell_{-1} = \infty$ means that a_n is identically 1. The only ξ for which $f^n(\xi) \in E$, $0 \le n < \infty$, is $\xi = +\infty$. Hence $\psi\{a_n\} = +\infty$.

ii) If $a_0 = 2$, then $a_n = 4$ for $n \geq 1$ and

$$\psi\{a_n\} = E_2 \cap f^{-1}[\bigcap_{n=0}^{\infty} f^{-n}E_4] = E_2 \cap f^{-1}(-\infty) = +0.$$

If $a_0 = 1$, then $a_\ell = 2$, $a_{n+\ell} = 4$, $n \geq 1$, where $\ell = \ell_{-1}$. Hence $\psi\{a_n\} = \bigcap_{n=0}^{\ell-1} f^{-n}E_1 \cap f^{-\ell}[E_2 \cap f^{-1} \bigcap_{n=0}^{\infty} f^{-n}E_4]$

$$= [\ell,+\infty] \cap f^{-\ell}\{+0\} = \ell.$$

iii) Let $a_0 = 2$. From the definitions of f, f_I it follows that $\bigcap_{n=0}^{\infty} f^{-n}E_{a_n} = \bigcap_{n=0}^{\infty} f_I^{-n}I_{b_n}$ where $b_n = (-1)^n \ell_n$, $0 \leq n \leq N-1$,

$$b_N = \begin{cases} +0, & N \text{ even} \\ -0, & N \text{ odd} \end{cases}, \quad b_n = \begin{cases} -\infty, & n > N \text{ and } N \text{ even} \\ +\infty, & n > N \text{ and } N \text{ odd.} \end{cases}$$

Since $\ell_{N-1} \geq 2$, it follows that $\{b_n\} \in \Omega(g)$ whenever $\{a_n\} \in \Omega(f_E)$. We conclude from Theorem 1 that $\psi\{a_n\} = \psi\{b_n\} = [\ell_0,\ldots,\ell_{N-1}]$. If $a_0 = 1$, then we obtain

$$\psi\{a_n\} = \bigcap_{n=0}^{\ell-1} f^{-n}E_1 \cap f^{-\ell}[\bigcap_{n=0}^{\infty} f^{-n}E_{a_{\ell+n}}]$$

$$= [\ell,+\infty] \cap f^{-\ell}[\ell_0,\ldots,\ell_{N-1}] = \ell + [\ell_0,\ldots,\ell_{N-1}].$$

iv) The proof is similar to that of iii) and is omitted.

To state Theorem 8.3, we introduce the f'_E-expansion of $\eta \in E$. This is just the f_E-expansion of η with 1's and 4's interchanged. If $\{a_n\}$ is the f'_E-expansion of η, then

$$\{a_n\} \in \Omega'(f_E), \quad \eta = \psi\{a_n\} = \bigcap_{n=0}^{\infty} f_E^{-n}E'_{a_n}, \quad \text{where } \Omega'_a(f_E),\ E'_n$$

are obtained from $\Omega(f_E)$, E_n by interchanging 1 and 4.

Theorem 8.3. $\Omega(T_R) = \Omega_a(T_R)$ and $T_R = \phi^{-1}\circ\sigma\circ\phi$. Let $\{a_n\} = \phi(\xi_0,\eta_0)$, $(\xi_0,\eta_0) \in R$ and $\{a_n\}^+ = \{a_n\}_{n\geq 0}$, $\{a_n\}^- = \{a_{-n-1}\}_{n\geq 0}$. $\{a_n\}^+$, $\{a_n\}^-$ are respectively the f_E and f'_E-expansions of ξ_0 and η_0.

Proof. To prove the theorem, we show that

i) $\psi\{a_n\}$ is a point in R whenever $\{a_n\} \in \Omega_a(T_R)$ and $\psi\{a_n\} = \psi\{a_n\}^+, \psi\{a_n\}^-)$;

ii) ψ maps $\Omega_a(T_R)$ onto R.

Observe that $\{a_n\}^+ \in \Omega_a(f_E)$, $\{a_n\}^- \in \Omega'_a(f'_E)$ when $\{a_n\} \in \Omega(T_R)$. The symbol ψ has thus been used for three different maps, the domain of each being clear from context.

i) Since $T_R(\xi,\eta) = (f_E(\xi),\cdot)$, $T_R^{-1}(\xi,\eta) = (\cdot,f_E(\eta))$, we have

$$(8.1) \qquad p_\xi\circ T_R^n = f_E^n\circ p_\eta, \quad p_\eta\circ T_R^{-n} = f_E^n\circ p_\eta, \quad n \geq 0.$$

For $\{a_n\} \in \Omega_a(T_R)$, $\{a_n\}^+ \in \Omega_a(f_E)$ and $\{a_n\}^- \in \Omega'_a(f_E)$. Let $\xi_0 = \psi\{a_n\}^+$, $\eta_0 = \psi'\{a_n\}^-$. It follows from (8.1) that

$$(8.2) \qquad \bigcap_{n=0}^{\infty} T_R^{-n} R_{a_n} = \bigcap_{n=0}^{\infty} T_R^{-n} p_\xi^{-1} E_{a_n} = p_\xi^{-1} \bigcap_{n=0}^{\infty} f_E^{-n} E_{a_n} = p_\xi^{-1}(\xi_0),$$

$$(8.3) \qquad \bigcap_{n=-1}^{-\infty} T_r^{-n} R_{a_n} = \bigcap_{n=0}^{\infty} T_R^{n} R'_{a_{-n-1}} = \bigcap_{n=0}^{\infty} T_R^{n} p_\eta^{-1} E'_{a_{-n-1}} = p_\eta^{-1} \bigcap_{n=0}^{\infty} f_E^{-n} E'_{a_{-n-1}} = p_\eta^{-1}(\eta_0).$$

Hence $\psi\{a_n\} = p^{-1}(\xi_0) \cap p_\eta^{-1}(\eta_0)$. We show that $(\xi_0,\eta_0) \in R$, so that $\psi\{a_n\} = (\xi_0,\eta_0)$ is a point in R. Assume first that both ξ_0 and η_0 are irrational, i.e. their f_E and f'_E-expansions are non-terminating. Then $\xi_0 \in \mathrm{Int}(p_\xi R_{a_0})$,

$\eta_0 \in \mathrm{Int}(p_\eta R'_{a_{-1}})$. As $a_{-1} \to a_0$, $\mathrm{Int}(p_\eta R'_{a_{-1}}) \subset \mathrm{Int}(p_\eta R_{a_0})$

Hence $(\xi_0, \eta_0) \in \mathrm{Int}\, R_{a_0} \subset R$.

Assume next that at least one of the numbers ξ_0, η_0 is rational or $\pm\infty$, i.e. the sequence $\{a_n\}$ terminates in one direction with either 1's or 4's. We consider the case $a_n = 1$ for n sufficiently large, the argument for the remaining cases proceeding in analogous manner. Suppose $a_{-1} \neq 1$, $a_n = 1$, $n \geq 0$. The f_E-expansion of ξ_0 is 1...1..., i.e. $\xi_0 = +\infty$. Since $\{a_n\}$ satisfies the transmission rules T and is not in the list L, the first three digits of the f-expansion of η_0 are 344 but the expansion is not 34...4... nor 34421...1... . We conclude from Theorem 8.2 that

$-\frac{1}{2} < \eta_0 < -0$. Hence $(\xi_0, \eta_0) \in U_{-0} \subset R$. In general, a_n cannot be identically 1, so $\exists\, N \ni a_{-N-1} \neq 1$, $a_n = 1$, $n \geq N$. Hence $\psi\{a_{N+n}\} \in R$ and $\psi\{a_n\} = T_R^{-N}\psi\{a_{N+n}\} \in R$.

ii) Let $(\xi,\eta) \in \mathbb{R}$ and $\{a_n\} = \phi(\xi,\eta)$. We show that $\{a_n\} \in \Omega_a(f)$. Hence $(\xi,\eta) = \psi\{a_n\}$ and ψ maps $\Omega_a(f)$ onto R. Since $T_R(R_{a_n}) \cap R_{a_{n+1}} = \emptyset$ iff $a_n \to a_{n+1}$,

the transition rules T hold for $\{a_n\}$. We must show that $\{a_n\} \notin L$. We prove that $\{a_n\} \neq \ldots 1 \ldots 124431 \ldots 1 \ldots$, the remaining sequences of L being dismissed in similar manner. Suppose $\{a_n\}$ equals the above sequence with $a_{N-1} = 3$, $a_N = 1$. Then $T_R^N(\xi,\eta) \in R$ and $T_R^N(\xi,\eta) = \psi\{a_{n-m}\}$. But $\Omega\{a_{n-m}\} = (\psi(1\ldots1\ldots), \psi'(34421\ldots1\ldots))$ $= (+,-\frac{1}{2}) \notin R$, a contradiction.

We now state the results for $f_{\tilde{I}}$ and T_P. We omit the proofs which are similar to those of Theorem 8.2 and 8.3.

<u>Theorem 8.4</u>. $\Omega(f_{\tilde{I}}) = \Omega_a(f_{\tilde{I}})$ and $f_{\tilde{I}} = \phi^{-1} \circ \sigma \circ \phi$. $\psi = \phi^{-1}$ is given by

$$\psi\{a_n\}=\begin{cases}\infty_k & \text{if } a_0 = u_k\\ +0\,(-0) & \text{if } a_0 = +0\,(-0)\\ \operatorname{sgn} a_0\cdot[|a_0|,\ldots,|a_n|] & \text{if } |a_0|,\ldots,|a_n| \in Z^+ \text{ and } a_{n+1} = +0\\ \operatorname{sgn} a_0\cdot[|a_0|,\ldots,|a_n|,\ldots] & \text{if } \forall\, |a_n| \in Z^+\\ k + \psi\{a_{n+|k|}\} & \text{if } a_0 = d_k\,.\end{cases}$$

To state Theorem 8.5, we introduce the $f'_{\tilde{I}}$-expansion of $\eta \in \tilde{I}$. Let $\tilde{I}'_a = p_\eta(T_P P_a)$, $a \in A$. Then $\tilde{I}'_a = \tilde{I}_{\pi(a)}$, where π is some fixed permutation of A. If $\{a_n\}$ is the $f_{\tilde{I}}$-expansion of η, then $\{a'_n\} = \{\pi(a_n)\}$ is defined to be the $f'_{\tilde{I}}$-expansion of η.

<u>Theorem 8.5</u>. $\Omega(T_P) = \Omega_a(T_P)$ and $T_P = \phi^{-1}\circ\sigma\circ\phi$. If $\{a_n\} = \phi(\xi,\eta)$, $(\xi,\eta) \in P$ then $\{a_n\}^+$, $\{a_n\}^-$ are respectively the $f_{\tilde{I}}$ and $f'_{\tilde{I}}$-expansions of ξ and η.

We come to $\Omega(T_C)$. Unfortunately there is no $\Omega_a(T)$. However we show how to convert $\Omega(T_C)$ into $\Omega_a(T_R)$ by simple rules.

<u>Definition</u>. For $\{a_n\} \in \Omega(T_C)$ let $\{\bar{a}_n\} = \vartheta\{a_n\}$ be defined as follows:

i) $\bar{a}_n = a_n$ if $a_{n-k}, a_{n-k+1}, a_{n-k-2} \neq 1,2,1$ or $4,3,4$ for $0 \le k \le 2$.

ii) $$\bar{a}_n,\bar{a}_{n+1},\bar{a}_{n+2} = \begin{cases}2,4,3 & \text{if } a_n,a_{n+1},a_{n+2} = 1,2,1\\ 3,1,2 & \text{if } a_n,a_{n+1},a_{n+2} = 4,3,4.\end{cases}$$

$\vartheta\{a_n\} = \{\bar{a}_n\}$ is well defined because the blocks 1,2,1,2,1 and 4,3,4,3,4 do not occur in $\Omega(T_C)$. Actually, after 2,1 comes 1 and after 3,4 comes 4. This can be read off Figure 4.6 and can be traced to the geometrical fact that a geodesic cannot intersect another twice. Since $\vartheta\{a_n\}$ is defined in a shift invariant manner, we have $\sigma\vartheta\{a_n\} = \vartheta\sigma\{a_n\}$.

In Theorem 8.6, we write ϕ_C, ϕ_R instead of ϕ when acting respectivey on C, R.

Theorem 8.6. $\vartheta\circ\phi_C = \phi_R\circ\Phi$.

We remark that since ϕ_R, Φ are bijective maps, the same holds for $\vartheta\circ\phi_C$. This fact, together with ϕ_C being surjective, readily imply that ϕ_C and ϑ are also bijective maps.

Proof. Let $(\xi,\eta) \in C$, $(\overline{\xi},\overline{\eta}) = \Phi(\xi,\eta)$, $\{a_n\} = \phi_C(\xi,\eta)$, $\{\overline{a}_n\} = \phi_R(\overline{\xi},\overline{\eta})$. We must show that $\vartheta\{a_n\} = \{\overline{a}_n\}$. From Figure 6.2 it is clear that

i) $(\xi,\eta) \in C \cap R - (U_0 \cup V_0) \Rightarrow (\xi,\eta) \in R_2 \cap C_2$ for some i, $1 \le i \le 4$

ii) $(\xi,\eta) \in T_C^{-n} U_k$ iff $a_{n-k}, a_{n-k+1}, a_{n-k+2} = 1,2,1, \quad 0 \le k \le 2$

$(\xi,\eta) \in T_C^{-n} V_k$ iff $a_{n-k}, a_{n-k+1}, a_{n=k+2} = 4,3,4, \quad 0 \le k \le 2$

iii) $(\overline{\xi},\overline{\eta}) \in T_R^{-n} U_0 \Rightarrow \overline{a}_n, \overline{a}_{n+1}, \overline{a}_{n+2} = 2,4,3$

$(\overline{\xi},\overline{\eta}) \in T_R^{-n} V_0 \Rightarrow \overline{a}_n, \overline{a}_{n+1}, \overline{a}_{n+2} = 3,1,2$.

We consider separately two cases.

Case 1. $a_{n-k}, a_{n-k+1}, a_{n-k+2} \neq 1,2,1$ or $4,3,4$ for $0 \le k \le 2$. By ii), $T_C^n(\xi,\eta) \in C \cap R - (U_0 \cup V_0)$. From i) and the definition of Φ follows

$$T_R^n(\overline{\xi},\overline{\eta}) = \Phi T_C^{-n} \Phi^{-1}(\overline{\xi},\overline{\eta}) = T_C^n(\xi,\eta) \in R_{a_n} \cap C_{a_n} .$$

But by the definition of $\overline{a}_n$, we have $T_R^n(\overline{\xi},\overline{\eta}) \in R_{b_n}$. Hence $\overline{a}_n = a_n$, and this case agrees with part i) of the definition of ϑ.

Case 2. Let $a_n, a_{n+1}, a_{n+2} = 1,2,1$. By ii) $T_C^n(\xi,\eta) \in U_0$, so that $T_R^n(\overline{\xi},\overline{\eta}) \in \overline{U}_0$. By iii) $\overline{a}_n, \overline{a}_{n+1}, \overline{a}_{n+2} = 2,4,3$. Similarly, we show: if $a_n, a_{n+1}, a_{n+2} = 4,3,4$ then $\overline{a}_n, \overline{a}_{n+1}, \overline{a}_{n+2} = 3,1,2$. Hence this case agrees with part ii) of the definition of ϑ. We conclude that $\vartheta\{a_n\} = \{\overline{a}_n\}$.

We observe that if $\vartheta\{a_n\} = \{\overline{a}_n\}$, then $\overline{a}_n$ depends on

a_k, $|k-n| \le 2$, but a_n depends on all $\bar{a}_n$. This last assertion follows from the fact that arbitrarily small rectangles $\bigcap_{-N}^{N} T^{-n} R_{\bar{a}_n}$ can straddle $\partial C_1 \cap \partial C_2$ or $\partial C_3 \cap \partial C_4$. The geodesics of M, $\pi(\partial F)$ excepted, are in 1-1 correspondence with the σ-orbits of $\Omega(T_R)$. The significance of the sequence $\{a_n\} \in \Omega(T_R)$ for the given geodesic γ which it represents is obscured by the fact that the rectangular coordinates $\bar{\xi}$, $\bar{\eta}$ do not seem to lend themselves to any significant geometric interpretation. Nevertheless, we show that the a_n's can be derived from γ in geometric manner.

With any geodesic γ whose end points $\xi, \eta \neq$ rational, ∞, we associate two symbolisms, which we name M and S after Morse and Series.* Label the sides of the net N formed by the Γ-translates of the edges of F as follows. The outer sides of the right, left, and bottom edges of F_0 are labelled 1, 4, u. The outer side of the edge τs of τF, $\tau \in \Gamma$, receives the same label as the outer side of the edge s of F.

Definition. i) Let γ start off from a side of $F_0 = F$ pointing to its exterior and passing successively through the fundamental domains $\{F_n\}$, $-\infty < n < \infty$. Let γ leave F_n through the edge with outer side b_n. $\{b_n\}$ is called the M-sequence of γ. If γ leaves F through a vertex, then b_n, b_{n+1}, b_{n+2} are interpreted to be the same as for a geodesic sufficiently close to γ and satisfying $b_n = 1$ or 4.

ii) Consider those n for which $(b_n, b_{n+1}, b_{n+2}) = (1,u,1)$. For these n let γ_n' be a curve joining a point $p_n \in \text{Int } F_n$ to a point $p_{n+3} \in \text{Int } F_{n+3}$ as indicated in Figure 8.1. If $(b_n, b_{n+1}, b_{n+2}) = (4,u,4)$ then γ_n' is defined in similar fashion. Let γ' be the curve obtained from γ by replacing the geodesic arcs $\widehat{p_n, p_{n+3}}$ by γ_n'. Corresponding

*Morse [M] does not treat the modular surface but deals with compact surfaces of genus $g \ge 2$. He introduces the M-symbolism and something like our so-called S-symbolism defined below. Series [Se-a] also uses Morse's second symbolism, giving it another description.

to γ' form a sequence $\{\bar{b}_n\}$ as in i). $\{\bar{b}_n\}$ is called the S-sequence of γ.

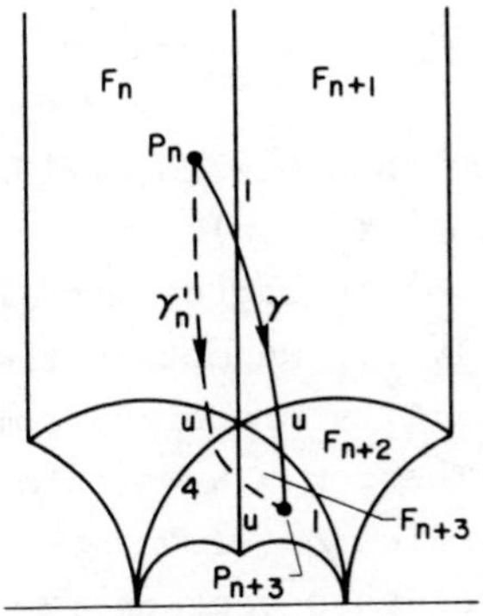

Figure 8.1

From Figure 8.1 we observe that $\{\bar{b}_n\}$ is obtained from $\{b_n\}$ by converting the strings lul into u4u and 4u4 into ulu.

We relate the sequences of $\Omega(T_C)$, $\Omega(T_R)$ respectively to the M- and S-sequences.

Theorem 8.7. Let the geodesic γ have initial unit tangent vector which projects into C, the projection having (ξ,η) and $(\bar{\xi},\bar{\eta})$ for its respective curvilinear and rectilinear coordinates. Assume that $\xi,\eta \neq$ rational, ∞. Let $\{a_n\} = \phi_C(\xi,\eta)$, $\{\bar{a}_n\} = \phi_R(\bar{\xi},\bar{\eta})$. Let

$$b_n = \begin{cases} a_n, & \text{if } a_n = 1 \text{ or } 4 \\ u, & \text{if } a_n = 2 \text{ or } 3, \end{cases}$$

$\bar{b}_n$ being defined analogously in terms of $\bar{a}_n$. Then $\{b_n\} =$ M-sequence of γ, $\{\bar{b}_n\}$ = S-sequence of γ.

Proof. That $\{b_n\}$ = M-sequence of γ follows from the definition of M-sequences and the way that we have defined coordinates on C. By Theorem 8.6, $\{\bar{a}_n\}$ is obtained from $\{a_n\}$ by converting the strings 121 into 243 and 434 into 312. Hence $\{\bar{b}_n\}$ is obtained from $\{b_n\}$ by converting the strings lul into u4u and 4u4 into ulu. Since the S-sequence of γ is obtained from the M-sequence of γ in similar manner, we conclude that $\{\bar{b}_n\}$= S-sequence of γ.

9. Factor Map

In this section we show how to derive ergodic properties of a two dimensional map $T_P(\xi,\eta)$ from those of the one dimensional continued fraction factor map $f(x) = (\frac{1}{x})$ and vice versa. In Theorems 9.1, 9.2 we obtain the invariant measure of f and its reversibility property from the invariant measure of the flow. In Theorem 9.6 we obtain the ergodicity of G_t from ergodic properties of f.

For the purpose of this section it is sufficient and convenient to replace P by an invariant subset differing from P by a set of measure zero. We delete from the coordinate space $\tilde{E} \times \tilde{E}$ all points (ξ,η) for which either coordinate is rational or infinite. As a result the complications due to boundary behavior disappear. We denote previously defined sets with these points deleted by their assigned letters with a dot above. Let

$$\dot{P} = P \cap \{(\xi,\eta) : \xi,\eta \text{ irrational}\}$$

$$\dot{I}^+ = \{\xi : 0 < \xi < 1, \quad \xi \text{ irrational}\}.$$

Thus $\dot{P} = \dot{S} \cup -\dot{S}$ where $\dot{S} = \{(\xi,\eta) : 0 < \xi, \ \eta < 1, \ \xi,\eta$ irrational$\}$ and $T_{\dot{P}}$ is the restriction of T_P to $\dot{P}$. Since P and $\dot{P}$ differ only by a set of measure zero, T_P and $T_{\dot{P}}$ have identical ergodic properties. To take advantage of the symmetry of the action of the $T_{\dot{P}}$ on $\dot{P}$, we define

$$(9.1) \qquad T_{\dot{S}}(\xi,\eta) = \left(\left(\frac{1}{\xi}\right), \frac{1}{[\frac{1}{\xi}]+\eta}\right), \qquad (\xi,\eta) \in \dot{S}.$$

It is readily verified that $T_{\dot{S}}$ is a 1-1 map from $\dot{S}$ onto itself, with

$$(9.2) \qquad T_{\dot{S}}^{-1}(\xi,\eta) = \left(\frac{1}{[\frac{1}{\eta}]+\xi}, \left(\frac{1}{\eta}\right)\right).$$

If we identify $(\ldots a_{-2},a_{-1};a_0,a_1,\ldots)$ with $(\xi,\eta) = ([a_0,a_1,\ldots],[a_{-1},a_{-2},\ldots])$, then

$$T_{\dot{S}}(\ldots a_{-2},a_{-1};a_0,a_1,\ldots) = (\ldots a_{-1},a_0;a_1,a_2,\ldots)$$

and

$$T_{\dot{S}}^{-1}(\ldots a_{-2},a_{-1};a_0,a_1,\ldots) = (\ldots a_{-3},a_{-2};a_{-1},a_0\ldots).$$

Let $q(\xi,\eta) = (|\xi|,|\eta|)$ which maps $\dot{P}$ onto $\dot{S}$. On $\dot{S}$ we obtain the $T_{\dot{S}}$-invariant measure $m_S = m_P q^{-1}$. In ξ,η coordinates

$$dm_S = \frac{1}{\log 2}\,\frac{d\xi d\eta}{(1+\xi\eta)^2}. \tag{9.3}$$

Let $S_2 = \{1,-1\}$, $m_2(1) = m_2(-1) = \frac{1}{2}$, and endow $\dot{S}\times S_2$ with the measure $m_S \times m_2$. Let $T_2(\varepsilon) = -\varepsilon$, $\varepsilon = \pm 1$. The map $(\xi,\eta) \to (q(\xi,\eta),\operatorname{sgn}\xi)$ is an isomorphism between $\dot{P}$ and $\dot{S}\times S_2$, $T_{\dot{P}}$ being conjugate to $T_{\dot{S}} \times T_2$. On $\dot{I}^+$ define the measure $\mu = m_S p_\xi^{-1}$. The map f is a countable to one map of $\dot{I}^+$ onto itself. We have

Theorem 9.1.

i) μ is f-invariant, i.e. $\mu(f^{-1}) = \mu(E)$ for any measurable subset $E \subset \dot{I}^+$.

ii) $d\mu = \frac{1}{\log 2}\,\frac{d\xi}{1+\xi}$, i.e. μ is the Gauss measure.

Proof.

i) $T_{\dot{S}}(\xi,\eta) = (f(\xi),\cdot)$ so that

$$p_\xi \circ T_{\dot{S}} = f \circ p_\xi \tag{9.4}$$

hence

$$(9.5)\qquad \mu(f^{-1}E) = m_S(p_\xi^{-1}f^{-1}E) = m_S(T_{\dot S}^{-1}p_\xi^{-1}E)$$

$$= m_S(p_\xi^{-1}E) = \mu(E)$$

ii) For $E \subset \dot{I}^+$, $p_\xi^{-1}(E) = E \times \dot{I}^+$.

Hence

$$(9.6)\qquad \mu(E) = m_S(E\times\dot{I}^+) = \frac{1}{\log 2}\int_E d\xi \int_0^1 \frac{d\xi}{(1+\xi\eta)^2}$$

$$= \frac{1}{\log 2}\int_E \frac{d\xi}{1+\xi}.$$

The Gauss measure has the following interesting reversibility property which we can easily demonstrate.

Theorem 9.2. Fix $n + 1$ positive integers $a_0,\ldots,a_n$. If

$$E_1 = \{\xi : \xi = [a_0,\ldots,a_n,\xi_{n+1},\ldots]\}$$

$$E_2 = \{\xi : \xi = [a_n,\ldots,a_0,\xi_{n+1},\ldots]\}$$

then

$$\mu(E_1) = \mu(E_2).$$

Proof. In formula (9.3) we can interchange ξ and η: so for $E \subset \dot{I}^+$ we have

$$(9.7)\qquad m_S(p_\xi^{-1}E) = m_S(p_\eta^{-1}E).$$

From (9.1) we get

$$(9.8)\qquad T_{\dot S}^{n+1}p_\xi^{-1}E_1 = p_\eta^{-1}E_2.$$

The desired result follows from (9.7) and (9.8).

We derive ergodic properties of G_t from those of $T_{\dot{S}}$ and those of $T_{\dot{S}}$ from those of f. Concerning the latter we have the next two theorems.

Theorem 9.3. f Is exact, in other words it has a trivial tail fied—i.e., if $A \in \bigcap_{n=1}^{\infty} f^{-n}\mathcal{B}_{\dot{I}^+}$ where $\mathcal{B}_{\dot{I}^+}$ denotes the field of Borel subsets of $\dot{I}^+$, then $\mu(A) = 0$ or 1.

A short proof of this can be found in [MPV; Lemma 4, p. 114].

Theorem 9.4. $T_{\dot{S}}$ is the natural extension of f, which means

i) $T_{\dot{S}}$ is one-to-one a.e.

and

ii) $\bigcup_{n=0}^{\infty} T_{\dot{S}}^{n}\mathcal{C}$

generates the Borel subsets of $\dot{S}$ where $\mathcal{C} = p_{\xi}^{-1}\mathcal{B}_{\dot{I}^+}$

Proof. As mentioned earlier, i) follows from the definition of $T_{\dot{S}}$. To prove ii) consider the partitions $\{\dot{I}_n = \dot{I}^+ \cap (\frac{1}{n+1},\frac{1}{n}) : n = 1,2,\ldots\}$ of $\dot{I}$ into intervals and $\mathcal{P} = \{p_{\xi}^{-1}\dot{I}_n : n = 1,2,\ldots\}$ of $\dot{S}$ into strips.

To show $\bigcup_{n=0}^{\infty} T_{\dot{S}}^{n}\mathcal{C}$ generates, it suffices to show that the common refinement of partitions $T_{S}^{-n}\mathcal{P},\ldots,T_{S}^{n}\mathcal{P}$ consists of rectangles, the largest of whose diameters decrease to zero as $n \to \infty$. This property follows from the fact that $T_{\dot{S}}$ contracts vertical distances and $T_{\dot{S}}^{-1}$ horizontal ones. Under iteration the rate of contraction can be shown to be exponential. □

We now apply the results of [Ro] about endomorphisms and automorphisms of a Lebesgue space. These are the objects we are investigating, the above terms referring respectively to almost everywhere many-to-one and one-to-one measure preserving transformations acting on measure spaces which are measure theoretically the same as the unit interval.

<u>Definition</u>. An automorphism T is said to be a <u>Kolmogorov automorphism</u> if there exists a sub-σ-algebra $\mathcal{C}$ of the family $\mathcal{B}$ of Borel sets such that

i) $\mathcal{C}\ E \subset T\,\mathcal{C}$

ii) $\bigcup_{n=-\infty}^{\infty} T^n\,\mathcal{C}$ generates $\mathcal{B}$

iii) $\bigcap_{n=-\infty}^{\infty} T^n\,\mathcal{C}$ is trivial.

<u>Theorem 9.5</u> [Ro]. An endomorphism is exact if and only if its natural extension is Kolmogorov.

From Theorems 9.3-9.5 we obtain the following:

<u>Corollary</u>. [AA, §§10, 11] $T_{\dot{S}}$ is a Kolmogorov automorphism. In particular, all powers are ergodic especially $T_{\dot{S}}^2$.

Finally, the ergodicity of G_t results from the following equivalences.

<u>Theorem 9.6</u>. The following are equivalent

i)	G_t	is ergodic
ii)	T_C	"
iii)	T_R	"
iv)	$T_{\dot{P}}$	"
v)	$T_{\dot{S}} \times T_2$	"
vi)	$T_{\dot{S}}^2$	"

<u>Proof</u>. The equivalence of ii)-iii) and iv)-v) follow from conjugacy. The equivalence of i)-ii), iii)-iv), v)-vi) follows from elementary set considerations.

Finally, the ergodicity of f may be obtained from that of G_t: for by Theorem 9.6, the ergodicity of G_t implies that of T_S^2. Since f^2 is a factor of $T_{\dot{S}}^2$, f^2 is ergodic, which implies the same for f.

10. Conclusion

We end this work with some after thoughts and a conjecture.

In §8 we introduced various symbolisms. The Morse symbolism (M-sequences) has a natural geometrical interpretation but they are not easily specified; on the other hand, the Series symbolism (S-sequences), is unnatural but easily specified. Another way of saying this is that the space $\Omega(T_C)$ is natural but not easily specified, while $\Omega(T_R)$ is unnatural but easily specified. Still another: T_C is natural but hard to prove ergodic, while T_R is unnatural but easy to prove ergodic.

Interpreting Figure 7.2 in light of the results of 9, we come up with the rather striking fact that by coordinatizing the points of $\dot{B}$ with $(\tilde{\xi},\tilde{\eta})$ the cross section map $T_{\dot{B}}$ is the Cartesian product $T_2 \times T_{\dot{S}}$, where $T_{\dot{S}}$ is the natural extension of the continued fraction map.

In §9 we fulfilled the promise of giving another derivation of the Gauss measure for the continued fraction map. We got it from the invariance of the hyperbolic measure with respect to the geodesic flow on the modular surface by means of a sequence of natural reductions. Our derivation of the invariance of $\frac{d\xi}{1+\xi}$, like that of Gauss's, relies on <u>a fortuitous step</u>. Gauss's depends on telescoping of a series, ours on the existence of a map T_R which is conjugate to T_C and has an obvious one dimensional factor related to the continued fraction map by inducing.

Finally, we present a conjecture arising from this work. It concerns finding a specific $u \in M$ such that $\lim_{T\to\infty} \frac{1}{T} \int_0^T f(G_t u)\,dt = \int_M f d\bar{m}$ for all continuous f on M of compact support. For such u the orbit $G_t u$ is called generic. Let ζ be the number constructed in [AKS] which is normal to the continued fraction expansion. Consider the point $(\tilde{\xi}_0,\tilde{\eta}_0) \in P$ where $\tilde{\xi}_0 = \tilde{\eta}_0 = \zeta$. Let $(\xi_0,\eta_0) = \Phi^{-1}\psi^{-1}(\tilde{\xi}_0,\tilde{\eta}_0)$.

<u>Conjecture</u>. $G_t\bar{\pi}(\xi_0,\eta_0,0)$ is generic.

The difficulty in proving this conjecture lies in the fact that the height function for the cross section B is unbounded.

References

[AF] R. L. Adler and L. Flatto, Cross section maps for the geodesic flow on the modular surface, Ergodic Theory and Dynamical Systems (to appear).

[AKS] R. L. Adler, M. Keane, and M. Smorodinsky, A construction of a normal number for the continued fraction transformation, J. of Number Theory 13 (1981), 95-105.

[AW] R. L. Adler and B. Weiss, The ergodic infinite measure preserving transformation of Boole, Israel J. of Math. 16 (1973), 263-278.

[AK] W. Ambrose and S. Kakutani, Structure and continuity of measurable flows, Duke Math. J. 9 (1942), 25-42.

[AA] V. I. Arnold and A. Avez, Ergodic Problems of Classical Mechanics, W. A. Benjamin, Inc. New York, 1968.

[A] E. Artin, Ein Mechanisches System mit quasiergodischen Bahnen, Abh. Math. Sem., Univ. Hamburg 3 (1924), 170-175.

[B] P. Billingsley, Ergodic Theory and Information, John Wiley & Sons, Inc., New York (1965).

[Bi] G. D. Birkhoff, Dynamical Systems, AMS Colloquium publications, vol. 9 (1927), reprinted (1966).

[BS] Bowen and C. Series, Markov maps for Fuchsian groups, IHES publications 50 (1979).

[CL] E. A. Coddington and N. Levinson, Theory of Ordinary Differential Equations, McGraw-Hill Book Company, Inc. New York (1955).

[HW] G. H. Hardy and E. M. Wright, Theory of Numbers, 4th edition, Oxford Univ. Press, London (1962).

[H-1] G. A. Hedlund, A metrically transitive group defined by the modular group, Amer. J. Math. 57 (1935), 668-678.

[H-2] _____, The dynamics of geodesic flows. Bull. Amer. Math. Soc. 45 (1939), 241-261.

[Ho] E. Hopf, Ergodic theory and the geodesic flow on surfaces of constant negative curvature, Bull. Am. Math. Soc. 77 (1971), 863-877.

[K] S. Kakutani, Induced measure preserving transformations, Proc. Imp. Acad. Tokyo 19 (1943), 635-641.

[L] J. Lehner, Discontinuous Groups and Automorphic Functions, AMS, Providence, R.I. (1964).

[M] M. Morse, Symbolic dynamics, Institute for Advanced Study Notes, by Rufus Oldenburger, Princeton (1966) (unpublished).

[Mo] J. Moser, Stable and Random Motions in Dynamical Systems, Annals of Math Studies 77, Princeton Univ. Press, Princeton, NJ (1973).

[MPV] J. Moser, E. Phillips, and S. Varadhan, Ergodic Theory, A Seminar, Lecture Notes, New York Univ., NY (1975).

[N] J. Nielsen, Untersuchungen zur Topologie der geschlossenen Zweiseitigen Flächen, Acta Math. 50 (1927), 189-358.

[O] D. Ornstein, The isomorphism theorem for Bernoulli flows, Advances in Math 10 (1973), 124-142.

[OW] D. Ornstein and B. Weiss, Geodesic flows are Bernoullian, Israel J. Math 14 (1973), 184-198.

[R] A. Renyi, Representations for real numbers and their ergodic properties, Acta Math. Akad, Sci. Hungar, 8 (1957), 477-493.

[Ro] V. A. Rohlin, Exact endomorphisms of a Lebesgue space, Izv. Akad. Nauk, SSSR Ser. Mat. 25 (1961), 499-530, Russian, Amer. Math. Soc. Transl., Series 2, vol. 39 (1964), 1-37, English.

[S] F. Schweiger, Some remarks on ergodicity and invariant measures, Mich. Math. J. 22 (1975), 181-187.

[Se-1] C. Series, Symbolic dynamics for geodesic flows, Acta Math. 146 (1981), 103-128.

[Se-2] ______, On coding geodesics with continued fractions, Proc. Ergodic Theory Conf., Plans sur Bex (1980), ed. Pierre de la Harpe, Springer (to appear).

Roy L. Adler
IBM Thomas J. Watson Research Center
Yorktown Heights, New York 10598

Leopold Flatto
Bell Laboratories
Murray Hill, New Jersey 07974

ERGODIC THEORY OF FRAME FLOWS

M. Brin*
University of Maryland

1. Introduction

Let M^n be a smooth n-dimensional Riemannian manifold and let T_1M^n be the manifold of unit tangent vectors on M^n. The geodesic flow $g^t : T_1M^n \to T_1M^n$ translates every vector $v \in T_1M^n$ by the parallel translation along the unique geodesic determined by v at distance t. The frame flow f_k^t acts in the space $St_k(M^n)$ of orthonormal ordered k-frames $w = \{x, v_1, \ldots, v_k\}$, where $x \in M^n$, $v_i \in T_1M^n$, $(v_i, v_j) = \delta_{ij}$, $1 \le i,j \le k$. The flow f_k^t translates every frame $w \in St_k(M^n)$ along the geodesic determined by the first vector of the frame at distance t. It is clear that $St_1(M^n) = T_1M^n$. Denote by p_k the natural projection $St_k(M^n) \to St_1(M^n)$, by $p_{k,m}$, $1 \le m \le k \le n$, the projections $St_k(M^n) \to St_m(M^n)$, $p_{k,m}(x, v_1, \ldots, v_m, \ldots, v_k) = (x, v_1, \ldots, v_m)$, and by $\pi : St_1M^n \to M^n$ the projection $\pi(x,v) = x$. If M^n is oriented, the space $St_n(M^n)$ has two connected components—the sets of positively and negatively oriented n-frames, each of the components being isomorphic with the space $St_{n-1}(M^n)$. The manifold $St_k(M^n)$ is a fiber bundle over $St_1(M^n) = T_1(M^n)$ with projection p_k and structure group $SO(n-1)$. There is a natural global right action of the group $SO(n-1)$ in $St_k(M^n)$, namely for every orthogonal matrix $(a_{ij}) = A \in SO(n-1)$ and any k-frame $w = (x, v_s, \ldots, v_k)$ we put

$$Aw = (x, v_1, \sum_{i=1}^{n} v_1 \cdot a_{i2}, \sum_{i=1}^{n} v_1 \cdot a_{i3}, \ldots, \sum_{i=1}^{n} v_i \cdot a_{ik}).$$

---

*Supported by NSF Grant #MCS79-03046.

Each fiber of the bundle $p_k : St_k(M^n) \to St_1(M^n)$ is mapped isometrically onto itself by A. This action obviously commutes with the frame flow f_k^t, $k \geq 2$, i.e., the following diagram commutes for every t and every $A \in SO(n-1)$,

(1.1)
$$\begin{array}{ccc} f_k^t : St_k(M^n) & \longrightarrow & St_k(M^n) \\ A \big\downarrow & & \big\downarrow A \\ f_k^t : St_k(M^n) & \longrightarrow & St_k(M^n). \end{array}$$

By definition the frame flow is an extension of or a skew product over the geodesic flow, hence the diagram

(1.2)
$$\begin{array}{ccc} f_k^t : St_k(M^n) & \longrightarrow & St_k(M^n) \\ p_k \big\downarrow & & \big\downarrow p_k \\ g^t : St_1(M^n) & \longrightarrow & St_1(M^n) \end{array}$$

commutes.

The geodesic flow preserves the natural Liouville measure ν in $St_1(M^n)$ which is the product of the Riemannian volume on M^n and the Lebesgue measure on the unit sphere S^{n-1}. Let $v \in St_1(M^n)$, then $f_k^t|p_k^{-1}(v)$ is an isometry of $p_k^{-1}(v)$ onto $p_k^{-1}(g^t v)$ which preserves the Legesgue measure λ_k in the fiber ($SO(n-1)$ acts transitively in the fiber and λ_k is the projection of the Haar measure on $SO(n-1)$). Therefore, the frame flow f_k^t preserves the product measure μ, $d\mu = d\nu \times d\lambda_k$. If M^n is compact, then so is $St_k(M^n)$, $k = 1,2,\ldots,n$, and all measures involved are finite.

In this paper we give a survey of results and ideas related to the frame flows on compact manifolds of negative curvature which are described in the following papers [Br1, Br2, BG, BK, BP]. The geodesic flow on a compact manifold of negative curvature is an Anosov flow [A]. Being a group extension of the geodesic flow [Br2], the frame flow inherites the topological and ergodic properties of the geodesic flows under certain assumptions (see Section 2). In this survey we reproduce the proofs of several important theorems and lemmas, give sketches of some arguments and provide references for the rest of the statements.

I am grateful to A. Katok who read this paper and made several useful remarks.

2. Statement of main results

For every $k < n-1$ the flow f_k^t is a factor of the flow f_{n-1}^t, therefore, if f_{n-1}^t is topologically transitive, ergodic, or Bernoulli (with respect to μ), then so is f_k^t. That is why below we study mainly the flow f_{n-1}^t. Let M^n be a smooth compact connected manifold. Denote by A the set of negatively curved C^3-metrics on M^n and denote by A_o the set of metrics from A for which the flow f_{n-1}^t is Bernoulli. Observe that the Bernoulli property implies ergodicity and topological transitivity.

2.1. Theorem [Brl]. If A is not empty then A_o is open and dense in A (see Section 5, Lemmas 5.4 and 5.5).

2.2. Theorem [BP]. Every metric of constant negative curvature belongs to A_o (see Section 6, Proposition 6.3).

2.3. Theorem [BG]. If n is odd and $\neq 7$, then $A_o = A$. (See Section 5, Lemmas 5.6, 5.7 and 5.8.)

2.4. Theorem [BK]. Let n be even and $\neq 8$ and let the sectional curvature be pinched between -1 and -0.99. Then the flow f_{n-1}^t is Bernoulli (see Section 6).

2.5. Theorem [BG], [BP]. For every even $n > 2$ there exists a Riemannian n-dimensional manifold of negative curvature such that every flow f_k^t has first integrals, $k = 2,3,\dots,n-1$.

2.6. Conjecture. If for every 2-plane in the tangent bundle TM the sectional curvature lies strictly between -1 and

$-\frac{1}{4}$, then the flow f^t_{n-1} is Bernoulli.

2.7. Remark. There are examples of metrics for which the sectional curvature K satisfies the non-strict inequality $-1 \le K \le -\frac{1}{4}$ and the frame flow has first integrals. For every point on the manifold in these examples there are 2-planes in the tangent space at this point such that the sectional curvature for the first plane is equal to -1 and is equal to $-\frac{1}{4}$ for the second one.

2.8. Definition. Let $x \in M^n$; for every piecewise smooth curve β starting and ending at x the parallel translation along β induces an isometry of $T_x M^n$. The set of all such isometries is called the holonomy group of M^n.

2.9. Conjecture. If the holonomy group for a compact manifold of negative curvature is $SO(n)$, then the frame flow f^t_{n-1} is ergodic and Bernoulli.

2.10. Theorem [Br2]. If M^n has negative curvature, then the ergodic component of the frame flow containing a frame $w \in St_{n-1}(M^n)$ is a smooth compact subbundle $Q(w)$ of the bundle $St_{n-1}(M^n) \to T_1 M$. For every $w' \in St_{n-1}(M^n)$ the intersection $Q(w) \cap p^{-1}_{n-1}(w')$ is an orbit of the left action of a closed subgroup $G \subset SO(n-1)$, the projection $p_{n-1} : Q(w) \to T_1 M$ is "onto" and the partition into ergodic components is invariant under the right action of $SO(n-1)$ described in Section 1. (See Lemma 5.2.)

3. Stable and unstable foliations and the ergodic decomposition

From now on we assume that M^n is a compact manifold of strictly negative curvature. The geodesic flow g^t on such a manifold is an Anosov flow [A], it has three invariant foliations W^t_g, W^s_g and W^u_g. The leaves of the first foliation W^t_g are are the trajectories of g^t. Let $v \in T_1 M^n$, and let $\gamma_v(t)$ be the geodesic determined by v.

Let H_∞ be the universal cover of H^n, H_∞ be the sphere at ∞. Then every geodesic $\gamma_v(t)$ has two ends $\gamma_v(\infty)$, $\gamma_v(-\infty) \in H_\infty$ (see E1). Denote by $S^+(v)$ the stable horosphere of v, i.e., the horosphere passing through $x = \pi(v)$ and centered at $\gamma_v(+\infty)$, and denote by $S^-(v)$ the unstable horosphere of v, i.e., the horosphere centered at $\gamma_v(-\infty)$. The leaves of the stable foliation W_g^s are the stable manifolds for g^t, the stable manifold $W_g^s(v)$ of a unit vector v is the set of vectors v' with support on $S^-(v)$ and such that $\gamma_{v'}(\infty) = \gamma_v(\infty)$. The unstable foliation and unstable manifolds are defined in a similar way. The flow g^t exponentially contracts the stable manifolds and exponentially stretches the unstable manifolds.

Denote by W_f^t the foliation formed by the trajectories of $f^t = f_{n-1}^t$ and let W_f^p be the foliation formed by the vertical fibers $p_{n-1}^{-1}(v)$, i.e., the sets of frames with same first vectors.

<u>3.1. Definition</u>. Two foliations W_1 and W_2 are called <u>integrable</u> if $\bigcup_{v' \in W_1(v)} W_2(v') = \bigcup_{v' \in W_2(v)} W_1(v')$ for every v.

It is clear that the foliations W_f^t and W_f^p are integrable.

<u>3.2. Proposition</u>. The frame flow $f_{n-1}^t = f^t$ has two invariant foliations W_f^s and W_f^u such that:

(i) $\dim W_f^s(v) = \dim W_f^u(v) = n - 1$, and hence
$\dim W_f^s + \dim W_f^u + \dim W_f^t + \dim W_f^p = \dim St_{n-1}(M^n)$;

(ii) W_f^s is the stable foliation for f^t, each leaf $W_f^s(w)$ is exponentially contracted by f^t for $t > 0$, and $p_{n-1}(W_f^s(w)) = W_g^s(p_{n-1}(w))$, the projection is one-to-one on each leaf;

(iii) W_f^u is the unstable foliation for f^t, each leaf $W_f^u(w)$ is exponentially contracted by f^t for $t < 0$, and $p_{n-1}(W_f^u(w)) = W_g^u(p_{n-1}(w))$, the projection is one-to-one on each leaf;

(iv) the foliations W_f^s, W_f^u, W_f^t, W_f^p are transversal, and every pair except for W_f^s and W_f^u is integrable.

Proof. Let $w \in St_{n-1}(M^n)$, $v = p_{n-1}(w)$ and $v' \in W_g^s(v)$. The distance between $g^t v$ and $g^t v'$ measured along the leaf $W_g^s(g^t v)$ decays exponentially as $t \to \infty$. Therefore, the fibers $p_{n-1}^{-1}(g^t v)$ and $p_{n-1}^{-1}(g^t v')$ exponentially approach each other. For every $v \in T_1 M^n$ and real t the flow f^t induces an isometry $p_{n-1}^{-1}(v) \to p_{n-1}^{-1}(g^t v)$ which depends smoothly on v and t. Thus, the difference between the isometries $f^t : p_{n-1}^{-1}(g^t v) \to p_{n-1}^{-1}(g^{t+t_1} v)$ and $f^t : p_{n-1}^{-1}(g^t v') \to p_{n-1}^{-1}(g^{t+t_1} v')$ decays exponentially (we use here the smoothness of f^t). Therefore, there is a unique frame $w' \in p_{n-1}^{-1}(v')$ such that the distance between $f^t(w)$ and $f^t(w')$ tends to 0 (exponentially). We put $W_f^s(w) = \bigcup_{v' \in W_g^s(v)} w'(v')$. The differentiability of $W_f^s(w)$ follows from the exponential decay of $W_g^s(v)$ (see [Br2]). Another way of constructing the stable manifolds is to treat f^t as a partially hyperbolic flow (see [BP]). The unstable manifolds are constructed in a similar way, and statements (i) through (iv) follow easily. The proposition is proved.

Let W be a foliation whose leaves are smooth and depend continuously on the point they pass through. Let $v' \in W(v)$ and consider two submanifolds $U \ni v$ and $U' \ni v'$ transversal to $W(v)$. There exist neighborhoods $V \subset U$, $V \ni v$, and $V' \subset U'$, $V' \ni v'$, and there exists a continuous bijective mapping $\varphi : V \to V'$ such that $\varphi(v_1) = V' \cap W(v_1)$.

3.3. Definition. The foliation W is called absolutely continuous if for every two transversals V and V' the mapping φ is absolutely continuous with respect to the

Riemannian volumes on V and V'.

The following statement is a version of the Fubini theorem for absolutely continuous foliations.

3.4. Proposition. Let A be a measurable set which consists mod 0 of entire leaves of an absolutely continuous foliation W, and let V be a transversal to the leaves of W. Then for almost every point $v \subset V$ either $W(v) \subset A$ mod 0 or $W(v)$ belongs mod 0 to the complement of A.

See [BP], §3, for the proof.

3.5. Proposition. The stable and unstable foliations of the frame flow on a manifold of negative curvature are absolutely continuous.

See [BP], §3, for the proof.

3.6. Remark. If the leaf of a foliation W depends differentiably in the C^1-topology on the point it passes through, then W is obviously an absolutely continuous foliation, since every mapping φ constructed above is differentiable and, therefore, absolutely continuous. Unfortunately, even the stable and unstable foliations for the geodesic flow may be not differentiable, and of course the same is true for the stable and unstable foliations of the frame flow (however, the foliations W_g^s and W_g^u are differentiable provided the sectional curvature lies between -1 and $-\frac{1}{4}$).

A well known argument which goes back to E. Hopf shows that, if f^t is a measure preserving flow which has an absolutely continuous invariant stable or unstable foliation W, then for almost every ergodic component C of f^t and for almost every leaf $W(v)$ the following alternative is valid: either almost every point of $W(v)$ (with respect to the Lebesgue measure on $W(v)$) belongs to C or almost every point of $W(v)$ belongs to the complement of C.

3.7. Proposition. Let ξ_e be the ergodic decomposition for

f^t and denote by $\nu(W_f^s)$ and $\nu(W_f^u)$ the measurable hulls of the partitions into stable and unstable leaves respectively. Then $\xi_e \le \nu(W_f^s) \wedge \nu(W_f^u)$. I.e., every set measurable with respect to ξ_e consists mod 0 of entire stable and unstable manifolds.

See [BP], §5, for the proof.

3.8. Proposition. Let ξ_p be the Pinsker partition for f^t. Then $\xi_p \le \nu(W_f^s) \wedge \nu(W_f^u)$.

See [BP], §5, and [S], Theorems 4.2 and 5.2, for the proof.

Thus the ergodicity of f^t (and the K-property) would follow from the non-existence of non-trivial measurable subsets of $St_{n-1}(M^n)$ consisting mod 0 of entire stable and unstable manifolds. We shall show later that the foliations W_f^s and W_f^u have this property under additional assumptions (see Section 2).

4. Transitivity group and ergodicity

In this section we describe the partition $\nu(W_f^s) \wedge \nu(W_f^u)$, i.e., the subalgebra of sets measurable with respect to both the partition into stable manifolds and the partition into unstable manifolds for f^t.

4.1. Definition (see [BP], §4, and [Brl]. A pair of foliations W_1 and W_2 on a manifold V is called transitive if for every two points $v, v' \in V$ there are points $v_1, v_2, \ldots, v_k \in V$, $v_1 = v$, $v_k = v'$, such that $v_{i+1} \in W_1(v_i)$ or $v_{i+1} \in W_2(v_i)$, $i = 1,2,\ldots,k-1$.

It seems natural to assume that, if a pair of foliations W_1, W_2 is transtitive and if each of them is absolutely continuous, then $\nu(W_1) \wedge \nu(W_2) = \pi$, where π is the trivial partition consisting of just one element which is the entire manifold. Unfortunately, there are reasons to believe that, in general, the transitivity assumption is not sufficient. On the other hand, there are examples when this assumption is not necessary. However, in the special case of frame flows on manifolds of negative curvature, or more general, of group extensions of Anosov systems, the transitivity of the stable and unstable foliations implies that the intersection of their measurable hulls is trivial (see [Br2]).

4.2. Definition. Let F be a metric space and μ be a Borel measure on F. Denote by $b_r(x)$ the ball of radius r centered at x and let A be a measurable set. A point x is called a point of density of A if for every $\varepsilon > 0$ there is an $r_o > 0$ such that $\frac{\mu(A \cap b_r(x))}{\mu(b_r(x))} > 1 - \varepsilon$ for every $r \geq r_o$.

4.3. Lemma. Let A be a measurable subset of $St_{n-1}(M^n)$ which consists mod 0 of entire stable and unstable manifolds of f^t and let w be a point of density of A. Then every point $w' \in W_f^s(w)$ (or $w' \in W_f^u(w)$) is a point of density of A.

Proof. The foliations W_f^t and W_f^p being integrable, let W_f^o be the smallest foliation containing both, i.e., $W_f^o(w) = \bigcup_{-\infty<t<\infty} f^t(W_f^p(w))$. The foliation W_f^o is differentiable and is integrable with both W_f^s and W_f^u. Denote by W_f^{so} the integral hull of W_f^s and W_f^o, $W_f^{so}(w_1) = \bigcup_{w \in W_f^s(w_1)} W_f^o(w)$.

Take a leaf $W_f^{os}(w_1)$ and consider two leaves $W_f^o(w_2)$, $W_f^o(w_3) \subset W_f^{os}(w_1)$. Let $\psi : W_f^o(w_2) \to W_f^o(w_3)$ be the succession mapping $\psi(w_4) = W_f^o(w_3) \cap W_f^s(w_4)$. By the construction of the stable foliation for every two such leaves the mapping ψ is an isometry. The leaf $W_f^{os}(w)$ is foliated by the stable leaves $W_f^s(\overline{w})$, and since the succession mapping ψ is an isometry, this foliation of $W_f^{os}(w)$ is absolutely continuous.

Since A consists mod 0 of entire unstable manifolds, there is a set A' which differs from A by a set of measure

0 and consists of entire unstable manifolds. The foliation W_f^{os} is absolutely continuous since both W_f^o and W_f^s are. Therefore, almost every leaf $W_f^{os}(w_1)$ is "good" in the sense that almost every leaf $W_f^s(w_2) \subset W_f^{os}(w_1)$ either belongs mod 0 to A' or belongs mod 0 to its complement. Let now w be a point of density of A (and, hence, of A'). For almost every point $w_1 \in W_f^u(w)$ the leaf $W_f^{os}(w_1)$ is "good." By decreasing ε and r in Definition 4.2 we can find a "good" leaf $W_f^{os}(w_1)$ lying arbitrarily close to w and such that the relative measure of A' in the ball $B_r^{os}(w_1)$ on the leaf $W_f^{os}(w_1)$ is greater than $1 - \gamma$, where $\gamma \to 0$ as $\varepsilon \to 0$. Let now consider $w' \in W_f^s(w)$ and consider the point $w_2 = W_f^u(w') \cap W_f^{os}(w_1)$. Since the succession mapping ψ is isometric (and, hence, measure preserving), the relative measure of A' in $B_r^{os}(w_2)$ is greater than $1 - 2\gamma$. The point w_2 is arbitrarily close to w' and for every $w_3 \in A' \cap B_r^{os}(w_2)$ the leaf $W_f^u(w_3)$ entirely belongs to A'. Therefore, the relative measure of A' (and, hance, of A) in $B_{r/2}(w')$ is greater than $1 - \beta$ for some β, $\beta \to 0$ as $\varepsilon \to 0$. Thus w' is a point of density of A. A similar argument goes through if $w' \in W_f^u(w)$. The lemma is proved.

Observe that any measurable set coincides mod 0 with the set of its point of density.

Let $v' \in W_g^s(v)$. Denote by $P(v,v') : p_{n-1}^{-1}(v) \to p_{n-1}^{-1}(v')$ the isometry given by the stable leaves $W_f^s(w)$, $w \in p_{n-1}^{-1}(v)$, and make the same notation if $v' \in W_g^u(v)$. Consider now the set S of finite sequences $v_o, v_1, \ldots, v_k \in T_1M^n$ such that $v_o = v_k = v$ and every pair (v_i, v_{i+1}), $i = 0, \ldots, k-1$, belongs either to the same stable or the same unstable manifold of the geodesic flow.

<u>4.4. Definition</u>. For every sequence $s = \{v_o, v_1, \ldots, v_k\} \in S$ consider the isometry I(s) of $p_{n-1}^{-1}(v)$ given by the composition

$$I(s) = \prod_{i=o}^{k-1} P(v_i, v_{i+1}).$$

The set of these isometries forms a subgroup $H(v)$ of $SO(n-1)$. The closure $\overline{H(v)}$ is called the <u>transitivity group</u> at v (see also [Br2]).

Obviously every two transitivity groups $H(v)$ and $H(v')$ are conjugate by an inner automorphism of $SO(n-1)$.

<u>4.6. Proposition</u>. If the transitivity group coincides with $SO(n-1)$, then the frame flow is ergodic and Bernoulli.

<u>Proof</u>. First we show that the Pinsker partition ξ_p is trivial. Let A be a set of positive measure which is measurable with respect to this partition. Since the stable and unstable foliations of the geodesic flow g^t are transitive (see [A]), Lemma 4.3 implies that the set of density point of A contains a union of left cosets of $H(v)$ in each fiber $p_{n-1}^{-1}(v) \simeq SO(n-1)$. This union is measurable for almost every fiber and has positive measure. Moreover, $H(v)$ is dense in $SO(n-1)$, therefore, the union is $SO(n-1)$ mod 0 and $A = St_{n-1}(M^n)$. Thus f^t is a K-flow (see Proposition 3.8) (and, hence, is ergodic).

Since f^t is an isometric extension of g^t, it follows from [R] that f^t is Bernoulli. The proposition if proved.

5. <u>Ergodic components</u>

The following lemma reduces the questions under consideration to the topology of fiber bundles.

<u>5.1. Lemma</u>. Let M^n be a compact connected manifold of negative curvature. If the frame flow $f_{n-1}^t = f^t$ is not ergodic (or is ergodic but is not Bernoulli), then the structure group of the fiber bundle $St_{n-1}(M^n) \to T_1M^n$ can be reduced to a proper closed subgroup $H \subset SO(n-1)$.

<u>Proof</u>. Suppose f^t is not ergodic, then the ergodic decomposition ξ_e is non-trivial. Since f^t commutes with the right action of $SO(n-1)$ in $St_{n-1}(M^n)$, the partition ξ_e is invariant under this action. For almost every fiber $p_{n-1}^{-1}(v)$ the partition ξ_e induces a measurable partition

$\xi_e(v)$ of $p_{n-1}^{-1}(v) \simeq SO(n-1)$ invariant under the right action of $SO(n-1)$. Since $\xi_e(v)$ is invariant under the right action of $SO(n-1)$, it is a partition of $SO(n-1)$ into the left cosets for a subgroup H. The measurability of $\xi_e(v)$ implies that H is closed.

Let $w \in p_{n-1}^{-1}(v)$ and consider the element Hw of the partition $\xi_e(v)$. For every set $A \subset St_{n-1}(M^n)$ denote

$$W^s(A) = \bigcup_{w' \in A} W_f^s(w') \quad \text{and} \quad W^u(A) = \bigcup_{w' \in A} W_f^u(w').$$

We set

$$Q(w) = W^u(W^s(Hw)).$$

An argument from [Br2] (see Theorem 1) shows that $Q(w)$ is a differentiable submanifold of $St_{n-1}(M^n)$. The submanifolds $Q(w)$ for different $w \in p_{n-1}^{-1}(v)$ form a partition of $St_{n-1}(M^n)$ invariant under the right action of $SO(n-1)$. Besides, $p_{n-1}(Q(w')) = T_1M^n$ for every w' and every $Q(w')$ is compact, since it intersects each fiber $p_{n-1}^{-1}(v')$ by a compact set (which depends continuously on v').

Thus, $Q(w)$ is a subbundle of $St_{n-1}(M^n) \to T_1M^n$ and the structure groups can be reduced to H.

If f^t is not Bernoulli, then it is not a K-flow (see [R]). In this case the Pinsker partition is not trivial. Since the Pinsker partition is also invariant under the right action of $SO(n-1)$, arguing like above we again get a partition into left cosets with respect to a subgroup $\bar{H}$ in every fiber $p_{n-1}^{-1}(v)$ (actually $\bar{H}$ is the transitivity group) and conclude that the structure group can be reduced. The lemma is proved.

The following lemma describes the ergodic components explicitly.

5.2. Lemma. Let $w \in St_{n-1}(M^n)$, denote by $C(w)$ the smallest set consisting of entire leaves of the foliations W_f^s and W_f^u and containing w, and put $B(w) = \bigcup_{t=-\infty}^{\infty} f^t(C(s))$.

Then the closure of $B(w)$ is the ergodic component $Q(w)$ (see Lemma 5.1) containing w.

For the proof see [Br2], Proposition 2. The ergodicity of f^t on each set $\overline{B(w)}$ follows from the transitivity of the pair of foliations W_f^s and W_f^{ut} in the set $B(w)$. The fact that $B(w)$ is a smooth compact submanifold is proved in the same way as in the previous lemma. Since $B(w)$ consists of entire stable and unstable leaves, it is a subbundle in $St_{n-1}(M^n)$ (see [Br2]). This proves Theorem 2.10.

5.3. Remark. The closures of the sets $C(w)$ introduced in Lemma 5.2 are exactly the elements of the Pinsker partition ξ_p.

5.4. Lemma. The set of C^3-metrics on M^n of negative curvature for which the frame flow f^t is ergodic (or is Bernoulli) is open.

Proof. We will prove only the statement concerning the Bernoulli property of f^t. The second part of the lemma is proved similarly.

Let f^t be Bernoulli, then the Pinsker partition ξ_p is trivial. Lemma 5.2 and Remark 5.3 show that the transitivity group is the whole of $SO(n-1)$ in this case and, hence, for every $\varepsilon > 0$ one can find a finite subset $G(v) \subset H(v)$ which is an ε-net in $SO(n-1) \simeq p_{n-1}^{-1}(v)$ for some $v \in T_1M$. Since the stable and unstable manifolds of the frame flow depend continuously on the Riemannian metric, we can change the set $G(v)$ continuously with the metric. Note that if ε is small enough, then the group generated by any ε-net in $SO(n-1)$ is dense in $SO(n-1)$. Thus, the transitivity group for a sufficiently small perturbation of the metric is $SO(n-1)$. Proposition 4.6 concludes the proof of the lemma.

5.5. Lemma. For any $r \geq 2$ every C^r-metric of negative curvature on M^n can be perturbed in such a way that the transitivity group for the perturbed metric is $SO(n-1)$.

For the proof see Proposition 3.1 of [Br1]. The

construction consists of several consecutive steps. At each step the dimension of the transitivity group is increased at least by 1. The succesive perturbations are local, each of them is concentrated in a small neighborhood on M^n; but such a local change of the metric affects the geodesic flow and the frame flow globally because the geodesics passing through the neighborhood in all directions are affected. Therefore, special precautions are necessary not to spoil at every step what was achieved at the previous one.

Theorem 2.1 follows now from Lemmas 5.4 and 5.5 and from Proposition 4.6.

We prove Theorem 2.3 now.

5.6. Lemma. Let $X \to S^q$ be a fibration over S^q with fiber S^p. If this fibration admits a structure group G which act non-transitively in S^p, then there is a section $S^q \to X$.

For the proof see [BG], Lemma 4.1, and [G].

5.7. Lemma. If n is odd, then the structure group of the bundle $St_{n-1}(M^n) \to T_1M^n$ acts transitively in $S^{n-2} \simeq p_2^{-1}(v)$.

Proof (see [BG], Corollary 4.2). By restricting the bundle $St_2(M^n) \to T_1M^n$ to the unit tangent sphere S^{n-1} at a point in M^n, we get the bundle St_2^n, of 2-frames in $\mathbb{R}^n$ with support at the origin, over S^{n-1} with fiber S^{n-2}. Lemma 5.6 shows that if the structure group of this restriction is not transitive, then there is a section. The bundle $St_2^n \to S^{n-1}$ is isomorphic to the unit tangent bundle T_1S^{n-1}. A section of T_1S^{n-1} is a non-zero vector field on S^{n-1}. For n odd and $n-1$ even such a field cannot exist. The lemma is proved.

Let St_{n-1}^n denote the set of $(n-s)$-frames with support at the same point $x \in M^n$.

5.8. Lemma. If n is odd and $n \neq 7$, then the structure group of the bundle $SO(n-1) = St_{n-s}^n \to S^{n-1}$ cannot be reduced to a proper subgroup $H \subset SO(n-1)$ which acts transitively in the fiber S^{n-2}.

For the proof see [BG], Proposition 5.1.

Thus, if n is odd, then by Lemma 5.7 the structure group of the bundle $St_{n-1}(M^n)$ must act transitively on S^{n-2}. If, in addition, $n \neq 7$, then Lemma 5.8 shows that the structure group must coincide with $SO(n-1)$. Theorem 2.3 follows now from Lemma 5.1.

5.9. Remark. Lemma 5.7 implies also that, if n is odd, then the 2-frame f_2^t is ergodic and Bernoulli.

6. Constant curvature and pinching

Let $M^n = M$ be a manifold of constant negative curvature and let $\widetilde{M}$ be the universal cover. We are going to show now that the transitivity group coincides with $SO(n-1)$. There are different ways to prove this; we choose the argument which can be generalized for the case of the curvature close to constant.

Let $x \in \widetilde{M}$ and $v_1 \in T_x\widetilde{M}$, $\|v_1\| = 1$. Denote by $\gamma_{v_1}(t)$ the geodesic determined by v and parameterized by the arc length. The geodesic $\gamma_{v_1}(t)$ has two ends at infinity $\gamma_{v_1}(\infty)$ and $\gamma_{v_1}(-\infty)$. Take now $v_2 \in T_xM$, $\|v_2\| = 1$, $v_2 \perp v_1$, and consider the point $\gamma_{v_2}(\infty)$.

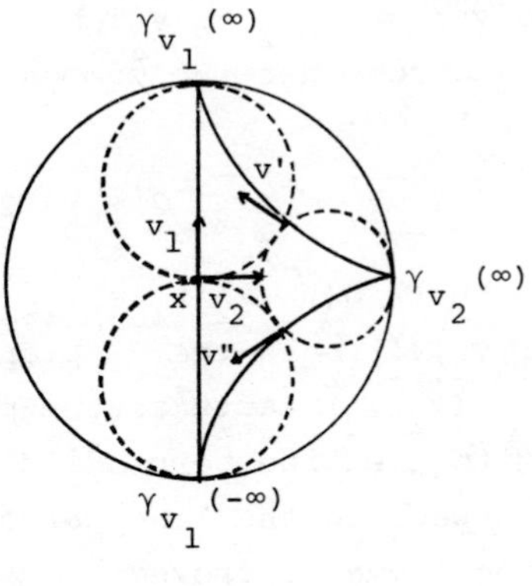

Figure 1

For a $v \in T_x M^n$ denote by $S^+(v)$ the horosphere passing through x and centered at $\gamma_v(\infty)$ and denote by $S^-(v)$ the horosphere passing through x and centered at $\gamma_v(-\infty)$. Consider now the vector v' such that $\pi(v') \in S^+(v_1)$, $\gamma_{v'}(\infty) = \gamma_{v_1}(\infty)$, $\gamma_{v'}(-\infty) = \gamma_{v_2}(\infty)$ (see Fig. 1). Let v'' be such that $\pi(v'') \in S^-(v_1)$, $\gamma_{v''}(\infty) = \gamma_{v_1}(-\infty)$, $\gamma_{v''}(-\infty) = \gamma_{v_2}(\infty)$ (see Fig. 1). Since $v' \in W_g^s(v_1)$, we have the isometry $P_{v_1v'}: p_{n-1}^{-1}(v_1) \to p_{n-1}^{-1}(v')$ (see Section 4 for notations). We also have the isometries $P_{v'v''}: p_{n-1}^{-1}(v') \to p_{n-1}^{-1}(v'')$ and $P_{v''(-v_1)}: p_{n-1}^{-1}(v'') \to p_{n-1}^{-1}(-v_1)$. Thus, for every $v_2 \in T_x\widetilde{M}$, $\|v_2\| = 1$, $v_2 \perp v_1$, we get the isometry $P(v_2) = P_{v''(-v_1)} \circ P_{v'v''} \circ P_{v_1v'}: p_{n-1}^{-1}(v_1) \to p_{n-1}^{-1}(-v_1)$.

6.1. Lemma. The isometry $P(v_2)$ is induced by the reflection of $T_x\widetilde{M}$ with respect to the $(n-2)$-plane perpendicular to the 2-plane spanned by v_1 and v_2.

Proof. It follows directly from the description of stable and unstable manifolds given in Proposition 3.2 that $P(v_2)$ is the parallel translation along the infinite triangle $(\gamma_{v_1}(\infty), \gamma_{v_2}(\infty), \gamma_{v_1}(-\infty))$, and the lemma follows immediately.

Take now two vectors $v_2, v_2' \in T_x\widetilde{M}$, $\|v_2\| = \|v_2'\|$, $v_2 \perp v_1$, $v_2' \perp v_1$, $v_2 \neq v_2'$, and consider the composition

$$Q(v_2, v_2') = P(v_2') \circ P(v_2).$$

It is easy to see that $Q(v_2,v_2')v_1 = v_1$ and $Q(v_2,v_2')v = v$ for every $v \perp (v_1, v_2, v_2')$. In the 2-plane spanned by v_2 and v_2' the isometry $Q(v_2,v_2')$ acts as the product of the reflection with respect to the line perpendicular to v_2 and the reflection with respect to the line perpendicular to v_2'. Thus, the following lemma is proved.

6.2. Lemma. The isometry $Q(v_2, v_2')$ rotates the plane

(v_2, v_2') by the angle $2\cdot\measuredangle(v_2, v_2')$ and leaves invariant every vector $v \perp (v_2, v_2')$.

The following proposition imples the ergodicity and the Bernoulli property of the frame flow f^t on a compact manifold of constant negative curvature.

6.3. Proposition. If M^n is of constant negative curvature, then the transitivity group (see Definition 4.4) is $SO(n-1)$.

Proof. Consider two frames at x: $w = (x, v_1, u_2, u_3, \ldots, u_{n-1})$ and $w' = (x, v_1, u_2', u_3', \ldots, u_{n-1}')$. It is enough to show that there is a composition of isometries $P(v, v')$ which sends w to w'. First we take the plane (u_2, u_2') and use Lemma 6.2 to find a pair of vectors v_2, v_2' in that plane such that the successive parallel translation $Q_2 = Q(v_2, v_2')$ along the corresponding infinite triangles sends u_2 to u_2'. Observe that $Q(v_2', v_2')v_1 = v_1$. Then we take the vectors Q_2u_3 and u_3' and find a pair of triangles such that the corresponding isometry Q_3 sends Q_2 to u_3' and fixes u_2' (note that $u_2' \perp u_3'$). And so on. The product $Q_{n-1} \circ Q_{n-2} \circ \cdots \circ Q_2$ sends w to w'. The proposition is proved.

Theorem 2.2 follows from Propositions 6.3 and 4.6.

Now we give a sketch of proof of Theorem 2.4; for complete proof cf [BK].

6.4. Lemma. Let n be even and $\neq 6$ and Let H be a subgroup of $SO(n+1)$ acting transitively on S^n.

Then $H = SO(n+1)$.

See [O] for the proof (dimension 6 is excluded because the exceptional group $\mathfrak{G}_2$ acts transitively on S^6).

Therefore, it is enough to show that under the pinching assumption of Theorem 2.4, the transitivity group acts transitively on the sphere S^{n-2}.

Consider again the picture shown in Fig. 1. The point x is special for the infinite triangle $(\gamma_{v_1}(\infty), \gamma_{v_2}(\infty), \gamma_{v_1}(-\infty))$. We have three horospheres centered at the vertices of the triangle and pairwise tangent, the two horospheres centered at $\gamma_{v_1}(\infty)$ and $\gamma_{v_1}(-\infty)$ being tangent at x. The triangle has this property due to the fact that $v_2 \perp v_1$. In case the curvature is non-constant we cannot expect to get the same picture—three pairwise tangent horospheres, two of them passing through x, which is necessary to get elements of the transitivity group at (x, v_1). However, it is easy to see that for every infinite triangle there is a unique triple of horospheres centered at the vertices and pairwise tangent. Thus, given $v_1 \in T_x\widetilde{M}$ we must find out which vectors $v_2 \in T_x\widetilde{M}$ have the property that two of the three horospheres corresponding to the triangle $(\gamma_{v_1}(\infty), \gamma_{v_1}(-\infty), \gamma_{v_2}(\infty))$ pass through x. Let $S^+_{v_1}(t)$ and $S^-_{v_1}(t)$ be the two families of horospheres centered at $\gamma_{v_1}(\infty)$ and $\gamma_{v_2}(\infty)$ respectively, $S^+_{v_1}(t) \cap S^-_{v_1}(-t) = \gamma_{v_1}(t)$. Consider the Busemann functions $F^+(y)$ and $F^-(y)$, $F^+(y) = t$ if $y \in S^+_{v_1}(t)$ and $F^-(y) = t$ if $y \in S^-_{v_1}(t)$. Denote $\Pi = \{y \in \widetilde{M} | F^+(y) = F^-(y)\}$. In the constant curvature case Π is the $(n-1)$-plane perpendicular to v_1. In the general case Π is an $(n-1)$-dimensional surface which is partitioned into the sets $\Pi_t = \{y \in \Pi | F^+(y) = F^-(y) = t\}$. As $t \to \infty$, Π_t "aproaches" the absolute. One can show (see [E2]) that Π_t tends to some set Π_∞ as $t \to \infty$, Π_∞ lies on the absolute and is homeomorphic to S^{n-2}. Every point $\alpha \in \Pi_\infty$ has the property we need: two of the horospheres corresponding to the triangle $(\gamma_{v_1}(\infty), \gamma_{v_1}(-\infty), \alpha)$ are tangent at x. Consider now the geodesic connecting x and α and let $v(\alpha)$ be the unit vector tangent to this geodesic at x. It is easy to see that $v(\alpha)$ cannot be parallel to v_1, hence, we can project $v(\alpha)$ on the plane perpendicular to v_1. Let $v(\alpha)$ be the projection and set $v_2(\alpha) = \frac{\widetilde{v(\alpha)}}{\|\widetilde{v(\alpha)}\|}$. Denote by $P(\alpha)$ the isometry of $T_x\widetilde{M}$ induced by the parallel translation along the infinite triangle $(\gamma_{v_1}(\infty), \alpha, \gamma_{v_1}(-\infty))$ and let $P_c(v_2(\alpha))$ (see Lemma 6.1) be the isometry of $T_x\widetilde{M}$ induced by the parallel translation with constant curvature along the infinite triangle $(\gamma_{v_1}(\infty), \gamma_{v_1}(-\infty), \gamma_{v_2(\alpha)}(\infty))$.

6.5. Lemma. If the angular distance between $P(\alpha)u$ and $P_c(v_2(\alpha))u$ is strictly less than $\frac{\pi}{2}$ for every $u \in T_x\widetilde{M}$, $\|u\| = 1$, and for every $\alpha \in \Pi_\infty$, then the set $\bigcup_{\alpha\in\Pi_\infty} P(\alpha)u$ contains an open neighborhood for some $u \in T_x\widetilde{M}$.

See [BK], Proposition 2.9, for the proof. If n is even, then the mapping $S^{n-2} \to S^{n-2}$ given by $v_2 \to P_c(v_2)u$, $u \perp v_1$, has degree 0 although almost every point has two preimages. The proof from [BK] uses index and homotopy arguments.

Obviously, if $\bigcup_{\alpha\in\Pi_\infty} P(\alpha)$ contains an open neighborhood, then one of the orbits of the transitivity group on S^{n-2} contains an open neighborhood, which implies that the group is transitive on S^{n-2}. The following proposition finishes the proof of Theorem 2.4.

6.6. Proposition. If the sectional curvature of M^n is pinched between -1 and -0.99, then the angular distance between $P(\alpha)u$ and $P_c(v_2(\alpha))u$ is less than $\frac{\pi}{2}$ for every $\alpha \in \Pi_\infty$ and every $u \in T_x\widetilde{M}$, $\|u\| = 1$.

See [BK], Section 3, for the proof.

7. Kähler manifolds

Let M^{2n} be a compact Kähler manifold and let J be the operator of almost complex structure on M^{2n}. Denote by (u,v) the scalar product in TM^{2n}, and consider the functions $h_{ij} = (v_i, Jv_j)$ defined for every frame $w = (x,v_1,\dots,v_k) \in St_k(M^{2n})$, $k \geq 2$. Since J is invariant under the parallel translation, the functions h_{ij} are invariant under f^t. Thus, if M^{2n} is a Kähler manifold of dimension >2, then the frame flow is not ergodic. Compact Kähler manifolds of negative curvature can be obtained as factors of complex hyperbolic spaces by cocompact lattices (see [Bo]). This proves Theorem 2.5.

However, it turns out that is some cases the function h_{ij} are the only first integrals of the frame flow. Denote by $Xc_k(M^{2n}) = \{(x,v_1,v_2,\dots,v_k) \mid v_1 \perp v_j$ and $v_i \perp Jv_j\}$ the space of unitary k-frames.

7.1. Proposition. If M^{2n} is a compact Kähler manifold of negative curvature, then the frame flow f_k^t in the space of unitary frames $Sc_k(M^{2n})$ is ergodic provided $n = 2$ or n is odd and $k \le n$.

See [BG] for the proof.

If $n > 2$ is even, then a further reduction of the structure group is possible, e.g. when M^{2n} carries a quaternion structure.

REFERENCES

[A] D. V. Anosov, Geodesic flows on closed Riemannian manifolds of negative curvature, Proc. Steklov Inst. Math., v. 90 (1967).

[Bo] A. Borel, Compact Clifford-Klein forms of symmetric spaces, Topology, v. 2 (1963), 111-122.

[Br1] M. Brin, Topological transitivity of one class of dynamical systems and flows of frames on manifolds of negative curvature, Functional Anal Appl., v. 9 (1975), 8-16.

[Br2] _____, Topology of group extensions of Anosov systems, Math. Notes of the Acad. of Sci. of the USSR, v. 18 (1975), 858-864.

[BG] M. Brin and M. Gromov, On the ergodicity of frame flows, Invent. Math., v. 60 (1980), 1-7.

[BK] M. Brin and H. Karcher, Frame flows on manifolds with pinched negative curvature, preprint.

[BP] M. Brin and Ya. Pesin, Partially hyperbolic dynamical systems, Math. of the USSR-Izvestija, v. 8 (1974), 177-218.

[E1] P. Eberlein, Geodesic flows on negatively curved manifolds, I, Ann. of Math. (2), v. 95 (1972), 492-510.

[E2] _____, preprint.

[G] M. Gromov, On a geometric Banach's problem, Izvestija AN SSSR, ser. mat., v. 31 (1967), 1105-1114 (in Russian).

[O] A. L. Onisçik, On Lie groups transitive on compact manifolds III, Mathematics of the USSR-Sbornick, v.4 (1968), 233-240.

[R] D. J. Rudolph, Classifying the isometric extension of a Bernoulli shift, J. d'Analyse Mathematique, v. 34 (1978), 36-60.

[S] Ya. G. Sinai, Dynamical systems with countably multiple Lebesgue spectrum II, Amer. Math. Soc. Translation (2), v 68 (1968), 34-88.

PRODUCTS OF INDEPENDENT RANDOMLY PERTURBED MATRICES

Eric V. Slud

Abstract. The almost sure limit π_1 of $n^{-1}\log\|A_nA_{n-1}\cdots A$ proved by Furstenberg and Kesten (1960) to exist for strictl stationary random sequences of $k \times k$ matrices A_i, is sho to be stable under small independent orthogonal perturbation of A_i when the A_i are independent identically distribute matrices which almost surely commute and take on only finite many values.

Introduction. Let $\{A_n\}_{n=1}^{\infty}$ be an independently and identica ly distributed sequence of random $k \times k$ matrices. Then a theorem of Kesten and Furstenberg (1960), usually proved now as a corollary of Kingman's (1973) Subadditive Ergodic Theorem implies for any norm $\|\ \|$ on matrices that as $n \to \infty$ the almost sure limit π_1 of $n^{-1}\log\|A_n \cdot A_{n-1} \cdots A_1\|$ exists and is constant. However, there seems to be no generally computable way to determine $\pi_1 = \pi_1(\mu)$ from the probability law μ of A_1 when the matrices A_n do not commute almost surely.

If $\mu = L(A_1)$ is a probability law on the $k \times k$ matrices in $SL(k,\mathbb{R})$ such that (i) $\int \|g\| d\mu(g) < \infty$, and (ii) the smallest closed subgroup G of $SL(k,\mathbb{R})$ containing the support of μ is non-compact and has no reducible subgroups of finite index, then Furstenberg (1963) shows that $\pi_1 > 0$. This is the best available information on π_1 unless the random walk $\{\psi_n\}_{n=1}^{\infty} \equiv \{A_n \cdot A_{n-1} \cdots A_1 \underline{v}/\|A_n \cdots A_1 \underline{v}\|\}_{n=1}^{\infty}$ has a uniq invariant measure ν on S^{k-1}. In that case Furstenberg gi the expression $\pi_1 = E(\int_{S^{k-1}} \log \rho(\underline{x}) d\nu(\underline{x}))$, where for a gi $x \in S^{k-1} \subset \mathbb{R}^k$, $\rho(\underline{x})$ is the random variable $\|A_1\underline{x}\|_2$. Let ν_A denote the law on S^{k-1} of $A\underline{x}/\|A\underline{x}\|_2$ when ν is the of $\underline{x} \in S^{k-1}$ and $A \in SL(k,\mathbb{R})$, it follows also in the ca of unique invariant measure that ν is determined by the tegral equation

$$\nu = \int \nu_A \cdot d\mu(A).$$

A. Katok has recently suggested as a model problem for the random perturbation of smooth dynamical systems, to find general conditions on the law μ of A_1 under which $\pi_1(\mu_\varepsilon) \to \pi_1(\mu)$ as $\varepsilon \to 0$, where μ_ε is a measure on $S^{k-1} \simeq O(k)$ defined by $\mu_\varepsilon = \mu * \lambda_\varepsilon = \int_{O(k)} \mu \circ g \, d\lambda_\varepsilon(g)$, λ_ε = uniform (Haar) measure on an ε-neighborhood of the identity in $O(k)$. In the present note, we show how $\pi_1(\mu_\varepsilon) \to \pi_1(\mu)$ can be proved for two special examples when $k = 2$.

Acknowledgement. This note was stimulated by and owes its existence to the interest of A. Katok. It is a pleasure to acknowledge his many valuable comments and insights.

Example 1. $k = 2$, $\varepsilon \geq 0$; the law $\mu_\varepsilon = \mu * \lambda_\varepsilon$ on $SL(2,\mathbb{R})$ is

$$\text{given by } A_n = \begin{cases} \begin{pmatrix} 2 & 0 \\ 0 & \frac{1}{2} \end{pmatrix} \begin{pmatrix} \cos\theta_n & \sin\theta_n \\ -\sin\theta_n & \cos\theta_n \end{pmatrix} & \text{with probability } \frac{1}{2} \\[2ex] \begin{pmatrix} \cos\theta_n & \sin\theta_n \\ -\sin\theta_n & \cos\theta_n \end{pmatrix} & \text{with probability } \frac{1}{2}, \end{cases}$$

where ν_n are independently and identically distributed uniform random angles in $(-\varepsilon,\varepsilon)$.

We define a random walk $\{\psi_n\}_{n=0}^{\infty}$ as above by fixing arbitrary $\psi_0 \in S^1 \subset \mathbb{R}^2$ and putting $\psi_{n+1} \equiv A_{n+1}\psi_n / \|A_{n+1}\psi_n\|_2$ for $n \geq 0$. It is obvious that for all $n \geq \pi/\varepsilon$ the probability density of ψ_n is continuous and strictly positive on S^1 (uniformly in ψ_0). Hence there exists a unique invariant measure for $\{\psi_n\}$. After changing variables by $\varphi_n \equiv \arg(\psi_n) \in (-\pi,\pi]$ and remarking

$$\varphi_{n+1} = \begin{cases} \varphi_n + \theta_{n+1} & \text{with probability } \frac{1}{2} \\[1ex] \tan^{-1}\left(\frac{1}{4}\tan(\varphi_n + \theta_{n+1})\right) & \text{with probability } \frac{1}{2}, \end{cases}$$

we define ν_ε to be the unique stationary law for the Markov chain $\{\varphi_n\}$ on $(-\pi,\pi]$. The integral equation for stationarity becomes

$$(1.1) \qquad \nu_\varepsilon = \frac{1}{2}\nu_\varepsilon * \lambda_\varepsilon + \frac{1}{2}(\nu_\varepsilon * \lambda_\varepsilon)_f$$

where λ_ε is again uniform measure on $(-\varepsilon,\varepsilon)$ and $(\quad)_f$ denotes image measure under $f(s) = \tan^{-1}(\frac{1}{4}\tan(s))$.

It is easy to see from (1.1) that ν_ε must have an everywhere positive smooth density h_ε on $(-\pi,\pi]$. Writing ℓ_ε for the density of λ_ε on $(-\pi,\pi]$ and defining convolution with respect to addition mod 2π, we compute from (1.1):

$$(1.2) \qquad \begin{aligned} h_\varepsilon(\varphi) &\equiv L_\varepsilon(h_\varepsilon)(\varphi) \\ &= \frac{1}{2} h_\varepsilon * \ell_\varepsilon(\varphi) + \frac{2}{\cos^2\varphi + 16\sin^2\varphi} h_\varepsilon * \ell_\varepsilon(f^{-1}(\varphi)). \end{aligned}$$

Now the linear operator L_ε on $L^1(S^1,\lambda)$ defined by (1.2) takes probability densities to probability densities and fixes the unique density h_ε. Moreover, since the Markov chain $\{\varphi_n\}$ is invariant (in law) under the reflections $\begin{cases}\varphi \to -\varphi \\ \varphi \to \pi-\varphi\end{cases}$ mod$(-\pi,\pi]$, so are ν_ε and h_ε. Finally, among all probability densities g on $(-\pi,\pi]$ invariant under the above reflections, L_ε preserves the set of g which are monotone decreasing on $[0,\frac{\pi}{2}]$. This is evident from (1.2) if we remark that f preserves $[0,\frac{\pi}{2}]$.

As $\varepsilon \to 0$, it follows from (1.1) that any weak-limiting measure for ν_ε must be invariant under f, and therefore must be concentrated on $\{0,\pm\frac{\pi}{2},\pi\}$. However, by (1.2) $h_\varepsilon(0) = \frac{5}{2} h_\varepsilon * \ell_\varepsilon(0)$, $h_\varepsilon(\frac{\pi}{2}) = \frac{5}{8} h_\varepsilon * \ell_\varepsilon(\frac{\pi}{2})$. By the remarks following (1.2), $h_\varepsilon(0) = h_\varepsilon(\pi)$, $h_\varepsilon(\frac{\pi}{2}) = h_\varepsilon(-\frac{\pi}{2})$, and for each $\varepsilon > 0$ the uniquely determined h_ε is monotone decreasing on $[0,\frac{\pi}{2}]$. Thus we have proved (if we identify π and $-\pi$)

$$(1.3) \qquad \nu_\varepsilon \overset{w}{\to} \frac{1}{2}\delta_0 + \frac{1}{2}\delta_\pi \quad \text{as} \quad \varepsilon \to 0.$$

But, $\rho(0) = \rho(\pi) \equiv \|A_1\binom{1}{0}\|_2 = \begin{cases} 2 & \text{with probability } \frac{1}{2} \\ 1 & \text{with probability } \frac{1}{2}. \end{cases}$

By our formula for $\pi_1(\mu_\varepsilon)$,

$$(1.4) \quad \lim_{\varepsilon\to 0} \pi_1(\mu_\varepsilon) = \frac{1}{2}\log 2 + \frac{1}{2}\log 1 = \frac{1}{2}\log 2 = \pi_1(\mu_0).$$

<u>Example 2</u>. $k = 2$, small $\varepsilon \geq 0$, $\{\theta_n\}$ as before; now $\mu_\varepsilon = L(A_n)$ is given by

$$A_n = \begin{cases} \begin{pmatrix} 4 & 0 \\ 0 & \frac{1}{4} \end{pmatrix}\begin{pmatrix} \cos\theta_n & \sin\theta_n \\ -\sin\theta_n & \cos\theta_n \end{pmatrix} & \text{with prob. } \frac{1}{2} \\ \begin{pmatrix} \frac{1}{2} & 0 \\ 0 & 2 \end{pmatrix}\begin{pmatrix} \cos\theta_n & \sin\theta_n \\ -\sin\theta_n & \cos\theta_n \end{pmatrix} & \text{with prob. } \frac{1}{2}. \end{cases}$$

Again we define Markov transition on S^1 by $\psi_{n+1} \equiv A_{n+1}\psi_n/\|A_{n+1}\psi_n\|_2$ for $n \geq 0$, and if $\varphi_n \equiv \arg(\psi_n) \in (-\pi,\pi]$, the transition for $\{\varphi_n\}$ is

$$\varphi_{n+1} = \begin{cases} f_1(\varphi_n + \theta_{n+1}) & \text{with probability } \frac{1}{2} \\ f_2(\varphi_n + \theta_{n+1}) & \text{with probability } \frac{1}{2}, \end{cases}$$

where $f_1(\varphi) = \tan^{-1}(\tan(\varphi)/16)$ and $f_2(\varphi) = \tan^{-1}(4\tan(\varphi))$. Just as in Example 1, there is a unique stationary measure ν_ε for $\{\varphi_n\}$ with smooth density and

$$(2.1) \quad \nu_\varepsilon = \frac{1}{2}(\nu_\varepsilon * \lambda_\varepsilon)_{f_1} + \frac{1}{2}(\nu_\varepsilon * \lambda_\varepsilon)_{f_2}.$$

It follows immediately from (2.1) that if ν' is any weak-limiting measure for a subsequence ν_ε as $\varepsilon \to 0$, then $\nu' = 2^{-n}\sum_{j=0}^{n}\binom{n}{j}(\nu')_{f_1^j \circ f_2^{n-j}}$ and ν' is concentrated on $\{0, \pm\frac{\pi}{2}, \pi\}$. In order to conclude that in fact ν' is concentrated on $\{0,\pi\}$, we require a more detailed argument.

We first define a Markov chain with state space $\mathbb{R}$:

$S_n \equiv \cot(\varphi_n)$ has transition $S_{n+1} \equiv \begin{cases} 16\dfrac{S_n - \tan\theta_{n+1}}{1+S_n \tan\theta_{n+1}} & \text{with prob. } \frac{1}{2} \\ \dfrac{1}{4}\dfrac{S_n - \tan\theta_1}{1+S_n \tan\theta_{n+1}} & \text{with prob. } \frac{1}{2}. \end{cases}$

Our idea will be to subdivide the interval $(-\pi,\pi]$ into three regions

$$E_1 = \{\varphi : |\cot(\varphi)| \geq \cot \delta_1^*(\varepsilon)\},$$

$$E_2 = \{\varphi : \tan \delta_1^*(\varepsilon) < |\cot(\varphi)| < \cot \delta_1^*(\varepsilon)\}$$

$$E_3 = \{\varphi : |\cot(\varphi)| \leq \tan \delta_1^*(\varepsilon)\},$$

and to find a number n^* of transition steps such that $\Pr\{\varphi_{n^*+1} \notin E_1 | \varphi_1 \in E_3\}$ and $\Pr\{\varphi_n \in E_3$ for some $n \leq n^* + 1 | \varphi_1 \in E_1\}$ are both small when ε is sufficiently small. This will be accomplished through the Strong Law of Large Numbers and uniform bounds on $|S_{n+1}/S_n|$ holding for $S_n \in \cot^{-1}(E_2)$.

(2.2) If $\varepsilon > 0$ is sufficiently small and $\delta_1 \equiv \tan^{-1}(20 \tan \varepsilon)$, then whenever $|S_n| \in (\tan \delta_1, \cot \delta_1)$, with conditional probability 1, $|S_{n+1}| > |S_n|$ implies $|S_{n+1}| \geq 14|S_n|$ and $|S_{n+1}| < |S_n|$ implies $|S_{n+1}| \geq |S_n|/7$.

<u>Proof</u>. One need only verify that for $S \in (\tan \delta_1, \cot \delta_1)$, $16 \dfrac{S-\tan \varepsilon}{1+S \tan \varepsilon} \geq 14S$ and $\dfrac{1}{4} \dfrac{S-\tan \varepsilon}{1+S\tan \varepsilon} \geq S/7$.

An immediate and useful corollary of (2.2) is

(2.3) If $\varepsilon > 0$ is sufficiently small and $s \in (100 \tan \delta_1, \frac{1}{100} \cot \delta_1)$, then $\Delta(S) \equiv \text{a.s. inf } \{S_{n+7} | \sum_{k=0}^{6} \chi_{(S_{n+k+1} > S_{n+k})} \geq 3, S_n = S\} > \frac{8S}{7}$.

We now define $\delta_1^*(\varepsilon)$ asymptotically much larger than δ_1 and much smaller than 1 such that $\nu_\varepsilon(E_2) \to 0$ as $\varepsilon \to 0$. This is possible because ν_ε is asymptotically as $\varepsilon \to 0$

concentrated near $0, \pm\frac{\pi}{2}, \pm\pi$. Our exact statement is

(2.4) There exists $\delta_1^*(\varepsilon) \geq 100\delta_1^{1/2}$ such that both $\delta_1^*(\varepsilon)$ and $\nu_\varepsilon(E_2) \to 0$ as $\varepsilon \to 0$.

Our main estimates are contained in (2.5), (2.6):

(2.5) For fixed $\gamma > 0$ there exists $L = L(\gamma)$ so large that for all sufficiently small ε and all $S_0 \in (L \tan \delta_1, L^{-1} \cot \delta_1)$, $\Pr\{S_1, S_2, \ldots, S_{m-1} \in (\tan \delta_1, \cot \delta_1),\ S_m \geq \cot \delta_1$ for some $m \leq 99 \log(1/\varepsilon)\} \geq 1-\gamma$.

(2.6) For fixed $\gamma > 0$, small $\varepsilon > 0$, and any $S \in (\frac{1}{8}, 8)$, $\Pr\{S_1, S_2, \ldots, S_m \geq \tan \delta_1^*(\varepsilon)$ for all $m \leq 100 \log(1/\varepsilon) \mid S_0 = S\} \geq 1 - \gamma$.

<u>Proofs</u>. Let $\{\xi_j\}_{j=1}^\infty \subset \{0,1\}^\infty$ be independent Bernoulli $(\frac{1}{2},\frac{1}{2})$ variables defined by $\xi_j = 1$ iff $S_j = 16 \frac{S_{j-1} - \tan \theta_j}{1 + S_{j-1} \tan \theta_j}$, 0 otherwise. By (2.2), the probability in (2.5) is $\geq \Pr \sum_{j=1}^k \xi_j \geq 3k/7$ for $\frac{\log L}{\log 7} \leq k \leq [99 \log \varepsilon^{-1}]\}$ which can be made arbitrarily close to 1 by Kolmogorov's Strong Law of Large Numbers if first L is chosen sufficiently large and then ε is chosen sufficiently small. For the same reason, $\Pr\{S_m \geq \cot \delta_1$ before $S_m \leq \tan \delta_1^*$ if either happens for $m \leq 100 \log \varepsilon^{-1} \mid S_0 = S\} \geq \Pr\{\sum_{j=1}^k \xi_j \geq 3k/7$ for $\frac{\log((\cot \delta_1^*)/8)}{\log 7} \leq k \leq 100 \log \varepsilon^{-1}\}$ can for arbitrary fixed $M > 100/\log 20$ be made $\geq 1 - \gamma/M$ by taking ε small enough. Finally, since $\min\{m : S_m \geq \cot \delta_1 \mid S_0 = S \in (\frac{1}{8}, 8)\} \geq \frac{-\log(8 \tan \delta_1)}{\log 20} \sim \frac{\log \varepsilon^{-1}}{\log 20}$, the probability is at least $1 - \gamma$ that $S_m \geq \tan \delta_1^*$ for all $m \leq 100 \log \varepsilon^{-1}$.

Here we have made use of the Strong Markov property for $\{S_n\}$ to say that <u>each</u> time the random walk S_n hits the interval $(\frac{1}{8}, 8)$ there is a probability at least $1-\gamma/M$ that it returns to $[\cot \delta_1, \infty)$ —using up at least $(\log \varepsilon^{-1})/\log 20$

transition steps—before hitting $[0, \tan \delta_1^*]$. We use the Strong Markov property again in making the remark that for fixed L and any $S \in (0, \tan \delta_1^*)$,

$$P\{\min\{m : |S_m| \geq L \tan \delta_1\} \geq \log \varepsilon^{-1} | S_0 = S\} \to 0 \quad \text{as} \quad \varepsilon \to 0.$$

This follows from the fact that any succession $\xi_{j+1} = \xi_{j+2} = \cdots = \xi_{j+k} = 1$ following $S_j \geq 0$, for which $\theta_{j+1}, \theta_{j+2}, \ldots, \theta_{j+k}$ are all $\geq \frac{\varepsilon}{2}$ and k is at least $\frac{\log(20\ L)}{\log 14} + 2$, implies $S_{j+k} \geq L \tan \delta_1$. Of course the probability that such a succession occurs in the course of $\log \varepsilon^{-1}$ steps is nearly 1 when L is fixed and ε is made small.

Now let $n = n^*(\varepsilon) \equiv [100 \log \varepsilon^{-1}]$, and consider the distribution of φ_n given the initial distribution ν_ε for φ_0. On the one hand, ν_ε is a stationary distribution, so that $\nu_\varepsilon = L(\varphi_n)$. However, by (2.5), (2.6) and the remarks making use of the Strong Markov property, for sufficiently small ε and any fixed $\gamma > 0$, $\Pr\{\varphi_n \in E_3 | \varphi_0 = \varphi \in E_3\} \leq 2\gamma$ and $\Pr\{\varphi_n \in E_3 | \varphi_0 = \varphi' \in E_1\} \leq \gamma$. Therefore, $\nu_\varepsilon(E_3) \leq 2\gamma\nu_\varepsilon(E_3) + \gamma\nu_\varepsilon(E_1) + \nu_\varepsilon(E_2)$, and it follows that

$$\nu_\varepsilon \xrightarrow{w} \frac{1}{2}\,\delta_0 + \frac{1}{2}\,\delta_\pi \quad \text{as} \quad \varepsilon \to 0, \tag{2.7}$$

just as in Example 1; and again by the formula for $\pi_1(\mu_\varepsilon)$,

$$\lim_{\varepsilon \to 0} \pi_1(\mu_\varepsilon) = \frac{1}{2} \log 4 + \frac{1}{2} \log \frac{1}{2} = \frac{1}{2} \log 2 = \pi_1(\mu_0). \tag{2.8}$$

Concluding remarks. It is easy to see that the argument in Example 2 is in no way restricted to 2×2 matrices or to two-point laws $L(A_1)$. In fact, if $\mu = L(A_1)$ is a probability law on $SL(k,\mathbb{R})$ that $\mu \times \mu(\{(A,B) \in SL(k,\mathbb{R})^2 : AB = BA\}) = 1$ and the support of μ is finite, then the method of Example 2 shows that $\pi_1(\mu_\varepsilon) \to \pi_1(\mu)$ as $\varepsilon \to 0$, where $\mu_\varepsilon = \mu * \lambda_\varepsilon$ is defined in the Introduction.

REFERENCES

Furstenberg, H., "Non-commuting random products," T.A.M.S. (1963), 377-428.

Furstenberg, H. and H. Kesten, "Products of random matrices," Ann. Math. Stat. 31 (1960), 457-469.

Kingman, J. F. C., "Subadditive ergodic theory," Ann. Prob. 1 (1973), 883-899.

Department of Mathematics
University of Maryland
College Park, Maryland

On large norm periodic solutions of some differential equations

Paul H. Rabinowitz

Introduction

This paper is concerned with the existence of periodic solutions of large norm for a class of general Hamiltonian systems as well as a related family of second order Hamiltonian systems. The nature of the results presented here is if the nonlinear terms in the system satisfy appropriate conditions for large values of their arguments, then the systems possess arbitrarily large periodic solutions of arbitrary period.

To be more precise, let $z \in \mathbb{R}^{2n}$, $H : \mathbb{R}^{2n} \to \mathbb{R}$, and consider the general Hamiltonian system

$$\dot{z} = \mathcal{J} H_z(z) \tag{0.1}$$

where $z = (p, q)$, $p, q \in \mathbb{R}^n$ and $\mathcal{J} = \begin{pmatrix} 0 & -\mathcal{I} \\ \mathcal{I} & 0 \end{pmatrix}$, $\mathcal{I}$ denoting the $n \times n$ identity matrix. For $a, b \in \mathbb{R}^j$, let $(a, b)_{\mathbb{R}^j}$ denote the usual Euclidean inner product in $\mathbb{R}^j$. Our first result is

Theorem 0.2: Let $H \in C^1(\mathbb{R}^{2n}, \mathbb{R})$ and satisfy

(h_1) There is an $r > 0$ and $\mu > 2$ such that for all $|z| \geq r$, $0 < \mu H(z) \leq (z, H_z(z))_{\mathbb{R}^{2n}}$

(h_2) There is an $s \geq \mu$ and constants $a_1, a_2 \geq 0$ such that for all $z \in \mathbb{R}^{2n}$,

$$|H(z)| \leq a_1 |z|^s + a_2 .$$

Then for any $T, R > 0$, there exists a T periodic solution $z(t)$ of (0.1) with $\|z\|_{L^\infty} \geq R$.

Thus the behavior of $H(z)$ near ∞ as expressed by (h_1), (h_2) guarantees the existence of large periodic solutions of (0.1) having any prescribed period. Since by (h_1), for all sufficiently large c, $H^{-1}(c)$ bounds a starshaped region in $\mathbb{R}^{2n}$, it follows from results of

[0] that $H^{-1}(c)$ contains a periodic solution of (0.1). However unlike Theorem 0.2, these results do not imply the existence of large norm solutions of (0.1) having a prescribed period. Hypothesis (h_1) implies that there are constants $a_3, a_4 \geq 0$ such that

$$H(z) \geq a_3|z|^{\mu} - a_4 \tag{0.3}$$

for all $z \in \mathbb{R}^{2n}$. There is a version of Theorem 0.2 without (h_2) in [1] but the proof given there is not complete. Hypotheses (h_2) can surely be weakened but whether it can be eliminated is not clear. For second order Hamiltonian systems, no such bound is needed. Restricting ourselves to the simplest such case, let $V: \mathbb{R}^n \to \mathbb{R}$ and consider

$$\ddot{q} + V_q(q) = 0 \quad . \tag{0.4}$$

We will prove

<u>Theorem 0.5</u>: Let $V \in C^1(\mathbb{R}^n, \mathbb{R})$ and satisfy

(V_1) There is an $r > 0$ and $\mu > 2$ such that for all $|q| \geq r$, $0 < \mu V(q) \leq (q, V_q(q))_{\mathbb{R}^n}$.

Then for any $T, R \geq 0$, (0.4) has a T periodic solution $q(t)$ with $\|q\|_{L^\infty} \geq R$.

The proofs of Theorems 0.2 and 0.5 will be carried out in §1 and §2 respectively. These proofs parallel the argument of [1] but are somewhat more streamlined. Roughly the idea is to pose (0.1) and (0.4) as variational problems in an appropriate infinite dimensional space, obtain critical points of approximating finite dimensional problems, use (h_1) and (h_2) to get upper and lower bounds for the corresponding critical values, and use these bounds to solve (0.1) and (0.4).

Similar ideas can also be employed to establish the existence of time periodic solutions of semilinear wave equations of the form

$$\begin{cases} u_{tt} - u_{xx} + f(x,u) = 0 , & 0 < x < \ell \\ u(0,t) = 0 = u(\ell,t) & . \end{cases} \tag{0.6}$$

However rather stringent growth conditions must be imposed on f.

§1. The proof of Theorem 0.2

To begin, for convenience we make a change of variables $t \to 2\pi t T^{-1} \equiv \tau$ so (0.1) becomes

$$\frac{dz}{d\tau} = \lambda \mathscr{J} H_z(z) \tag{1.1}$$

with $\lambda \equiv T(2\pi)^{-1}$. Now we seek 2π periodic solutions of (1.1). Let $E = (W^{\frac{1}{2},2}(S^1))^{2n}$, the Hilbert space of $2n$-tuples of 2π periodic functions which possess a derivative of order $\frac{1}{2}$. For

$$z = \sum_{-\infty}^{\infty} a_j e^{ij\tau} \in E,$$

where $a_{-j} = \bar{a}_j \in \mathbb{C}^{2n}$, the usual norm is

$$\sum_{-\infty}^{\infty} (1 + |j|)|a_j|^2 .$$

For z a C^1 2π periodic function, let

$$A(z) \equiv \int_0^{2\pi} (p, \frac{dq}{d\tau})_{\mathbb{R}^n} \, d\tau ,$$

the so-called action integral of z. It is easy to see that $A(z)$ is a bounded quadratic form on C^1 in the E norm and therefore extends to E. Let

$$I(z) \equiv A(z) - \lambda \int_0^{2\pi} H(z)\, d\tau .$$

Then $H \in C^1$ and (h_2) imply that $I \in C^1(E, \mathbb{R})$ and any critical point of I on E is a solution of (0.1). (See e.g. [2]).

For technical reasons, instead of working with I and H, a modified problem will be treated. Before introducing it however, it is convenient to re-norm E. Thus let $e_1, \cdots, e_{2n}$ denote the usual Euclidean basis for $\mathbb{R}^{2n}$ and set

$$\begin{cases} \varphi_{jk} = (\sin j\tau)\, e_k - (\cos j\tau)\, e_{k+n} \\ \psi_{jk} = (\cos j\tau)\, e_k + (\sin j\tau)\, e_{k+n} & j = 0,1,2,\cdots, \\ \theta_{jk} = (\sin j\tau)\, e_k + (\cos j\tau)\, e_{k+n} & 1 \le k \le n \quad . \\ \zeta_{jk} = (\cos j\tau)\, e_k - (\sin j\tau)\, e_{k+n} \end{cases}$$

These vectors are orthogonal in the usual L^2 sense. Let

$$E^+ \equiv \text{span}\,\{\varphi_{jk}, \psi_{jk} \mid j \in \mathbb{N}, \quad 1 \le k \le n\} \,,$$

$$E^- \equiv \text{span}\,\{\theta_{jk}, \zeta_{jk} \mid j \in \mathbb{N}, \quad 1 \le k \le n\}$$

and $$E^0 = \text{span}\,\{\varphi_{0k}, \psi_{0k} \mid 1 \le k \le n\} \quad .$$

It is easy to verify that E^+, E^-, E^0 are respectively the subspaces of E on which A is respectively positive definite, negative definite, and null. Moreover $E = E^+ \oplus E^- \oplus E^0$ and if $z \equiv z^+ + z^- + z^0 \in E$, $A(z) = A(z^+) + A(z^-)$. It is therefore convenient to put an equivalent norm on E defined by

$$\|z\|^2 = A(z^+) - A(z^-) + |z^0|^2 \quad .$$

Thus E^+, E^-, E^0 are mutually orthogonal subspaces of E in the inner product associated with this norm.

To set up the modified problem, let $K > 0$ and $\chi_K(x)$ be a C^∞ real valued function such that $\chi_K(x) \equiv 1$ for $x \le K$; $\equiv 0$ for $x \ge K+1$; and $\dfrac{d\chi_K(x)}{dx} < 0$ for $x \in (K, K+1)$. Set

$$H_K(z) = \chi_K(|z|)\, H(z) + (1 - \chi_K(|z|))\, \sigma |z|^s \quad . \tag{1.2}$$

Then $H_K \in C^1(\mathbb{R}^{2n}, \mathbb{R})$ and satisfies (h_1) with μ replaced by $\nu = \min(\mu, s)$ provided that

$$\sigma \ge \max_{K \le |z| \le K+1} \frac{|H(z)|}{|z|^s} \tag{1.3}$$

which choice we henceforth make. Note also that by (h_2) we can assume that σ is independent of K. Thus H_K also satisfies (h_2) with a_1 replaced by $\overline{a_1} \equiv \max(a_1, \sigma)$. Now set

$$I_K(z) \equiv A(z) - \lambda \int_0^{2\pi} H_K(z)\, d\tau \ .$$

We will obtain critical points of I_K restricted to certain finite dimensional subspaces of E and use them to get solutions of (0.1). Thus let

$$E_m^+ \equiv \text{span}\,\{\varphi_{jk}, \psi_{jk} \mid 1 \le j \le m,\ 1 \le k \le n\} \ ,$$

$$E_m^- \equiv \text{span}\,\{\theta_{jk}, \zeta_{jk} \mid 1 \le j \le m,\ 1 \le k \le n\} \ ,$$

$E_m = E_m^+ \oplus E_m^- \oplus E^0$, and consider $I_K\big|_{E_m}$. Symmetry properties of this functional will be exploited to find critical points. For $\theta \in [0, 2\pi]$ and $z \in E_m$, let $g_\theta(z) = z(\tau + \theta)$. Clearly $g_\theta(z) \in E_m$. Observe also that $I_K(g_\theta(z)) = I_K(z)$ for all $\theta \in [0, 2\pi]$, i.e. I_K is equivariant with respect to the S^1 action induced by this family of translations. (See [1]).

To use these symmetries, an index theory is required. Let $\mathcal{E}_m$ denote the collection of subsets of E_m that are invariant under $\{g_\theta \mid \theta \in [0, 2\pi]\}$. Thus $B \in \mathcal{E}_m$ if and only if $g_\theta(z) \in B$ for all $z \in B$ and $\theta \in [0, 2\pi]$. Observe that E_m^+, E_m^-, and E^0 are invariant subspaces of E_m. Furthermore E^0 is the set of fixed points for the above S^1 action, i.e. $g_\theta(z) = z$ for all $\theta \in [0, 2\pi]$ if and only if $z \in E^0$. A mapping $\varphi : E_m \to E_m$ is called equivariant if $\varphi(g_\theta) = g_\theta(\varphi)$ for all $\theta \in [0, 2\pi]$. Let $f(X, Y)$ denote the family of continuous maps from X to Y. Lastly B_ρ denotes a ball of radius ρ about 0 in E_m and $L^\perp$ denotes the orthogonal complement (in E_m) of a subspace L.

Lemma 1.4: There is an index theory, i.e. a mapping $i : \mathcal{E}_m \to \mathbb{N} \cup \{\infty\}$ such that for all $B, D \in \mathcal{E}_m$,

1°. $i(B) < \infty$ if and only if $B \cap E^0 = \emptyset$

2°. If $f \in C(B, D)$, where f is equivariant, then $i(B) \le i(D)$

3°. $i(B \cup D) \le i(B) + i(D)$

4°. If L is an invariant subspace of E_m and $L \subset (E^0)^{\perp}$, then $i(L \cap \partial B_1) = \frac{1}{2}\dim L$

5°. If L is an invariant subspace of E_m, $E^0 \subset L$, $\dim L \geq 2(j+n)$, and $B \in \mathcal{E}_m$ such that $i(B) \geq 2mn - j + 1$, then $B \cap L \neq \emptyset$.

Proof: The definition of index and proofs of 1° - 4° can be found in [3]. Property 5° is equivalent to Lemma 4.2 of [1].

The index theory of Lemma 1.4 and minimax arguments from the calculus of variations can now be employed to obtain critical values of $I_K|_{E_m}$. To do so some families of sets are needed. Let

$$V_{mk} \equiv E^0 \oplus E_m^- \oplus \operatorname{span}\{\varphi_{ij}, \psi_{ij} \mid 1 \leq i \leq k,\ 1 \leq j \leq n\} . \tag{1.5}$$

Thus V_{mk} is an invariant subspace of E_m with $\dim V_{mk} = 2n + 2mn + 2nk$. Next set $\overline{\lambda} \equiv -2\pi\lambda a_2$ and

$$\Gamma_m \equiv \{h \in C(E_m, E_m) \mid h \text{ is an equivariant homeomorphism of } E_m \text{ onto } E_m \text{ with } h(z) = z \text{ if } I_K(z) \leq \overline{\lambda}\} . \tag{1.6}$$

Note that $\Gamma_m \neq \emptyset$ since $h(z) \equiv z \in \Gamma_m$. Finally define

$$c_{mk} = \inf_{h \in \Gamma_m} \sup_{z \in V_{mk}} I_K(h(z)), \qquad 1 \leq k \leq m . \tag{1.7}$$

Since $I_K(z) \to -\infty$ as $z \to \infty$ in E_m (via (0.3)), $h(z) = z$ for $h \in \Gamma_m$ and z large so in fact the "sup" in (1.7) can be replaced by "max".

We will show that c_{mk} is a critical value of $I_K|_{E_m}$. The following lemma paves the way for this result.

<u>Lemma 1.8</u>: There is a constant $R_k > 0$ and independent of m and K such that

$$c_{mk} \geq R_k + \overline{\lambda} \tag{1.9}$$

and $R_k \to \infty$ as $k \to \infty$.

Proof: Let $Z_{mk} \equiv V_{mk} \oplus \text{span}\{\varphi_{k1}, \psi_{k1}\}$. Then Z_{mk} is an invariant subspace of E_m and $\dim Z_{mk} = 2mn - 2nk + 2$. We claim

$$(1.10) \qquad h(V_{mk}) \cap \partial B_\rho \cap Z_{mk} \neq \emptyset$$

for all $h \in \Gamma_m$ and $\rho > 0$. Indeed since h is a homeomorphism of E_m onto E_m, (1.10) is equivalent to

$$(1.11) \qquad V_{mk} \cap h^{-1}(\partial B_\rho \cap Z_{mk}) \neq \emptyset .$$

By 2° and 4° of Lemma 1.4,

$$i(h^{-1}(\partial B_\rho \cap Z_{mk})) = i(\partial B_\rho \cap Z_{mk}) = mn - nk + 1 .$$

Moreover V_{mk} contains E°. Hence we can invoke 5° of Lemma 1.4 to get (1.11). For $h \in \Gamma_m$ and $\rho > 0$, let $w \in h(V_{mk}) \cap \partial B_\rho \cap Z_{mk}$. Then

$$(1.12) \qquad \sup_{V_{mk}} I_K(h(z)) \geq I_K(w) \geq \inf_{\partial B_\rho \cap Z_{mk}} I_K .$$

Since h is arbitrary in Γ_m, (1.12) implies that

$$(1.13) \qquad c_{mk} \geq \inf_{\partial B_\rho \cap Z_{mk}} I_K$$

for any $\rho \geq 0$. Writing $z \equiv z^+ + z^- + z^0 \in E = E^+ \oplus E^- \oplus E^0$, by (h_2)

$$(1.14) \qquad I_K(z) = \|z^+\|^2 - \|z^-\|^2 - \lambda \int_0^{2\pi} H_K(z)\, d\tau$$

$$\geq \|z^+\|^2 - \|z^-\|^2 - \lambda(\overline{a}_1 \int_0^{2\pi} |z|^s\, d\tau - 2\pi a_2) .$$

For $z \in \partial B_\rho \cap Z_{mk}$, $z = z^+$ and (1.14) becomes

$$(1.15) \qquad I_K(z) \geq \rho^2 - \lambda \overline{a}_1 \int_0^{2\pi} |z|^s\, d\tau + \overline{\lambda} .$$

By the Gagliardo-Nirenberg inequality [4], there is a constant a_5 such that for all $z \in E$,

$$\|z\|_{L^s} \le a_5 \|z\|^{1-\frac{2}{s}} \|z\|_{L^2}^{\frac{2}{s}} . \tag{1.16}$$

Moreover for all $z \in Z_{mk}$, there is a constant a_6 independent of m and k such that

$$\|z\|_{L^2} \le a_6 k^{-\frac{1}{2}} \|z\| . \tag{1.17}$$

Combining (1.15) - (1.17) yields

$$I_K(z) \ge \rho^2 (1 - \lambda a_7 k^{-1} \rho^{s-2}) + \overline{\lambda} . \tag{1.18}$$

Choosing $\rho = \rho_k$ satisfying $1 = 2\lambda a_7 k^{-1} \rho^{s-2}$ gives (1.9) with $R_k = \frac{1}{2} \rho_k^2$.

The next lemma provides some standard variational existence tools. For $\Phi : E_m \to \mathbb{R}$ and $c \in \mathbb{R}$, let $\mathcal{K}_c = \{z \in E_m \mid \Phi(z) = c$ and $\Phi'(z) = 0\}$ and $\mathcal{A}_c = \{z \in E_m \mid \Phi(z) \le c\}$.

Lemma 1.19: Suppose $\Phi \in C^1(E_m, \mathbb{R})$ is equivariant with respect to $\{g_\theta \mid \theta \in [0, 2\pi]\}$ and satisfies the Palais-Smale condition, i.e. any sequence (z_ℓ) such that $\Phi(z_\ell)$ is bounded and $\Phi'(z_\ell) \to 0$ is precompact. Then for any $c \in \mathbb{R}$, for any invariant neighborhood $\mathcal{O}$ of $\mathcal{K}_c$, and any $\overline{\varepsilon} > 0$, there is an $\varepsilon \in (0, \overline{\varepsilon})$ and $\eta \in C([0,1] \times E_m, E_m)$ such that

1° $\eta(t, \cdot)$ is equivariant for all $t \in [0,1]$

2° $\eta(t, \cdot)$ is a homeomorphism of E_m onto E_m for all $t \in [0,1]$

3° $\eta(t, z) = z$ if $\Phi(z) \notin [c - \overline{\varepsilon}, c + \overline{\varepsilon}]$

4° $\eta(1, \mathcal{A}_{c+\varepsilon} \setminus \mathcal{O}) \subset \mathcal{A}_{c-\varepsilon}$

5° If $K_c = \emptyset$, $\eta(1, \mathcal{A}_{c+\varepsilon}) \subset \mathcal{A}_{c-\varepsilon}$.

Proof: Without 1°, the Lemma is a special case of results which can be found, e.g. in [5] or [6]. To also obtain 1°, one need only observe that there exists an equivariant locally Lipschitz continuous pseudo-gradiant vector field for Φ, [7] or [8]. Then the proofs of [5] or [6] also give 1°.

With the aid of the above lemmas, we can prove:

Lemma 1.20: For all $m \in \mathbb{N}$ and $1 \le k \le m$, c_{mk} is a critical value of $I_K|_{E_m}$.

Proof: By above remarks, $I_K \in C^1(E_m, \mathbb{R})$ and is equivariant with respect to $\{g_\theta \mid \theta \in [0,2\pi]\}$. Moreover (0.3) implies $I_K(z) \to \infty$ as $\|z\| \to \infty$ uniformly for $z \in E_m$. Consequently, if I_K is uniformly bounded along a sequence (z_ℓ), the sequence must be bounded and the Palais-Smale condition is trivially satisfied. Thus Lemma 1.19 is applicable here. If c_{mk} is not a critical value of $I_K|_{E_m}$, then by 5° of Lemma 1.19 (with $\bar{\varepsilon} = \frac{1}{2}R_k$), there is an $\varepsilon \in (0, \frac{1}{2}R_k)$ and $\eta \in C([0,1] \times E_m, E_m)$ such that

(1.21) $$\eta(1, \mathcal{A}_{c_{mk}+\varepsilon}) \subset \mathcal{A}_{c_{mk}-\varepsilon} .$$

Choose $h \in \Gamma_m$ such that

(1.22) $$\sup_{V_{mk}} I_K(h(z)) \le c_{mk} + \varepsilon .$$

By 1° and 2° of Lemma 1.19, $\eta(1,h)$ is an equivariant homeomorphism of E_m onto E_m. The choice of $\bar{\varepsilon}$ and (1.9) imply that

(1.23) $$c_{mk} - \bar{\varepsilon} \ge \frac{1}{2}R_k + \bar{\lambda} .$$

Thus if z is such that $I_K(z) \le \bar{\lambda}$, thus $I_K(z) \notin [c_{mk} - \bar{\varepsilon}, c_{mk} + \bar{\varepsilon}]$. Consequently by the definition of Γ_m, $h(z) = z$ and by 3° of Lemma 1.19, $\eta(1,h(z)) = z$. Hence $\eta(1,h) \in \Gamma_m$. But then by (1.7),

(1.24) $$\sup_{V_{mk}} I_K(\eta(1,h(z))) \ge c_{mk}$$

contrary to (1.21) and (1.22). Thus c_{mk} is a critical value of $I_K|_{E_m}$.

To continue, let z_{mk} denote a critical point of $I_K|_{E_m}$ corresponding to c_{mk}. To get a solution of (0.1), uniform (in m) bounds are needed for $\{z_{mk}\}$. The first step in obtaining such estimates is an upper bound for c_{mk}.

Lemma 1.25: There is a constant L_k independent of m and K such that $c_{mk} \le L_k$.

Proof: Since Γ_m contains $h(z) \equiv z$, (1.7) implies

$$c_{mk} \le \sup_{V_{mk}} I_K(z) . \tag{1.26}$$

As was noted earlier, $I_K(z) \to -\infty$ as $\|z\| \to \infty$ so there is a point $\hat{z} \in V_{mk}$ at which I_K attains its supremum. Writing

$$\hat{z} = \|\hat{z}\|_{L^2} (\zeta \cos \omega + \hat{\zeta} \sin \omega) \tag{1.27}$$

where $\zeta \in E^0 \oplus E_m^-$, $\hat{\zeta} \in E_m^+$, $\omega \in [0, 2\pi]$, and $\|\zeta\|_{L^2} = 1 = \|\hat{\zeta}\|_{L^2}$, and substituting (1.27) into I_K shows

$$\bar{\lambda} \le c_{mk} \le I_K(\hat{z}) . \tag{1.28}$$

Using (0.3) and simplifying terms in (1.28) yields

$$\|\hat{z}\|_{L^\nu}^\nu \le a_5 (k \|\hat{z}\|_{L^2}^2 + 1) \tag{1.29}$$

for some constant a_5 independent of m, k, and K. Thus (1.29) and the Hölder inequality give an upper bound for $\|\hat{z}\|_{L^2}$ depending only on k. Returning to (1.28), we find

$$c_{mk} \le \|\hat{z}\|_{L^2}^2 A(\hat{\zeta}) + 2\pi\lambda a_4 \le k a_6 \|\hat{z}\|_{L^2}^2 + 2\pi\lambda a_4 \tag{1.30}$$

via the L^2 bound for $\hat{\zeta}$ and the Lemma follows.

The next step in solving (0.1) is a K (and k) dependent bound on $\|z_{mk}\|_{W^{1,2}}$.

<u>Lemma 1.31</u> : There is a constant $N_k(K)$ depending on k and K but independent of m such that $\|z_{mk}\|_{W^{1,2}} \le N_k(K)$.

Proof: Since z_{mk} is a critical point of $I_K|E_m$,

$$(1.32) \qquad c_{mk} = I_K(z_{mk}) - \frac{1}{2} I_K'(z_{mk})z_{mk}$$

$$= \lambda \int_0^{2\pi} [\frac{1}{2}(z_{mk}, H_{Kz}(z_{mk}))_{\mathbb{R}^{2n}} - H_K(z_{mk})]\, d\tau$$

By Lemma 1.25 and (h_1) (for H_K), (1.32) implies that

$$(1.33) \qquad (\frac{1}{2} - \frac{1}{\nu})\lambda \int_0^{2\pi} (z_{mk}, H_{Kz}(z_{mk}))_{\mathbb{R}^{2n}}\, d\tau \le L_k + a_7 \quad .$$

For our later purposes note that (1.33) provides that an m and K independent upper bound for $\|(z_{mk}, H_{Kz}(z_{mk}))_{\mathbb{R}^{2n}}\|_{L^1}$. From (1.33) and (1.2), we conclude that

$$(1.34) \qquad \|z_{mk}\|_{L^s} \le a_8$$

where a_8 depends on k and K . Since

$$(1.35) \qquad I_K'(z_{mk})\varphi = 0$$

for all $\varphi \in E_m$, an appropriate choice of φ and (1.2) yields

$$(1.36) \qquad \|\frac{dz_{mk}}{d\tau}\|_{L^2} \le \lambda \|H_{Kz}(z_{mk})\|_{L^2} \le a_9(1 + \|z_{mk}\|^{s-1}_{L^{2(s-1)}}) \quad .$$

By the Gagliardo-Nirenberg inequality [4] if $z \in (W^{1,2}(S^1))^{2n}$,

$$(1.37) \qquad \|z\|_{L^{2(s-1)}} \le c\|z\|^a_{W^{1,2}} \|z\|^{1-a}_{L^s}$$

where $a = (s-2)\,[(s+2)(s-1)]^{-1}$. Consequently by (1.36) - (1.37) ,

$$(1.38) \qquad \|z_{mk}\|_{W^{1,2}} \le \|z_{mk}\|_{L^2} + \left\|\frac{dz_{mk}}{d\tau}\right\|_{L^2}$$

$$\le \|z_{mk}\|_{L^2} + a_{10}(1 + \|z_{mk}\|_{W^{1,2}}^{\frac{s-2}{s+2}}) \|z_{mk}\|_{L^s}^{(1-a)(s-1)} .$$

The bound (1.34) and simple estimates then give the $W^{1,2}$ bound for z_{mk}.

With the aid of these bounds, we can now get solutions to the modified equation:

$$(1.39) \qquad \frac{dz}{d\tau} = \lambda \mathcal{J} H_{Kz}(z) .$$

Lemma 1.40: For each $k \in \mathbb{N}$ and $K > 0$, (1.39) has a continuously differentiable 2π periodic solution $z_k(K)$ such that

$$(1.41) \qquad I_K(z_k(K)) \ge R_k + \overline{\lambda} .$$

Proof: The bounds of Lemma 1.31 imply for each $k \in \mathbb{N}$ and $K > 0$, a subsequence of z_{mk} converges as $m \to \infty$ weakly in $W^{1,2}$ and therefore strongly in L^∞ to a solution $z_k(K) \in W^{1,2}$ of (1.39). Since the right hand side of (1.39) is then continuous, $z_k(K) \in C^1$. The lower bounds (1.41) on I_K follow via (1.32) from (1.9) and the convergence of z_{mk} in L^∞.

The next lemma enables us to go from solutions of (1.39) to solutions of (0.1).

Lemma 1.42: For each $k \in \mathbb{N}$, there is a constant M_k independent of K such that $\|z_k(K)\|_{L^\infty} \le M_k$.

Proof: By (h_1), for all $z \in \mathbb{R}^{2n}$,

$$(1.43) \qquad H_K(z) \le \frac{1}{\nu}(z, H_{Kz}(z))_{\mathbb{R}^{2n}} + a_5$$

with a_5 independent of K. Choosing $z = z_k(K)$ and integrating yields

$$(1.44)\qquad \int_0^{2\pi} H_K(z_k(K))\,d\tau \le \frac{1}{\nu}\int_0^{2\pi} (z_k(K), H_{Kz}(z_k(K)))_{\mathbb{R}^{2n}}\,d\tau + 2\pi a_5 .$$

Equation (1.33) implies the right hand side of (1.44) is bounded independently of K. Since $z_k(K)$ satisfies the Hamiltonian system (1.39), $H_K(z_k(K))$ is independent of τ. Therefore (1.44) and (0.3) yield a K independent L^∞ bound for $z_k(K)$.

Completion of the proof of Theorem 0.2 : Choose $K(k) = M_k$ and set $z_k \equiv z_k(M_k)$ where M_k is given by Lemma 1.42. Then $H_{Kz}(z_k) = H_z(z_k)$ and z_k satisfies (0.1). Moreover $I_K(z_k) = I(z_k)$. Lastly if $\{\|z_k\|_{L^\infty}\}$ were uniformly bounded, the numbers

$$I(z_k) = \lambda \int_0^{2\pi} [\tfrac{1}{2}(z_k, H_z(z_k))_{\mathbb{R}^{2n}} - H(z_k)]\,d\tau$$

would also be bounded, contrary to (1.41). The proof is complete.

§2. The proof of Theorem 0.5

Since the proof of Theorem 0.5 parallels that of Theorem 0.2, we will be somewhat sketchy here. Note that no upper bound is required of V for Theorem 0.5, the reason being that we can work in a class of more regular functions than in §1 and get better lower bounds for critical values than in Lemma 1.8.

To begin, as in §1, we rescale the time variable and replace (0.4) by

$$(2.1)\qquad q'' + \lambda^2 V_q(q) = 0$$

with $\lambda = T(2\pi)^{-1}$ and q'' (resp. q') now denotes $\frac{d^2q}{d\tau^2}$ (resp. $\frac{dq}{d\tau}$).

An appropriate Hilbert space to employ here is $\hat{E} = (W^{1,2}(S^1))^n$ with norm

$$\|q\|_{\hat{E}}^2 \equiv \int_0^{2\pi} (|q'|^2 + |q|^2)\,d\tau .$$

The functional corresponding to (2.1) is

$$(2.2) \qquad \hat{I}(q) \equiv \int_0^{2\pi} [\tfrac{1}{2}|q'|^2 - \lambda^2 V(q)]\, d\tau \ .$$

Since $\hat{E}$ is compactly embedded in $(C(S^1))^n$ and $V \in C^1(\mathbb{R}^n, \mathbb{R})$, it follows that $\hat{I} \in C^1(\hat{E}, \mathbb{R})$.

The space E_m of §1 is replaced here by

$$\hat{E}_m = \text{span}\{(\sin j\tau)e_k, (\cos j\tau)e_k \mid 0 \le j \le m, \ 1 \le k \le n\}$$

and $\hat{E}_m = \hat{E}^0 \oplus \hat{E}_m^+$ where $\hat{E}^0 = \text{span}\{e_k \mid 1 \le k \le n\}$ and

$$\hat{E}_m^+ = \text{span}\{(\sin j\tau)e_k, \ (\cos j\tau)e_k \mid 1 \le j \le m, \ 1 \le k \le n\} \ .$$

We also replace $\mathcal{E}_m$ by $\hat{\mathcal{E}}_m$ defining the latter in the obvious fashion. An analogue of Lemma 1.4 holds for $\hat{\mathcal{E}}_m$.

For $m \in \mathbb{N}$ and $1 \le k \le m$, set

$$\hat{V}_{mk} \equiv \hat{E}^0 \oplus \text{span}\{(\sin j\tau)e_i, \ (\cos j\tau)e_i \mid 1 \le j \le k, \ 1 \le i \le n\}$$

and define $\hat{\Gamma}_m$ as in (1.6) with E_m replaced by $\hat{E}_m$ and I_K by $\hat{I}$. Finally set

$$(2.3) \qquad \hat{c}_{mk} \equiv \inf_{h \in \hat{\Gamma}_m} \ \sup_{q \in \hat{V}_{mk}} \hat{I}(h(q)) \qquad 1 \le k \le m \ .$$

The only significant structural changes from §1 in what follows are in obtaining lower bounds for $\hat{c}_{mk}$ and in getting good enough bounds for corresponding critical points q_{mk} so as to able to pass to a limit. Therefore we will carry out these steps in some detail.

Lemma 2.4: There is a constant α_k independent of m such that

$$(2.5) \qquad \hat{c}_{mk} \ge \alpha_k$$

where $\alpha_k \to \infty$ as $k \to \infty$.

Proof: Set $\hat{Z}_{mk} = \hat{V}_{mk}^{\perp} \oplus \text{span}\{(\sin k\tau)e_1, \ (\cos k\tau)e_1\}$. Arguing as in Lemma 1.8, we find

$$(2.6) \qquad \hat{c}_{mk} \geq \inf_{\partial B_\rho \cap \hat{Z}_{mk}} \hat{I}$$

so the proof reduces to obtaining lower bounds for the right hand side of (2.6) . Let $W(s)$ be a smooth function such that

$$(2.7) \qquad W(s) \geq \sup_{|q| \leq s} |V(q)| \ .$$

We can further assume W is monotone increasing in s . Thus $W(|q|) \geq V(q)$ and

$$(2.8) \qquad \hat{I}(q) \geq \int_0^{2\pi} [\tfrac{1}{2}|q'|^2 - \lambda^2 W(|q|)]\, d\tau$$

for all $q \in \hat{E}$. For $q \in (\hat{E}^0)^\perp$,

$$(2.9) \qquad \|q'\|^2_{L^2} \geq \tfrac{1}{2}\|q\|^2_{\hat{E}} \ .$$

Therefore for $q \in \hat{Z}_{mk} \cap \partial B_\rho$, by (2.8) - (2.9) ,

$$(2.10) \qquad \hat{I}(q) \geq \tfrac{1}{4}\rho^2 - \lambda^2 \int_0^{2\pi} W(|q|)\, d\tau \ .$$

Since

$$(2.11) \qquad W(s) \leq M + s^4 W(s)$$

where $M = \max\{W(s) \mid |s| \leq 1\}$, (2.10) implies that

$$(2.12) \qquad \hat{I}(q) \geq \tfrac{1}{4}\rho^2 - \lambda^2 \|W(|q|)\|_{L^\infty} \int_0^{2\pi} |q|^4\, d\tau - 2\pi\lambda^2 M \ .$$

For $q \in (\hat{E}^0)^\perp$, we have

$$(2.13) \qquad \|q\|_{L^\infty} \leq a_1 \|q'\|_{L^2} \leq a\|q\|_{\hat{E}} \ .$$

Moreover by the Gagliardo-Nirenberg [4] inequality, there is a constant a_2 such that for all $z \in \hat{E}$,

$$(2.14) \qquad \|q\|_{L^4} \leq a_2 \|q'\|^{1/4}_{L^2} \|q\|^{3/4}_{L^2} \ .$$

Also there is a constant a_3 independent of m and k such that for all $q \in \hat{Z}_{mk}$,

(2.15)
$$\|q\|_{L^2} \le a_3 k^{-1} \|q'\|_{L^2} .$$

Substituting (2.13) - (2.15) into (2.12) and using the monotonicity of W yields

(2.16)
$$\hat{I}(q) \ge \rho^2 \left(\frac{1}{4} - a_4 \rho^2 k^{-1} W(a\rho)\right) - 2\pi\lambda^2 M$$

for $q \in \partial B_\rho \cap \hat{Z}_{mk}$. Choosing $\rho = \rho_k$ such that $k = 8a_4 \rho_k^2 W(a\rho)$ we find

(2.17)
$$\hat{I}(q) \ge \frac{1}{8} \rho_k^2 - 2\pi\lambda^2 M \equiv \alpha_k .$$

Thus (2.5) obtains.

The analogues of Lemmas 1.19, 1.20, and 1.25 now show $\hat{c}_{mk}$ is a critical value of $\hat{I}|_{\hat{E}_m}$ and $\hat{c}_{mk}$ is bounded from above independently of m.

<u>Lemma 2.18</u>: If q_{mk} is a critical point of $\hat{I}$ corresponding to $\hat{c}_{mk}$, then there is a constant $\hat{M}_k$ independent of m such that

(2.19)
$$\|q_{mk}\|_{\hat{E}} \le M_k .$$

Proof: The m independent upper bound for $\hat{c}_{mk}$ and argument of Lemma 1.31 through (1.33) yield an m independent upper bound for

$$\int_0^{2\pi} (q_{mk}, V_q(q_{mk}))_{\mathbb{R}^n} \, d\tau .$$

By (V_1) and (0.3), this yields an upper bound for $\|q_{mk}\|_{L^\mu}$ and a fortiori for $\|q_{mk}\|_{L^2}$ depending only on k. Also

$$(2.20) \qquad \hat{c}_{mk} = \int_0^{2\pi} [\tfrac{1}{2} |q'_{mk}|^2 - \lambda^2 V(q_{mk})] \, d\tau$$

$$= (\tfrac{1}{2} - \tfrac{1}{\mu}) \|q'_{mk}\|^2_{L^2} + \int_0^{2\pi} [\tfrac{1}{\mu} |q'_{mk}|^2 - \lambda^2 V(q_{mk})] \, d\tau$$

$$\geq (\tfrac{1}{2} - \tfrac{1}{\mu}) \|q'_{mk}\|^2_{L^2} - a_5$$

via (V_1) and the fact that $\hat{I}'(q_{mk}) q_{mk} = 0$. Thus (2.20) combined with the L^2 bound on q_{mk} gives (2.19).

Passing to a limit as in §1 gives a 2π periodic solution q_k of (0.4) and Lemma 2.4 implies $\{ \|q_k\|_{L^\infty} \}$ forms an unbounded sequence thereby completing the proof of Theorem 0.5.

References

[0] Rabinowitz, P. H., Periodic solutions of Hamiltonian systems, Comm. Pure. Appl. Math., 31, (1978), 157-184.

[1] Rabinowitz, P. H., A variational method for finding periodic solutions of differential equations, Nonlinear Evolution Equations (edited by M. G. Crandall), Academic Press, (1978) p. 225-251.

[2] Benci, V. and P. H. Rabinowitz, Critical point theorems for indefinite functionals, Inv. math., 52, (1979), 336-352.

[3] Fadell, E. R. and P. H. Rabinowitz, Generalized cohomological index theories for Lie group actions with an application to bifurcation questions for Hamiltonian systems, Inv. math., 45, (1978), 139-174.

[4] Nirenberg, L., On elliptic partial differential equations, Ann. Sc. Norm. Sup. Pisa, 13(3), (1959), 1-48.

[5] Clark, D. C., A variant of the Ljusternik-Schnirelman theory, Ind. Univ. Math. J., 22, (1972), 65-74.

[6] Rabinowitz, P. H., Variational methods for nonlinear eigenvalue problems, Proc. Sym. on Eigenvalues of Nonlinear Problems, Edizioni Cremonese, Rome, 1974, 141-195.

[7] Ekeland, I. and J. M. Lasry, On the number of periodic trajectories for a Hamiltonian flow on a convex energy surface, to appear, Ann. of Math.

[8] Benci, V., A geometrical index for the group S^1 and some applications to the research of periodic solutions of O.D.E.'s, to appear Comm. Pure Appl. Math.

This research was supported in part by the Office of Naval Research under Contract No. N 00014-76-C-0300 and by the U.S. Army under Contract No. DAAG 29-75-C-0024. Any reproduction in part or in full for the purposes of the U.S. Government is permitted.

Department of Mathematics
University of Wisconsin
Madison, Wisconsin 53706

PROGRESS IN MATHEMATICS

Already published

PM 1 Quadratic Forms in Infinite-Dimensional Vector Spaces
Herbert Gross
ISBN 3-7643-1111-8, 431 pages, paperback

PM 2 Singularités des systèmes différentiels de Gauss-Manin
Frédéric Pham
ISBN 3-7643-3002-3, 339 pages, paperback

PM 3 Vector Bundles on Complex Projective Spaces
C. Okonek, M. Schneider, H. Spindler
ISBN 3-7643-3000-7, 389 pages, paperback

PM 4 Complex Approximation, Proceedings, Quebec, Canada, July 3-8, 1978
Edited by Bernard Aupetit
ISBN 3-7643-3004-X, 128 pages, paperback

PM 5 The Radon Transform
Sigurdur Helgason
ISBN 3-7643-3006-6, 202 pages, paperback

PM 6 The Weil Representation, Maslov Index and Theta Series
Gérard Lion, Michèle Vergne
ISBN 3-7643-3007-4, 345 pages, paperback

PM 7 Vector Bundles and Differential Equations
Proceedings, Nice, France, June 12-17, 1979
Edited by André Hirschowitz
ISBN 3-7643-3022-8, 255 pages, paperback

PM 8 Dynamical Systems, C.I.M.E. Lectures, Bressanone, Italy, June 1978
John Guckenheimer, Jürgen Moser, Sheldon E. Newhouse
ISBN 3-7643-3024-4, 300 pages, paperback

PM 9 Linear Algebraic Groups
T. A. Springer
ISBN 3-7643-3029-5, 304 pages, hardcover

PM10 Ergodic Theory and Dynamical Systems I
A. Katok
ISBN 3-7643-3036-8, 352 pages, hardcover

PM11 18th Scandinavian Congress of Mathematicians, Aarhus, Denmark, 1980
Edited by Erik Balslev
ISBN 3-7643-3034-6, 528 pages, hardcover

PM12 Séminaire de Théorie des Nombres, Paris 1979-80
Edited by Marie-José Bertin
ISBN 3-7643-3035-X, 408 pages, hardcover

PM13 Topics in Harmonic Analysis on Homogeneous Spaces
Sigurdur Helgason
ISBN 3-7643-3051-1, 142 pages, hardcover

PM14 Manifolds and Lie Groups, Papers in Honor of Yozô Matsushima
Edited by J. Hano, A. Marimoto, S. Murakami, K. Okamoto, and H. Ozeki
ISBN 3-7643-3053-8, 480 pages, hardcover

PM15 Representations of Real Reductive Lie Groups
David A. Vogan, Jr.
ISBN 3-7643-3037-6, 771 pages, hardcover

PM16 Rational Homotopy Theory and Differential Forms
Phillip A. Griffiths, John W. Morgan
ISBN 3-7643-3041-4, 264 pages, hardcover

PM17 Triangular Products of Group Representations and their Applications
S.M. Vovsi
ISBN 3-7643-3062-7, 150 pages, hardcover

PM18 Géométrie Analytique Rigide et Applications
Jean Fresnel, Marius van der Put
ISBN 3-7643-3069-4, 215 pages, hardcover

PM19 Periods of Hilbert Modular Surfaces
Takayuki Oda
ISBN 3-7643-3084-8, 144 pages, hardcover

PM20 Arithmetic on Modular Curves
Glenn Stevens
ISBN 3-7643-3088-0, 214 pages, hardcover

PM21 Ergodic Theory and Dynamical Systems II
A. Katok, editor
ISBN 3-7643-3096-1, 215 pages, hardcover

PM22 Séminaire de Théorie des Nombres, Paris 1980-81
Marie-José Bertin, editor
ISBN 3-7643-3066-X hardcover

PM23 Adeles and Algebraic Groups
A. Weil
ISBN 3-7643-3092-9, 136 pages, hardcover

PROGRESS IN PHYSICS

Already published

PPh1 Iterated Maps on the Interval as Dynamical Systems
Pierre Collet and Jean-Pierre Eckmann
ISBN 3-7643-3026-0, 256 pages, hardcover

PPh2 Vortices and Monopoles, Structure of Static Gauge Theories
Arthur Jaffe and Clifford Taubes
ISBN 3-7643-3025-2, 275 pages, hardcover

PPh3 Mathematics and Physics
Yu. I. Manin
ISBN 3-7643-3027-9, 111 pages, hardcover

PPh4 Lectures on Lepton Nucleon Scattering and Quantum Chromodynamics
W.B. Atwood, J.D. Bjorken, S.J. Brodsky, and R. Stroynowski
ISBN 3-7643-3079-1, 587 pages, hardcover

PPh5 Gauge Theories: Fundamental Interactions and Rigorous Results
P. Dita, V. Georgescu, R. Purice, editors
ISBN 3-7643-3095-3, 375 pages, hardcover